For the entertainment
of family, friends and fans.

Other Hank Tower novels available in bookstores, from www.amazon.com or as e-books on Kindle, Nook, Kobo and other e-book sources.

Death Visits The Caribbean
The Bone Dealers
The Bride Killer
Final Inheritance
Murder In Venice
The Death Chip
The Bennington Murders
Wall Street Killers

Go to www.charliehornfiction.com for previews.

THE DEADLY FARM BOY

PROLOGUE

(1982-1998)

At the age of eight he still answered to "Boy" when he was summoned to butcher a pig, behead a chicken or carve meat from a carcass he had hung in the smoke house. Between these and other chores he drifted purposelessly through 's hot summers unaware of the loneliness of the small farm he shared with his "mother." In winters he slept, mostly, and gazed mindlessly out drafty windows until snow had to be removed or wood had to be brought in or a plank in the roof had to be replaced or when some other household repair was needed.

At age ten during a fierce, Ozark lightning storm he was standing near the horse he had fed and watered since he was six when it was electrocuted by touching a wire fence struck by lightning. The thunder behind the bolt knocked him to the ground, but he didn't run to the farmhouse. He sat on the wet grass and watched the horse die, fascinated by its convulsions.

He saw no girls or boys his age or any other age. On those rare occasions when adults appeared, he would watch them unseen from an upstairs window of the farmhouse. He wasn't afraid, only curious, as a cat might be observing a new prey.

His vocabulary was small, for his weary "mother" was the only person he had ever heard speak and her waking hours were consumed by silent labor. If she had spoken more often to him, it would not have helped much; for she was not educated and said only what was necessary to survive on the isolated, unyielding

Arkansas farm. Her mind was too numb and her body too weary at the end of a day to consider conversation. She was satisfied with the few words necessary to wrench a living from the rocky, Ozark soil "The Lord has given us to bear." She had no time for or interest in learning more.

She was a good woman who read her Bible when she could. She was childless and a recent widow when she took in the boy as her own, having found him with his hands tied to the barn door. It was the desperate act of a young mother no longer able to support him in the inhospitable ecosystem of the Ozark Mountains. He was only two years old, dirty and skinny, but otherwise satisfactory. He showed no tears. She issued no pleas for help with his arrival; nor had she ever before it. She saw her circumstances as the will of her Christian God. She was not inclined to think beyond His will. That was in 1982.

She kept the boy a secret and when necessary explained to others that he was the parentless child of a departed cousin, a lie that caused her God-fearing soul uneasiness. But there was a practical reason behind the sin that she felt the Lord would understand and forgive; and the guilt soon passed. At fifty, she knew the grinding labors of the farm would soon overwhelm her; but, she thought, if I can manage for another six or seven years, this youngster will be strong enough to take over the minor chores and soon thereafter assume all of them but the cooking and gardening.

In 1996 he was a lean and muscular sixteen years of age when he found his "mother" lying on the dirt floor next to the tiny, three-legged stool she sat on to milk the cow. There was no sadness or fear in his heart. For many years he had lived with death, most of it delivered by his own hand. His mind was not affected as others might be. This death was just another part of a whole, nothing more. He dutifully pulled her corpse away from the cow's hind legs and settled it against a wall of the barn. The move wasn't one of kindness or respect. He would have moved a dead chicken had he found one where she lay. It was a reflexive response to protect the animal's wellbeing on which the two of them depended for milk and butter.

There was no phone and he had been told that the nearest farm was a two-hour walk, but reporting her death to someone was not in his thinking. His survival was at stake, for without her cooking and gardening, specialties he knew nothing about, he realized he was in danger. He knew what he had to do and if he didn't do it now, he would have to do it soon. Now seemed the better choice.

He took the .22 rifle he used to kill pigs and other animals and packed what little food there was in the kitchen into an empty flour bag. He had seen the car that the elderly owners of the distant farm used for going into town and socials and prayer meetings in the area's small, one-room church. The couple seemed ancient to his young eyes as he observed them from an upstairs window the few times when they called for some food or drink to bide them over. The two were sitting at a table they had fashioned from a large, wooden spool that once held electrical cable. They were eating plates of boiled vegetables from their garden when he shot them in the back of the head and took their food.

It took some time to learn how to master the car, but the empty farmyard allowed sufficient space for experimenting. In a short time, he was navigating the hills and gullies of a dirt road that led to a small roadside store and gas station. The proprietor filled the car's tank automatically and walked back into the store where the youngster was waiting with his rifle hidden behind him. He killed the man, emptied the cash register of several hundred dollars and bagged enough groceries for a week. He drove west for two days, stopping only for what he realized was necessary to propel the car. Finally, he abandoned it and the rifle in a collection of wrecks in an overgrown junk yard. With only a plastic bottle filled with water he started walking toward the bright lights on the horizon.

Hours later he was on the rim of where he bought a healthy meal, purchased new clothes at a Goodwill store and acquired a job cleaning floors and bathrooms in a small casino / motel on the fringe of town. Over the coming years he would listen as closely as a spy while customers conversed, recording every new word he heard and how it was said and the context in which it was spoken. He took his boss's orders obediently and when appropriate tried the new words on customers to confirm their meanings. All the while he gave fastidious attention to the business of the small casino, especially its Twenty-One table. His diligence produced an offer for a better job, but he turned it down, accepting a small raise instead. More information about his new world was needed before he would venture further into it.

Two years later with the help of a bribe he had a driver's license and for the first time in his eighteen years a recorded name – Jonah Flood, names he chose from mumblings he remembered from his "mother" when she read her Bible. But for the forged driver's license, he was a blank in the normal world. He had no birth certificate, no credit card, no bank account, no social security number – the owner paid him in cash – no tax return, no phone number, no computer, no wallet, no fingerprints or DNA on file, no address but the casino's when an address was necessary. He possessed only his clothes and the bills and change in his pockets. He never went to school and was never shown how to read. It was through his own ingenuity that he learned to understand signs and simple menus and the headlines of newspapers. He was a quick learner.

He had two God-given gifts that would always provide him with a satisfying livelihood. The first was a photographic memory that, among other things, let him remember cards used on a Twenty-One table. The second was a sociopathic mind that let him kill people without a trace of feeling. It was the Deity's second gift that would take Hank Tower within a millisecond of death.

CHAPTER 1
(Present)

I deal with dry periods by pondering things that would never cross my mind when I'm on a case. It helps mitigate the dangerous effects of not having a damned thing to do because not having a damned thing to do leads to drinking too much, irritating my beautiful mate, Carol, and kicking dogs and cats. To illustrate the need for diversion, two days ago at the bar of the Thirsty Tongue I dropped a glass which immediately sent its jagged parts skidding under banquettes and other unreachable spots. It set off a pondering of Newton's Second Law of Thermodynamics. Roughly translated, it says that everything in the Universe is exploding and unless you take a tight control of whatever you're doing, it will come apart.

The replacement drink brought with it a pondering closer to my business – murder. The public's view on murder is most surely influenced by TV where every murderer gets caught. Ah, if it were so. There are six thousand unsolved murders in the U.S. every year. So I ask myself, if the market is that large, why can't I get a case to catch one, a paying case, that is? I've the talent and a good resume for it.

I was about to order a third drink when I got a call on my cell from my friend, NYPD Police Captain Tom Holden. Tom and I are as close as our different roles permit. My words to the Mayor a couple of years ago were partly responsible for his promotion to Captain – a powerful position in New York. He knows this and gives me more moving room than he might give another New York PI. When I call him it is usually to report a dead body, sometimes two or three.

"Hank, are you on a case?"

"No."

"Interesting."

"Why?"

"In a few words?"

"Three, if possible. I'm meeting Arnie in a few minutes."

"Murder, murder, murder. Now, don't tell me you aren't involved."

"Really, I'm not."

Arnie is Arnie Macgregor, an ex-NYPD sergeant and my associate. We were leaving to see our office manager, Lydia, who was hospitalized.

"Then this may be a first. I'm calling you with a corpse instead of you calling me."

"Tom, I'm interested. Check that. I'm desperate. My mind's wandering about in trivia land. Carol is about to leave me. I'm drinking more than I should. Arnie can take only so much vacation without going nuts."

"You're in. But no holding back."

"I promise on the soul of my grandchildren, no holding back."

"You don't have any grandchildren."

"When I do, I promise on their souls I won't hold back."

"I'm serious, Hank."

"I am too. I won't hold back."

"Meet me for lunch at the restaurant in the Museum of Modern Art."

"You're into the art world?"

"It has tables where we can talk quietly. Yes, I'm in the art world."

"How about three o'clock. We're on our way to see Lydia. She's…"

"Two o'clock."

Two-o'clock it was. You don't argue with a New York Police Captain, especially when he has work for you.

My firm, Hank Tower and Associates, LLC, qualifies for the "S "on Associates by a factor of one. Besides me, there is the aforementioned Arnie Macgregor and Lydia Larson, our office manager. Now, after three years as a close threesome, Arnie and I were about to lose our warm, sharp-witted, sixty-three-year-old office and life manager to a creeping condition suddenly turned ugly. Lydia was in a hospital under an oxygen tent suffering from what the doctors called in laymen's terms collapsing lungs. In the past, she was able to weather milder forms of the problem, but this one was serious, and the prognosis was not good. Our competent, sometimes caustic, common-sense associate and friend was on the edge, according to the doctor in charge. We arrived at 1:00.

It was heart-wrenching seeing her imprisoned inside a plastic tent sprouting enough tubes to run an atomic reactor. Arnie and I stood silently at the side of her bed looking through the plastic, not knowing what to do, not able to converse with her. We could see she was breathing, but each inhale was such a struggle I wondered if she could manage another one. Her eyes were closed, her face was pale. A doctor came in. We looked at him apprehensively.

"Don't give up. She's responding better than we hoped. You're her employers?"

I nodded and stared an obvious question at him.

"If she makes it, she'll have to carry an oxygen bag."

He paused, looked up at Arnie's six-foot-six, then down to my six-foot-one.

"What do you do?"

"We're private detectives. Lydia is our office manager."

He rubbed his chin and said,

"Anything exciting could..."

"We will make other arrangements, doctor."

"I would recommend it."

"Do you have all her insurance data?"

"I believe so. Her niece and nephew were here earlier. I saw them at the Admin office."

"Here is my card. Please call for any reason. She's special to us."

He nodded. Arnie extended his catcher-mitt hand, swallowing the doctor's. Mine was smaller, but still larger than the doc's. While waiting for the elevator,

"Arnie, while I'm with Holden, find Lydia's nephew. What's his name?"

"Freddie."

"Mid-twenties, right?"

"Just went to twenty-seven. Lydia 'ad a birthday present for 'im on 'er desk last week."

"Let's hire him. Some of his feats with the computer were Houdinian. We could use his expertise on site instead of freelance."

"Aye, 'ank. I will. Lydia said 'e's independent-minded, doesn't care about money, just 'is computer."

"That's what we want. Tell him to bring his own computer and any other device he needs to max out. Mention half of Lydia's salary as a starter."

He smiled. "Aye. I might learn a few things from 'im."

"Good. There's a cab across the street. Take it. I want to walk a bit before meeting Tom. What do you know about art, Arnie?"

He looked surprised at the question, "Nothing."

"We may have to do some studying. Maybe not. We'll see"

I turned away from the hospital and started walking

toward Fifth Avenue.

Manhattan's Museum of Modern Art is on Fifty-third Street, a few steps west of Fifth Avenue. Carol visits it occasionally; I've never been there. I was directed by a young woman at the door to a separate way into the restaurant so I could avoid an entrance fee. A dollar here, a dollar there and over a year…A few moments later I spotted Tom sitting at a table for two snugged up against a floor-to-ceiling glass wall. The view opened to a small inner garden a few feet below with benches for quiet time and an array of sculptures to admire. Nice. It was exactly 2:00.

"Timeliness is one of my many fortes, Captain Holden. There is also, brightness, persistence, charm…"

"I don't have much time. If you want this job…"

"I do, but before we begin I must add an item to my list. I cannot live without money."

"I can pay you your regular fee and reasonable expenses, but the bonuses I've heard you earn are out of the question. There's a two-week limit on the assignment."

"Fair enough."

A waiter arrived. Tom ordered expansively for a man with a svelte figure and a City salary: lobster salad to start followed by roasted wild salmon. Then I realized he expected me to pay the check.

"Okay, I'm in the employ of the NYPD. What can I do?"

"Your involvement is my doing, Hank. You report to me and only me. If it got out that I hired…well, the PR would be awful."

"NYPD helpless; forced to hire talented PI…"

"Something like that."

"You know I'm loyal to our friendship."

"Yes. I'm counting on
it. Now..."

I listened to Tom's tale, fascinated by a part of the art world not familiar to me. I didn't expect a dissertation from the laconic Captain on the aesthetic value of art; or how a desirable piece can make collectors go funny; or the astronomical prices some pieces are getting as more and more billionaires bid up values. I certainly knew the prices some pieces were getting. On a wall only yards from where we sat hangs one of three versions of a painting by Edvard Munch called *The Scream.* One of the versions recently sold for over a hundred million. All this was familiar to me. It was the art restoration part of the art world that was new; specifically, how easy it was to steal a valuable piece being restored and murder the restorer; private restorers, that is, not those who are safely housed inside museums.

"Two private art conservators have been murdered; one here, another in Chicago," said Tom, examining the lobster salad sitting in front of him.

"So pass the word to those still alive."

He gave me a thanks-for-the-brilliance look and went on.

"They're no-witness killings. The murderer took a particular painting the conservator was working on and killed him, here and in Chicago. The owner of the painting gets the insurance and the private market gets a painting valued in the millions. Don't think you know anything about markets until you know about art markets. There are two of them and the clandestine one is vicious. A painting can disappear into the private collection of a wealthy person anywhere on the globe and never reappear."

I started to cringe at a difficulty I sensed. Tom answered it.

"Catching a hired killer is the toughest assignment

of all."

The waiter took away Tom's whistle-clean plate and my empty cup of soup.

"Especially when the killer's employer can be anywhere on earth," he added.

His roasted salmon and my *foie gras* tart arrived.

Something was on his mind that he was having difficulty with.

"Between the employer and the employed, it's usually easier to catch the employer."

"You expect more of these murders?"

"Yes. Think about it. It's an easy crime. Many of these conservators work at home or in a small, private studio. They're incredibly vulnerable. Two matching murders in two weeks says someone has discovered that."

"Have you staked out some of them?"

He frowned. "I can't justify it – one murder in one month in New York? We have nearly one a day. And if I could, I don't have that kind of manpower. But I'm certain there are going to be more killings because it's an ideal set up. And the prize has a double value. The owner's made whole or nearly so by insurance and the thief makes it available for sale in a market where nobody asks questions about how he got his masterpiece. There are no witnesses to interview. The conservator's dead."

"The boss behind the killing could be the painting's owner."

He nodded, fixed a studious look on me and speared a chunk of salmon. I nibbled away at the tart and sipped mineral water while he completed the salmon. He signaled for a busboy to remove the plates.

"One of my lieutenants had an idea we all thought was a good way to prevent more of these murders."

"I'm listening."

"He said we could plant knowledge about the discovery of a rare, slightly damaged painting worth millions, a Degas or Vermeer, say, that...that an experienced restorer would be working on here in Manhattan. Would you like a cup of coffee?"

"Tom..."

He made a sipping motion and flashed two fingers at the waiter.

"Tom."

Nothing.

"Then another lieutenant brought up your name and listed your many talents. I found it extremely satisfying hearing how much everyone else in the Department respects your intelligence, your physical abilities. It was a special moment for me."

"Tom."

The coffees arrived. He raised his cup to his lips and said,

"With the proper clothes...you're quick with a gun."

"You want me as bait."

"You might say that, yes."

"You might say that, he says."

I was getting hot. Not good policy with a police Captain, but this one – a friend! – could get me killed. What if the hit guy used a rifle? Or was a professional knife thrower? Or poisoned my wine? What if he posed as a customer? How in the hell would I know if a painting's owner was legit? I put these considerations to my freeloading lunch mate.

"It's possible, of course, that he would use other means, but the two victims so far were killed at close range with a nine-millimeter."

"Now isn't that comforting? And for this, for hanging my balls on an easel, I get my regular fee."

Carefully lowering his coffee cup to its saucer,

"Think of the public service."

"Horseshit."

He looked at me seriously.

"I know it's asking a lot, Hank, but we'll have a hidden backup for you. I can spare one stakeout. Yes, we need a bait, but not any bait, a smart bait, someone bright who can handle himself, someone who's handled danger before. I scanned the Department and couldn't find anyone who could match you. We'll outfit a studio with easels, give you a paint-smeared apron, some old paintings and other tools of the trade."

"What if the killer's boss doesn't see the plant?"

Tom relaxed. I had snapped at his hook.

"We're working with a person who knows people in the art world. He says he can mention that a multi-million-dollar painting has been found and is currently being restored for a rich customer. The grapevine will get it to the killer's boss."

'And who is this kindly person?"

"Someone who knows every rich guy in New York."

I looked at him, suspecting who it was.

"Name?"

"Edgar Corton. He was the last Mayor's right-hand man."

Edgar Corton, gourmet *par excellence,* my host for many an expensive lunch, my source for just about anything New York and a good friend. I hoped he wasn't aware that the police planned to use me as their tethered goat.

"Let me think about it overnight, Tom."

"Corton doesn't know about you."

I nodded and said,

"I'll call you tomorrow morning."

Risky, yes, but I was confident I could handle it. What I wanted to think about was how I could leverage this public service with my powerful friend and NYPD Captain.

CHAPTER 2
(1998-2000)

Jonah Flood was confident that he had the basic tools of life the farm had denied him. At eighteen, after two years of listening intently to conversations and practicing every word he heard and matching many of them to their printed forms, he was ready to ask for what he had wanted since he arrived at age sixteen – the Twenty-One table. The owner quickly agreed to his request. After all, Jonah had never missed a day's labor, never took a sick day or hinted for a vacation. His work was impeccable. He had a distant personality, but he was acceptable to the staff and always polite to customers. Plus, in all his sixty-three years, the owner had never seen anyone so intent on learning new things – and succeeding so quickly.

"Okay," he said, "you can be a Twenty-One dealer, Jonah. It's a good place to start because the rules are simple. If the total of your cards is under seventeen, you must take another card. If it is seventeen or over, you must stand pat."

Jonah had surmised that principle from watching the game. The game was far too simple for his acquisitive brain, but it didn't matter. His real interest was the customer side of the table. Here, there were no restrictions on the play except ignorance. Here was where the opportunities lay. Dealing day after day from a shoe filled with as many as four decks of cards was the ideal place to practice his card-counting in real time.

It was 1998 and the country had recovered well from

an earlier recession. People were vacationing. Business was good. For Jonah, it was time to leave. His departure was no surprise to the owner.

"I've expected it, Jonah. You're too smart for this desert outpost. I was hoping to put you on the craps table where your brain would get more use, but I understand."

Jonah went out the door without a handshake to a used car he had purchased with cash from his savings. He drove into Las Vegas and checked into a cheap motel just off the Strip. It was time to test his talent. His first stop was the Sands Hotel.

He walked around several Twenty-One tables noting how far the dealer had gotten into his cards. When he saw a shoe being refilled, he stood close enough to see the cards being played. When the shoe was half empty he would take a seat. His bets were necessarily modest; larger ones would come when he could afford them.

There were four other players at the table he chose and the cards played fast. He waited until he was sure he knew what remained in the shoe and put down a sizeable bet. The dealer turned over a seven and by Jonah's calculations he had a ten or a face-card in the hole. That would require him to stand pat at seventeen. Jonah held a ten and a nine. He stood pat. The dealer turned over his hole card. A queen. Jonah's nineteen won. He doubled his next bet.

He continued to win modest bets until the dealer refilled the shoe. He stayed for two more hands, purposely lost both in small amounts, and took his same formula to two other casinos. At the first casino he had won eight-hundred dollars; at the second casino he won seven hundred. At all three he won twenty-five-hundred dollars in less than three hours. The next day he repeated the procedure in three different casinos and was equally successful. He finished the circuit of the

Strip's casinos, then went downtown to the smaller, less extravagant establishments. He allowed for at least a week between visits to a particular casino and never stayed more than an hour at one of them. He always lost a few hands before he left. In six months, he had accumulated a hundred thousand dollars.

The birthdate he assigned himself on his forged driver's license was 1980. It was accurate, but a guess, for his "mother" never told him his age; nor did he have any reason to inquire about it. The birth-year made him eighteen, which was how old most people said he looked when he asked them to guess his age.

He bought a better used car with cash and drove north to Reno, Nevada, where he repeated the formula of never winning too much and never staying in one casino too long. When he reached what his license said would be twenty, he had two-hundred-thousand dollars in mostly hundred-dollar bills bundled inside a steel box welded to the underbelly of his car.

His next step started with a conversation in a bar in Lovelock, Nevada, a small town he was exploring about one-hundred-and-fifty miles northeast of Reno. The older man sitting at a bar two stools away from him had watched closely while Jonah played his cards in the casino.

"I'd like to buy you a drink, young man."

Jonah gave him a blank look. The man moved to the stool next to Jonah.

"I've been in the gambling business every day of my sixty years. You have the knack, son. I mean, you have the knack. What'll it be, another beer, something else?"

Jonah turned his head to the man and remained silent with an indifferent stare.

"Ah, come on. I don't mean no harm. I'm a fan. Jesse, make it one of those Rolling Rock beers for my rockin'-roll friend here – make it two. On me, Jesse."

The man raised his bottle to Jonah in respect.

"You're good. I can tell. I'm like a baseball scout. Yeah, like a baseball scout. I can see, smell and feel talent."

In a lowered voice,

"Now, tell me how you know what the dealer's holding damn near as well as he does."

No response. Only a disinterested stare.

"Okay, I'll guess. You got one of those brains that can remember everything. You was counting them cards. I'm right, aren't I? Now, do I care? Hell no! Does the owner care?"

He smiled devilishly at the question and pulled back from Jonah.

"I bet he does, yeah, I bet he does. Still what can he do?"

He looked at Jonah for an answer. Jonah simply looked at him.

"Well, he cain't do a thing legally. He's hog-tied, ain't he? Cause you ain't done nothin' wrong. All he can do is not let you play in his place anymore, right? That's all he can do."

The man sipped his beer and let out a burp. He was medium-size, jowly with a beer-belly.

In a low conspiratorial voice,

"He could let all the other owners know, too, couldn't he? He'd take a picture hidden like and send it around to all the rest of 'em."

The man looked at Jonah for an answer. Nothing.

"Now, do I care? No, no. I'm with you, son. I'm on your side. I ain't going to say anything. I want to take that gift of yours and make more money with it than you can scratch out of a casino. Probably easier on yer head, too. I bet it's so. Yeah, much easier. I'm talking poker. And your new friend, Sonny, that's me, is going to show you where the big games are."

Still nothing from Jonah. His free beer was untouched. Sonny continued unaffected.

"You need an agent that can find the suckers for you, like in that Paul Newman movie. 'Fast Eddie.' That was his name. That's it. You're my 'Fast Eddie.' Together, we'll make a million."

Jonah finally spoke.

"I have business tonight in Battle Mountain."

"Why that's Fate itself. I know ranchers there – five of them – that gather themselves every Friday night. Everyone of 'em think's he's God's best appointed poker player west of the Mississippi."

He stopped and looked hard at Jonah.

"It takes five thousand cash to ante in."

"I have it."

"Why shake my balls, I bet you do, and more! We won't need any of your money beyond the first play. From then on all the antes come from winnings. You're looking at a fortune."

Jonah had now turned his body full to Sonny, but the expression on his face was unknowable.

"You're thinking Sonny wants half the winnings for taking you to the fishing holes. Well, if that's what you think, you got Sonny wrong. He's a fair man. He knows there's no gain for him without your talent no matter how many damn fishing holes he knows about in this here country."

He paused and looked at Jonah with an earnest face.

"All Sonny wants – all Sonny deserves – is thirty percent of the winnings. Now is that fair? Is that a deal? All Sonny needs is a handshake."

Jonah extended his hand.

"Okay! We're partners. What time is it? Nine o'clock. The game starts at eleven. You got stamina? What's your name?"

Jonah said "George."

"George. Wonderful! George Washington. Father of our country, right? You got stamina, George? I have to know."

Jonah nodded. "Good, cause these games go beyond the dawn. I got one more question. My car's in repair. If we want to make the eleven o'clock game, we'll have to take yours. Battle is less than two hours. Your car okay?"

Jonah nodded.

"Quiet as a sleeping clam. Damned if you ain't. But what a brain! These guys will grunt over your young face like greedy pigs. Then they'll wet their pants trying to figure you out. Wonderful, just wonderful."

Sonny paid the bar bill and they went to Jonah's car. Jonah had paid no attention to the poker table at the small casino where he had cleaned bathrooms. The game was a blank to him. But by the time they were an hour out of Lovelock, Sonny had given him all the rules and hands from ace-high to five aces. "Five aces wins, if there's a wild card, but most of the time there ain't. A Royal Flush is the best you can get with no wild cards."

There was a second lecture on Texas Hold'em.

"Can't never tell when they'll play it, but most of the time it's the game I just told you."

Jonah remained silent through the entire lecture, waiting. Finally, the sixty-year-old dozed off with his head leaning against the passenger window. Jonah drove a mile or two while he snored then in quick motions tapped the accelerator, jerking the car abnormally. It woke Sonny.

"What's wrong?"

"Gas line. Trouble with it in Reno. I'll take a look."

He edged the car onto a flat space on the side of one of the few rises on an otherwise flat highway. The top of the rise dropped off into a thick forest of prickly pear bushes. Jonah went to the rear of the car and took the lug wench from the trunk.

In a toneless voice he said, "I need your help."

Sonny opened the car door and was pivoting himself onto his feet when Jonah crushed the back of his head with the wrench. The pivoting movement of his body and the force of the blow carried Sonny's body near the edge of the drop off. Jonah checked the highway and went quickly to him. He smashed the wrench onto his skull again and studied the dead promoter carefully. With his foot he sent him rolling down the incline into the thick scrub below. He wrapped the wrench in an old cloth and laid it in the trunk.

It was 10:30 at night. U.S. 80 was empty but for the occasional eighteen-wheeler barreling across the valley on its way west to Reno or east to Salt Lake City. Overhead the vast dome of a dark blue sky was sprinkled with a thousand blinking stars. In the distance the mountains crowned in snow, reflected the cold, silver light of the moon. Not far from the highway their foothills rose from a rolling carpet of dark grass waving in a breeze under the light of a half moon. As he approached town he passed a large billboard that would have made most people smile, "Battle Mountain. Voted the Arm Pit of America. Make Us Your Pit Stop." On the town's boundary was a smaller sign that read "Battle Mountain. Population 3,635."

Jonah eschewed a pit stop and continued east on U.S. 80 through Battle Mountain toward Salt Lake City. About halfway there he disposed of the lug wrench in a deserted spot and the bloody rag a few miles later.

Jonah was a blank-faced, uncaring loner, a trait Sonny might have recognized had he looked into his uninterested eyes. There was never a care for Sonny's promise of riches. The threat of exposure was why he accepted his proposal. To Jonah, Sonny's killing was no more than beheading a chicken or swatting a bothersome pest, an event done and forgotten. Like a fingernail, the self-named Jonah Flood was alive and dead at the same time.

CHAPTER 3
(Present)

I've stalked killers often since I left the spying business to become a PI and I still sleep above ground. Waiting for one to stalk me and staying above it is a different matter. In the former you're the hunter running the game; in the latter you're the hunted and the game is running you. In life the aggressor, if persistent, always wins. But there was a larger reason I took the assignment. The dull, grinding idleness of the past weeks was morphing into apathy. Rot was around the corner. I needed a game.

Restlessness of this kind can also lead to mistakes, which Arnie thought I had made when I told him I would accept Holden's assignment.

" 'ank, I need to be in the area. Ye 'ave no idea what this killer looks like. It could even be a lass. We need a camera on ye..."

"I'll handle it, Arnie." I paused. "I like the camera idea, though. I'll mention it to Holden"

"I can better the stake out, 'ank. Two are better than one."

I nodded. "How about Freddie Larson? Is he on board?"

"Aye. Excited and eager."

"Half Lydia's salary?"

"Aye. I think we should keep 'er on salary."

"I agree. Do you agree there's a pro behind the two art killings? Tom and I sort of accepted it without a discussion."

"Aye, I do. It's 'ard to fit a guy who can own expensive art as a 'ands-on murderer. Why would 'e risk a life sentence?"

Arnie looked at me with his Scotsman's eye.

"I would think finding the person who 'ired 'im would beg a larger fee."

"It would, but I'll never get it from Holden."

I called him.

"Tom, I need your permission to include Corton in what I'm doing."

"You're in?"

"Yeah, I'm in. I expect a full-dress funeral, gun salutes, crossed swords, speeches – the works – if this takes a bad turn."

"My money's on you."

"Corton is the one spreading the bait. He might have an idea about the guy behind the killer, if there is one. I need to include Edgar."

"The more people who know about this set up the more the killer will leave you alone."

I wasn't sure how to answer that, so I didn't.

"Corton is as discreet as a bishop."

"No other reason to include him, of course."

"Well, no."

"Like connections to wealthy art collectors concerned about keeping their paintings out of the black market."

"Well, that would be a service, of course. As you said, once a piece is stolen it could disappear forever."

"And the prevention thereof would deserve a fee."

"That's the American way."

A long pause. "Okay. Tell Corton, but that's it. It's you, Corton and me."

"And Arnie."

"Arnie's fine."

"Okay. Call me after you speak to him."

I hung up and dialed Edgar. As I knew, he suggested lunch at one of New York's finest. When Edgar worked for the former Mayor, he always treated me when we ate at his high-priced eateries. Now, he was employed somewhere else, meaning I might have to pick up my half.

"Edgar, the Palm is too noisy for what we have to discuss. Besides, it's a bit above my lunch budget."

"How's the art world?"

He was guessing, of course, but it had substance behind it. First, he gets a hush-hush call from Tom Holden to spread the word on a valuable painting that needs repairs, then after not hearing from me for months he suddenly gets a phone call.

"I have no idea. I need your help understanding it."

"Okay. Meet me at the Four Seasons. I'll get a table in the Pool Room where it's quiet."

"Edgar, you didn't hear my second concern, the one about lunch budgets."

"It's on me. I'll explain over a martini."

We hung up. I was talking to Arnie when our new hire, Freddie Larson tapped quietly on my office door. Arnie invited him in and angled an eye on me.

Freddie was completely bald but for a line of blond hair about an inch high running fore 'n aft down the center of his skull. Other than that, he appeared fairly normal to my semi-square sensibilities. The pockets of his cargo pants were sagging, most likely filled with the gadgets of his trade. His shirt, I was glad to see, had sleeves. There were no ear or nose rings. I could see the constrained smile on Arnie's face. He said,

"Freddie this is 'ank Tower, our employer."

I rose and took a limp-soft hand in mine. Pianists shake hands that way to protect their fingers from a macho crush. I supposed keyboard whizzes are entitled to the same protection.

"Welcome, Freddie."

"Thank you, Mr. Tower. I brought some equipment

with me. Mr. Macgregor said I could. It's in the hall."

"You'd better bring it in. We cleared the top of your aunt's desk for you, but haven't opened any drawers. I would leave them alone until we know for certain she can't return. Call us Hank and Arnie."

Arnie was standing near Freddie as Goliath might have stood near David preparing to flatten him. Freddie was a foot shorter than Arnie and had a build that suggested if Freddie had been David, Goliath would have prevailed. It was clear that the young man's talents were slinging cyber bolts, not lethal rocks. I detected no frivolity in his manner, only the tenseness of a runner ready to spring at the gun. I had the feeling he, much like me, would explode, if he were ever idled for a long period, only he played international chess, a much healthier outlet than pondering trivia and drinking.

"Do you want a hand with your equipment?"

Defensively, "No, no. I'll get it."

He scurried out into the hall. I walked after him.

"Let us know when you're ready for action."

Excited, "Do you have an assignment for me? I thought I might have to wait…"

"No. We promise no dust on your keys. Let me know when you're ready."

I went to the top of the staircase and turned back to Arnie.

"When he's set, ask him to compile a list of art restorers in the New York area. See if he can separate out those who work at home or in a studio rather than in a museum. Also, I need a list of art restoration terms and any other info about art restoration he can find. I'm off to see Edgar Corton."

"Aye, 'ank."

With a twinkle, "Maybe we can edge 'im into a full 'ead of 'air."

I smiled. "As long as more hair isn't a reverse Samson."

The Four Seasons is just off Park Avenue on Fifty-second Street. It's a royal in the pantheon of upscale Manhattan restaurants and draws an elite court to its tables. Jackets are required which in my case is *de rigueur* wherever I go. I carry a .38 holstered in the small of my back. I was led through a door on the left side of the Grill Room into a large dining space with a decorative pool in its center. Corton was at a table for two near a wall with a lake-size martini parked in front of him. I took a seat and ordered a pinot noir, slightly chilled, from Instant Waiter and smiled across at my friend.

"Edgar, it's truly good to see you. It's been too long."

His expression said it hadn't been that long at all. What was the fuss? I said,

"I'd say two months at least."

"You've been busy?"

"No! Bored as hell. Worried about my sanity. But I want to hear about you, now that your well-off benefactor is no longer Mayor."

"I joined a private wealth firm."

"Perfect. You know where every hundred million is in this town. Name?"

"Collin Brothers."

"Ah. Very private. And part of your remuneration is what we're doing here."

"Yes. I insisted."

"Well, yours truly isn't in the Collin league, but if he had access to wealthier clients…"

He almost smiled. A rarity.

"Clients with large art collections?"

"Or oil fields, banks, we don't discriminate."

The waiter arrived with menus, killing any further

conversation until Edgar emerged from his trance. He studied the offerings, asked a couple of questions and placed his order. I twirled my pinot and said I would have the same. Why second guess a pro? He returned to the present and said,

"I have mentioned to a few people that someone I know had one of his paintings damaged during Hurricane Sandy, a Renoir worth well over ten-million dollars. A corner of it was torn. It's being sent to a private art conservator here in the City. If he matches his past performances, the tear will be impossible to see."

"You didn't mention anything else."

"I mentioned that if they or anyone they knew had needs for such repairs, I knew the best restorer in the business."

"You know who that 'best in the business' is?"

"Knowing what Holden was up to, I had a feeling. Your call confirmed it."

I leaned back and sipped my pinot.

"I'll instruct my heirs not to hold you complicit in my demise. How many people did you speak to?"

"Four."

"Did any of them ask for my name, address?"

"Not yet."

He looked at me with concern. "Holden said there would be back up."

"That's what he told me. Arnie will also be in the shadows."

"Do they have a studio selected yet?"

"Haven't heard. Ten million seems low for a Renoir, Edgar. Some of the prices I've read about..."

"It is. They and their friends will know it's low."

I sipped the last of the pinot and declined another. We ate our matching meals quietly and rejected desserts. Edgar ordered coffee.

"Edgar, only you, Tom and Arnie are supposed to

know about the trap. I'm sure he explained that."

"Yes, he did."

"Collin Brothers, eh? With the same restaurant deal as before. I hope I'm around to enjoy some of them with you."

An almost-grin, "You will be."

I grunted and excused myself with a genuine thank you.

The curtain was edging up on the play.

Some months ago, I made a devastating mistake when I asked Carol to join me on a business trip to the Caribbean. Killers were involved, but I thought I could enjoy her company and still keep her safe from the unforeseen events that seem to plague my ventures. It didn't work. She was almost killed. We had a wedding planned for June twenty-first. She canceled it because of the terror she experienced, but mostly, I believe, because of my work. The horrible possibility that a future child of ours might experience something close to what she did overwhelmed her interest in marriage. When we returned she decided to live with Didi Harrington, a close friend, for a couple of weeks to sort things out. We're back together in our Greenwich Village apartment, but talk of a child or a wedding doesn't come up, as it did so often before the event. "Just us, Hank" is how she put it when she returned. If she had the slightest hint of what I had planned with Holden, she would bolt for a saner life. I wouldn't blame her. There's something inherently crazy about setting yourself up as a potential victim. But the need to challenge danger – and beat it – has been in my make-up since I balanced my way across a high bridge railing at age six. I have the same primal need to find and defeat an adversary as a mountain climber must have to climb a dangerous peak.

Carol knows criminality, which most likely exacerbated her fear for our future. Her first job after Journalism school was as a crime reporter for the *St. Louis Post Dispatch*, then for the *New York Post*, a tabloid owned by News Corp. The assignments often exposed her to the horrific results of nut cases carrying guns, but she never had face-to-face contact with a mental until our trip. Now, she's safely ensconced inside News Corp's building where she runs and owns part of a website she started called solve.it.ny.com.

I surfaced from the subway, bought a bottle of David Bruce pinot noir at my friendly wine shop and walked home. She arrived a half-hour later at 7:00 and hung her coat next to my .38 in the hall closet.

It was early November and New York was in its autumnal glory. The sky was a sharp blue spotted with drifting puffs of lumpy white clouds. The leaves of trees on some streets had turned color. But it was Central Park that took win, place and show. The Park has over twenty thousand trees in scores of varieties: maple, oaks, elms, sycamores. They were breathtaking in their multiple shades of orange, red and brown. Autumn is New York's finest season. Its brisk, clean air breaks the heat of the summer and puts a peppier step in your walk. It prepares you for winter.

Business talk had largely replaced any discussion of this kind between us. The romantic repartee, the gentle needling of each other was rare. Making love when it occurred was more dutiful than passionate. Perhaps all this will change, but it's nearly six months since the incident. Nothing was ever said about the fat sicko who tied her to a pole in his basement. I beat the shit out of him, but that helped me, not her.

She went to the sofa and flipped open her iPad on the coffee table. Staring at Google Analytics,

"Our traffic is up, but not much. We need those ads that were promised."

"Would you like a glass of pinot?"

"Uh? Oh, yes. Half full."

I poured accordingly.

"Grover said he bargained a lower price for us. So where are the ads?"

I sat across from the sofa in a matching chair and listened. Her eyes were still on the screen.

"We're scheduled for another quarterly meeting next week."

"The last one turned out okay. A twenty-five-thousand-dollar bonus, I recall."

Still fixed on the screen. "I'd be happy with that, but it won't be that much this time." She closed the lid and looked at me expressionless.

"I have zilch for dinner."

I sipped my pinot and looked at her. God, she's as beautiful as the first day we met, not an ounce of difference anywhere, not a smidgeon of change in complexion or hair or legs or waist or breasts or neck or ankles or eyes. No, the eyes have changed. Before the horror there was always a glint of seductive mischief in them when she looked at me. They seemed to say "Be on guard, Tower. I'm going to get you into bed." That was gone.

"Let me take you to dinner," was the best I could come up with.

"Good. I'll freshen up."

I watched her go down the hall to our bedroom.

CHAPTER 4
(2000-2002)

Far ahead of Jonah the lights of Salt Lake City were spreading a dim, orange glow across an immense expanse of sky. It suggested the remains of a devastating fire were smoldering beneath it. But what lay beyond the glow was a display of Nature that overwhelmed the manmade light. The Wasatch Mountain Range, a western extension of the Rockies, was flaunting a cold, glistening cape of snow across a massive bulk that reached as high as twelve thousand feet toward the sky. The majestic mountains stood as a barrier to any expansion to the east by the two million people of Greater Salt Lake City who lived on their western side.

It was 11:00 when Jonah noticed his car was low on gasoline. Tomorrow was safe enough for a refill, but Jonah himself also needed refilling. Eleven o'clock was past the bedtime he had lived with during his fourteen years on the farm. A few more years would pass before he would stop thinking he should retire before dark. Even in the ever-active casinos of Las Vegas and Reno he remained part slave to the old habit. To gamble until midnight, which he did occasionally, was a struggle he most certainly would have lost but for the bright lights, the discordant sounds of the slots and the crowds cheering for their bets at the craps tables.

He spotted a motel and pulled into the parking lot. It was a white, single story building shaped in an "L" with the office located on the short leg of it. A "Vacancy" sign hung askew in the office door. Three cars only a year or two away from the junk yard were parked nose first in front of separate rooms next to the office. A yellow light behind the Vacancy sign was the only other hint of life.

Jonah hit a bell on the counter to wake the man slumped in a chair behind it and with the aid of a hundred-dollar bill convinced the hairy, tattooed owner to give him an unregistered room for the night. He parked his two-year-old car directly in front of the door to his room and activated the electric charge he had rigged to the steel safe attached to its underbody. If anyone touched it, the charge was enough to knock them out for a moment and alert Jonah. So far that had never happened. His luggage was a small suitcase containing two shirts, underwear, an extra pair of trousers, shoes and toiletries.

Jonah was now years away from the farm. He had learned to speak his thoughts clearly and adequately and to read well enough not to appear unschooled. He had more money than most Americans and a gambling ability that allowed him to earn more almost at will. He was street smart, a quick learner and, as others would learn, had no feelings for other living things. He was also untraceable in today's connected world.

The incident occurred about 3:00 a.m. It wasn't the car's alarm going off that woke him – it was the stop-and-start scratching sound of something struggling on a gravel surface. He peered out the window and saw his car being pushed away from his door. He went to his suitcase and removed an Army .45 he had purchased in Nevada with two of his many hundred dollar bills. The whiskered, eighty-year-old seller said he didn't have to be bulls-eye accurate with it. The slug was powerful enough to shoot a man in the hand and still knock him down. "It was designed in World War II," he had explained. "to stop Japs wrapped in tape so thick the standard-issue side arm couldn't stop them from overrunning a position." Jonah accepted the sales pitch and bought the gun.

He went back to the window and watched. There were two men in denim overalls. Both had their backs to him. One was pushing and steering the car back from the door; the other was pushing it from the front. The gravel sound that woke Jonah was coming from the man trying to turn the car's front wheels to keep it on a straight line.

Jonah stepped across the wooden walkway paralleling the doors to the rooms and pressed the gun into the nape of the neck of the man pushing the front of the car. He froze. The other man glanced back over his shoulder, saw Jonah's extended arm and the gun at the end of it and fled across the highway into the darkness of the other side. Jonah let him go, took his prisoner's arm and walked him into his room. He pushed the man into a chair, shoved a piece of dirty underwear into his mouth and told him to empty his pockets. One side pocket had sixteen dollars and change in it; a back pocket held a black comb and crumpled tissues. The only light in the room came from a dim, exterior night-light edging its way through the slats of the window blinds. The broken light created burnt-yellow stripes across Jonah's face. To the would-be thief, the light was coming from a furnace in Hell and Jonah was its keeper. Jonah stared hard at the man, but not with anger. His eyes were as dark and bottomless as a panther's and equally disinterested in his quarry's life.

The man started to rise. Jonah shoved him back into the chair, then signaled with the muzzle of the .45 for him to go to the door. He pushed him toward the deserted end of the motel, the high end of its "L" shape, keeping the gun firmly against the thief's back. His chin was now trembling uncontrollably and urine had started to run down his left leg. He knew death was near. When he tried to speak or break away, Jonah pressed the gun's muzzle hard against his head.

He walked him about a quarter of a mile behind the motel into thick stands of trees and shrubs fed by rivulets of water winding their way through the underbrush. Jonah stopped the man and forced him to lie in a gully lined by tangles of ground vegetation. He pulled the underwear out of the man's mouth, pushed in the gun and fired. The result was far more damaging than when he killed a pig with a shot to the head from his .22 rifle; but otherwise he made no distinction between killing the man and killing a food animal. To Jonah, it was simply another way to prevent his identification. He shoved the underwear into his pocket and spread fallen limbs and thick vines over the body until it was buried. After listening for a couple of minutes, he proceeded back to his room, cleaned it, made the bed and quietly rolled his car to the highway before he started the motor, as the two thieves had tried to do.

It took two days for the thief who escaped Jonah's gun to decide conclusively that it was too dangerous for him to report his missing cohort. They both had police records in Utah and other states and his own record included a car theft that sent him to prison for a year. Answering the flurry of questions he knew the police would ask might link him to other thefts under investigation, some of which might actually be his. A second conviction would mean a prison term of several years, a thought that made him shudder. Let somebody else report his absence, I'm moving on, he decided. There weren't any others to report it. Both men were loners, drifters, who quickly sold their stolen goods and moved on to other venues. It would take two months before the body of the murdered man was exposed by a pet dog a guest let loose behind the motel.

A day after the murder Jonah ditched the two-year-old car in an abandoned junk yard and took a license plate from one of its derelicts. With his stash of cash he purchased another of a different color, year and make. It was a sensible precaution. Even though he had no feeling of wrongdoing, he knew the police would see it differently, if they could connect the killing to him. Down the road, unseen by anyone, he crawled under the new car and fastened his briefcase-size vault of hundred-dollar bills to the underbody.

A few miles away he found an all-night diner with gas pumps. He ate toast and eggs and bacon and filled the tank, paying for it in small bills. From there he drove south on U.S. 15 toward Provo, Utah, avoiding the mountains to the east until he found a secluded place where he could sleep in the back seat and safely dispose of the .45. Refreshed, he resumed his journey south to U.S. 70 where he turned east through Fishlake National Forest toward Grand Junction, Colorado. Along the way he would learn from a complaining diner cook that the only way you could gamble in Utah casinos was by playing bingo, an old folks' game, he said derisively. Jonah had seen bingo in Reno. It was another reason for him to leave Utah.

Now, he was in western Colorado where, again, at a diner he quizzed the short-order cook about gambling.

"Yeah, they're casinos with Twenty-One tables in Colorado. Black Hawk is a great one. They got more than one," he said. "But they have a limit. A hundred a play, I think."

Jonah knew he could parlay hundred dollar bets into a thousand or two, give back a couple of hundred and move onto another table or another casino. He paid for his cheeseburger and home fries and got directions toward the nearest Black Hawk from a nearby gas station attendant.

Once again the crowned majesty of the mountains,

the small freshets rushing down their jagged sides, the vast reach of a flawlessly blue sky passed by Jonah Flood without appreciation. His thoughts were on staying within the posted speed limits and acquiring a new gun. The concern for a weapon was not without merit. All his assets were in his pockets and the vault attached underneath it. He couldn't ask the police for help, if he were threatened. They would require personal data, of which he had none; nor could he ask anyone else for help; for he wanted no one to know or remember him. The years of street knowledge he had gained from Las Vegas, Reno and various spots in Utah told him that he was best off remaining an unknown entity beyond tracing by anyone in the official or unofficial world. He was a phantom and phantoms were loners who protected themselves.

He came upon a secluded, wood-frame, single-story building fronted by a long, narrow porch under a tin roof. Near its entrance was a large sign that read "See 'em there; eat 'em here!" It was held by a fifteen-foot figure of a smiling cowboy dressed in a large hat, leather chaps, boots and spurs. He was pointing a finger at two buffalos in a small corral twenty yards away. A smaller sign near it screamed in red "Guns! Ammo! Fireworks!"

Jonah drove his car across the empty, dusty lot in front of the building, parked and went directly to the gun section. The proprietor, a husky woman with brown, weathered skin saw him from the restaurant area and walked slowly in his direction. He saw her in a mirror and took three hundred-dollar bills from his pocket. Without turning, he spread them where she could see them on the counter top and pointed to a .22 caliber pistol that held six shots. The price tag said seventy-five dollars. She handed him the gun and took the cash. Jonah pointed to a small box of shells and she handed it to him. No charge for the shells; no questions about the gun. He was in and out of the store in less than five minutes without a word exchanged between buyer and seller.

U.S. 70 stretches all the way to Baltimore, but Jonah wasn't going nearly that far, not yet. The opportunities the rich and fertile Northeast held for a man of his talent were still years away. He drove and drove, always at or near the speed limit, through Glenwood Springs, Edwards, Vail, stopping only for gas and food and occasional naps in his back seat. His goal was a casino with Twenty-One tables and the short-order cook had told him there was one farther to the east. Dallying or sightseeing, no matter how spectacular the views, were not on his agenda. So he drove. Finally, he came upon a large billboard advertising a Colorado casino.

The name was different from the one the cook had mentioned, but perhaps that was good. He could work this one and move on to the other one. He found a downtrodden motel where he could pay cash without registering, set the alarm on his secret vault and retired. In the morning he refreshed himself and casually inspected the casino's layout. That night he returned when the tables were full and began his card-counting. He won eight-hundred dollars, lost a hundred of it and repeated the formula at another table and another. In two hours Jonah had won nearly three-thousand dollars. During his slow, nonchalant roaming from table to table, he was being watched from above by eyes far more established in the world of gambling than the departed Sonny's. They belonged to the man who would become Jonah's mentor, a man who over the coming years would involve the dead-eyed, twenty-two-year-old in his primary career and offer him profits that were many times what working the Twenty-One tables would provide him.

CHAPTER 5
(Present)

Carol finished her bathroom routine and went into the kitchen to lay out some breakfast items. I did my own thing and joined her at the small kitchen table she had set up. She poured two cups of coffee and said without much interest,

"Do you have a new case? You seem occupied."

"Yes. It shouldn't take me out of New York though. You're meeting with Boss Grover today about the bonus situation?"

Returning the coffee pot to its warmer, "Yes."

It was a halfhearted response to something I knew she considered very important.

I suppose there's no way to know when your unconscious is going to make itself heard. Perhaps it was Carol's desultory response that gave mine its voice. I've been absently aware of my hidden self's pestering for months, but when it tried to speak I suppressed it. The subject matter it wanted to bring up was too uncomfortable for my waking self to deal with. Not now, I had said, over and over. Then one day in an unsuspecting moment, the unconscious decides it can't handle the put down anymore and the question it had been wanting its owner to face for months pops out like one of those springs pressed inside a fake can of peanuts. She was sipping her coffee when mine popped out.

"Carol…"

Looking over her coffee at me,

"What?"

"Are you happy?"

Nothing, just a guarded look.

"It's been almost six months since you came back from Didi's and, well, I don't know if you're happy you did."

She lowered her head into what I took as the universal I'd-rather-not-talk-about-it position. Finally, she looked at me,

"Yes, sometimes."

I'm wobbly at this kind of stuff. I'd rather face a nut with a gun than go into deep emotional waters. Do what you do and I'll do what I do. Let's be happy; let's everybody be happy, is my wish. But, of course, Life doesn't work that way and whoever thinks it does is heading for trouble. The spring will eventually come out of the peanut can and when it does it can cripple such a person for life. My unconscious knew this truth better than my day-to-day mind.

She was waiting for me to say something.

"I know. That's what I feel. You're happy sometimes."

"Am I hurting you, Hank? If so, I will..."

"Don't say it. When I hurt it's because you're hurting. I want you to be happy full time."

I was remembering our first time in bed only a day after her near death because of my foolish decision. She had her arm over my naked chest, but her head was buried in her pillow. Loving me and afraid of me at the same time, afraid of what my job would bring, not just to her, to a child, if we had one.

"Carol, I can look for another way to earn a living."

She smiled. "You'd go nuts."

"A little maybe, but...but..."

She was softening. "But...but...no buts about it. You'd go nuts. I wouldn't want that for you and definitely not for me."

"I will, Carol. You're more important to me than..."

She got up from her chair and wiggled her way onto

my lap.

"It's fading, Hank. The nightmares are less and less. I've seen someone a few times and it's helped. He suggested another week or two. That's all. Stick with me."

"Stick with you! Good Lord, woman, I thought you wanted to unstick with me."

"No....I wish...well, maybe your assignments might be less dangerous, but I know that's part of it, isn't it?"

"A little."

Shit, it was all of it.

"Maybe if we had a child they would be less dangerous..."

I grabbed at it. "Yes, I could reduce..."

"And your new case, it's probably not very dangerous."

"No, of course not. Not at all."

She grinned. Then for the first time since we returned from that grotesque experience she took the initiative.

"I know bringing this up wasn't easy for you, but it helps me."

She pulled herself closer to me and kissed me softly under my ear. I turned her lips to mine and kissed her hard.

One of Mark Twain's best maxims is "When in doubt, tell the truth." So with respect to that wise man's insight, I justified the corollary, "When there's no doubt, tell a lie." Carol suspected my "No, of course not. Not at all." was a lie, but in deference to the moment, she said nothing. The challenge now was to undo the lie by staying alive.

Arnie and Freddie were waiting for me at the office. I looked at the big Scot with his full head of reddish hair, then at Freddie with the stubby, blond growth running down the center of his bare head. It looked like a missed row of corn stalks in a mowed field. He jumped up.

"Here is a list of all the art conservators in the New York area, Mr. Tow…Hank. I've starred those I was able to determine work at home or in small studios."

I took the paper. How in hell he did it I didn't ask.

"Good, Freddie, very good. Arnie and I will go over the list. In the meantime, take it easy. More stuff is coming, but not immediately."

Glancing down at his desk, "Read your book for a while."

The tome was upside down to me, but I could read the larger type in the title, "The Great Philosophers of…"

We have a cyber-intellectual in our midst. Arnie signaled me into my office with a half-grin on his face. He had seen me reading the title.

" 'ank, I took a call from a man who said a friend of a friend referred him to you. 'e wanted an appointment right away. 'e's on 'is way."

"Any idea why?"

He smiled. "Says 'e's an art collector."

"I've been told that the art world is close knit. Anything else?"

"No."

"Okay, we wait for our art dealer. Make a copy of this list for yourself. I'm calling Holden about my new quarters."

My Police Captain friend answered in a tone of moderate cheerfulness, the kind that oozes out after one accomplishes a goal.

"We have a studio for you in a townhouse. It's on the first floor so it's easy for the killer to get in."

"Thoughtful, Tom, thoughtful."

"West Eighties off Central Park West. Make sure Corton has the address."

"Oh, I will, I will. Otherwise how could the killer find me?"

"We'll have someone outside, Hank. I can only spare one man."

"Well, there's always a cow bell tied to the door and tacks on the floor."

He gave me the studio's address without comment.

"It'll be ready at three this afternoon."

"Do I bring my own paints?'

"No. All the gear will be there, including some cheap paintings and clothes."

"I've been assembling some remarks for my eulogy. You might want to rehearse them."

"There's only one man, Hank, but he's a good one."

"I'll need a key."

"One will be delivered to your office any moment."

"Arnie will be on watch."

"That's fine."

'Any recent developments, Tom?"

"Well..."

"I'm listening."

"Last night...about eleven there was an incident in Soho."

"An incident. You mean a robbery."

"No, a murder in a loft."

"An artist's loft?"

"Well, yes."

"The victim was restoring an expensive piece of art."

"Well, yes."

"Shot, most likely."

"Yeah."

"In the head. Quick death. No suffering?"

"No suffering."

"That's always a good thing, isn't it? Killer was professional most likely."

"Yeah."

"Probably the same one who killed the other artist here and in Chicago."

"Probably. Evidence points that way."

"Interesting. It's good that the killer is in town."

"Yeah."

"And that he kills humanely. No suffering, as you say."

"Yeah."

"A considerate killer."

"Yeah, Hank…"

"Oh, I'm still in the game. Wait…"

Freddie knocked on my door with a package. I opened it.

"I have the key, Tom."

I almost said, "The goat has its tether," but clicked off instead.

Our client-to-be, Hugh Patterson, we learned, had gotten my name from an artsy friend of a currency trader I crossed paths with on my last case. My involvement saved the trader from a fatal disaster, even though we were on opposite sides of the issue. The man obviously remembered me gratefully. Patterson had a small personal collection of modern art, but his primary role in the art world was as a dealer. He ran a gallery on Madison Avenue in the East Sixties, home to several upscale galleries and one of the highest rent neighborhoods in the highest rent county of America's thirty-one hundred, Manhattan. The man must sell some high-priced pieces.

He was aware of the murder of a New York art restorer. He told Arnie that he knew the victim. He was unaware of the murder in Chicago or the one in Soho just reported to me by Captain Tom Holden, the third one within a week. He stood a distinguished five-foot nine, had neatly combed, wavy, graying hair, heavy eyelashes and a pencil mustache with a gray tint. He was slim, but not muscular – more of a watch-the-weight type than someone who worked out regularly. He was impeccably dressed in a pressed, dark suit, an off-white, stiff-collared shirt, striped tie and expensive Italian shoes. I guessed he was sixty years old plus or minus five percent. While he and I spoke, Freddie cyber-vetted him in the outer office.

I introduced him to Arnie and waved him into the black, wooden armchair in front of my desk. In a deep voice that belied his rather delicate build he said,

"Gabriel wasn't a close friend, but we..." He stopped.

"Let me take that back. If I'm not honest with you, I can't expect you to be honest with me. We were intimate friends. I want his killer found and jailed. I don't trust the police to give his murder the proper attention. He wasn't a celebrity."

If I weren't looking at another fee, I would have defended the police against that remark. Instead, I returned a meaningless look.

"I can pay your regular fee, but I will also pay you a bonus, if the killer is found before the end of the year or..."

I raised my eyebrows and waited.

"...or if he's killed."

I explained our regular fee, then added,

"Please understand, Mr. Patterson, that we will do our best to find the killer, but if we find him before the police do, we must turn him over."

A bit embarrassed, "Oh, yes, I know. I wasn't suggesting..."

"Quite all right. If you and the victim were intimate, revenge is a natural thing. An eye for an eye is our nature. On the honesty subject, please know that Arnie and I are already working with the police to find Gabriel's killer. I don't see a conflict..."

"Nor do I! That's wonderful. You'll have access to their investigations. Is that right?"

"Yes, I will. Now, what kind of bonus do you have in mind, Mr. Patterson?"

"One-hundred-thousand dollars, if the murderer is either in custody or dead before midnight December thirty-first this year."

"That's about eight weeks from now."

"Yes."

"Any reason for that date?"

He lowered his head. "Yes, we met at a New Year's Eve party fifteen years ago when the millennium turned. It's a sentimental need to...to make his memory more real...more..."

"I understand. We will email you a contract detailing our fee and expenses and the bonus you offered. Now, I need to ask some questions."

He looked up eagerly.

"Gabriel was an art restorer, correct? Not a collector."

"That's right. He was well known in the conservation business. He worked on valuable paintings mostly from private collections that were damaged or found in an attic or had gotten dirty over time."

"Did he have some valuable paintings in his studio when he was killed?"

"One very valuable one. A Picasso."

"The killer took the painting. How valuable do you estimate it was...is?"

"Yes, he took it. Price? Oh, that always depends on how badly a buyer wants it."

"Take a guess."

"For a passionate collector I would price it at fifteen to twenty million."

"How many people do you think knew Gabriel had the painting?"

"I can't say. Gabriel was discreet regarding what he was working on, but the owner might have mentioned it to someone."

"These high-priced paintings are insured, correct?"

"Oh, yes. The conservator would insist on it before taking possession."

"Do you know if the owner has filed a claim?"

"No, I don't, but I'm sure he will."

"Who is the owner?"

"A Park Avenue couple, Gerald and Mona Harris."

"We haven't seen Gabriel's apartment yet. You've been there?"

"Many times."

"Easy entry?"

"Yes. It's one floor up with large windows. It's an old factory still being gentrified. Large, noisy elevators, an old rusty fire escape on the wall outside. Virtually anyone could get in, if they wanted to. The paintings were always stored out of sight except what he was working on. He might leave that one on the easel or a table top."

"If he wasn't working on the Picasso, the killer would have to find it."

"Yes, he would have to recognize it, of course. Gabriel's other assignments were nowhere near the value of the Picasso."

"The police believe it was a hired killer who was told to take a specific painting."

"All he would need is a picture of it. And time to find it, unless…"

"…unless he forced Gabriel to find it for him. How big is the Picasso?"

"In its frame about two feet by three feet."

"How would a killer know if the painting was done? Do you know if the work was finished?"

"No, I don't. He could force it out of Gabriel or be smart enough to know on his own. Or be told that it was done. The Harris's would know. If Gabriel were finished, he would have wanted to get paid as soon as possible."

"We'll call them. Are you aware of any insurance claims on issues like this, not murder, just a theft?"

"No, I'm not. Many high-value paintings are restored in museums where they're guarded."

"Why not this one?"

"It might have been too long a wait. The conservation departments of major museums are busy caring for their own artwork. They usually refer a private collector to a respected conservator. Gabriel or another freelance restorer would also charge less than a museum willing to take the assignment."

I thought about the one I would supposedly be working on. "What would you guess a restored Renoir would go for?"

"Oh, my. I'd have to see it, but if the repair was well done and it was one of his more famous pieces, the price could reach fifty million, maybe twice that. The world has more billionaires and multimillionaires today than ever in history. Many of them need to spend their money and art is benefiting. Some of the prices paid today would have been laughable only a decade ago."

"I have a list of over a hundred art restorers in the New York area. Does that sound right?"

"I would say it's about right. Nationally, it's many times that."

To confirm what he told Arnie, "Have you heard of an art conservator murdered in Chicago?"

"No."

I didn't mention the one in Soho; nor did he.

"Okay. We're on it. Give us two days and we'll have

a progress report. Here's my card. Arnie Macgregor is my alter-ego. You can share whatever you wish with him. He was a sergeant with New York's Finest before joining the firm and knows who's important and who's not. The young man outside just arrived."

"Mr. Tower, Gabriel needs my revenge."

"I understand, Mr. Patterson. So does society."

On that high-minded note we parted.

I turned to Arnie.

"Fifty-million-plus for a lost Renoir. That's a fat goat for the tiger out there."

"Aye, 'ank, 'tis indeed."

CHAPTER 6
(2002)

Had Jonah been a drinker he might not have been spotted gambling by his soon-to-be mentor; but he was not a drinker. Not only was there no alcohol on the farm, its mere existence was unknown to his "mother" and her nearest neighbors. His first exposure to "Demon Rum" was in the seedy Nevada casino/motel where he worked after dumping his stolen car in a junkyard. He considered it a strange lure and an even stranger spectacle – men and women sitting at a long counter facing scores of bottles of various shapes and colors, sipping various shaped and colored drinks. But the scene gradually blended into the casino's ambiance. If he had stopped for an occasional drink while roaming the tables in this new casino or accepted a free one while gambling, as others did, it might have changed the rest of his life. To the man looking down through the one-way ceiling he would have appeared as a typical customer undeserving of special notice.

But Jonah was focused intensely on the tables, working his formula. He would win a thousand or so then lose a hundred or two and always leave a table when the dealer refilled his shoe with multi-decks of cards. The routine caught the experienced eye of the man on the other side of the ceiling. The young man was clearly counting cards, he mused. That's not easy, not easy at all, but he let Jonah continue to play and watched with a growing admiration.

Jonah had accumulated nearly five-thousand dollars before two husky men appeared behind him at the

Twenty-One table. One of them nodded to the dealer and the next round of cards excluded Jonah. The taller man said politely,

"We'd like you to come with us. Someone wants to meet you."

Jonah gave his permanently blank stare to the speaker and then to the other man. The encounter would have sent a flash of danger up most spines, but Jonah had never known fear. His response was simple curiosity. He pocketed his chips and nodded nonchalantly to the taller man. The three walked through the crowded mass of gamblers all of whom were too fixated on their game or slot machine to notice anything unusual about two burly men in dark suits escorting one with an untucked shirt through the tables.

They took an elevator up one level. The shorter one pressed a buzzer. A solid wood door opened, revealing a room with a beamed ceiling, a shiny wooden floor and a massive bay window framing the towering, snow-topped Rocky Mountains in the distance. The two men led Jonah to the front of a large mahogany desk.

Behind it sat Isa Hajjar, a sixty-year-old, lean, handsome, well-tailored Lebanese man versed in every gambling trick known to modern man. He owned the casino and parts of an unknown number of others. He stood to greet Jonah, gave a disarming smile and signaled one of the escorts to give him a chair. Jonah took it and stared disinterestedly at the man. Isa said to Jonah in the pleasant way of a gracious host,

"Well, sir, you certainly know your way around this business. I must thank our legislators for putting a hundred-dollar limit on our bets. I might have had to sell everything I own to keep up with you. May I ask your name?"

It was 2002 and Jonah, according to his forged driver's license, had just turned twenty-two. His six years of worldly experience since leaving the farm at sixteen had educated him somewhat in the art of conversation, if short sentences are given weight. He would never develop an ease with words; nor would he ever see any need to do so. His instincts always told him immediately where he stood in a situation. If he sensed a threat, he would handle it without words.

"Jonah Flood."

"I'll call you Jonah. Now, Jonah, these eyes and ears have been in this business since they left their mother's lap. My compliments. You are a master card counter. The way you moved from table to table, purposely leaving a little behind at each, watching when the shoe was refilled. I must say again," raising his hands to the ceiling in mock gratitude, "Thank you Denver for putting a limit on bets."

Isa narrowed his eyes and returned to Jonah, studying him, waiting for a denial or a protest. But neither came. Jonah simply looked at him unflinchingly. Isa's instincts picked up something in Jonah's vacant look. This was not an ordinary young man. He didn't stir, blink or show any sign of worry, yet he is in a closed room with two tough men watching him while he faces an accuser. He's a prisoner at their mercy and not an eyelash moves, not a breath breathes harder. I bet his pulse is no higher than when he sleeps, thought Isa. Normally, when he suspected a person of card counting, he would ask that the winnings be retuned and order the person not to return to the casino. Something held him back this time. His business nose smelled something that might be useful.

"Have you ever been a dealer, Jonah?"

In a flat tone, "Yes, in Nevada. I prefer playing instead of dealing."

Isa broke into a wide smile. "I bet you do. I bet you

do."

Then Isa's face darkened as he explained the usual routine in situations like this. Jonah rose from his chair unperturbed and started for the door. Both men quickly blocked it. Jonah turned to Isa and said,

"Tell them to move or I will kill them."

Isa looked at the taller man. He indicated Jonah had no weapon. But Isa sensed danger. He opened the flat drawer under his desktop and put his hand over the butt of a revolver. The taller man moved toward Jonah, pointing for him to sit back down. Jonah stood firm. The man reached for him and with an arm that had chopped tons of wood and lifted hundreds of pounds of pigs Jonah seized the man's right arm, twisted it behind his back and jerked it up. A crack and a scream pierced the room. Jonah held the man firmly in front of him as a shield. The other man froze in place, gazing at his partner's contorted face.

Jonah to Isa, "Tell him to get out of my way."

Isa's hand was still on the hidden revolver. With his other hand he waved the second man away from the door. Jonah held the injured man close to him. He was moaning in excruciating pain. His arm was now dangling grotesquely at his side, then Jonah pushed him into a wall and walked toward the door.

"Wait, Jonah!"

He turned to Isa with the same blank face.

"Leo, take Carl to a doctor. Leave me with Jonah and close the door behind you."

Leo hesitated.

"Go. I'll be okay."

Carl's scream had changed to a flurry of ferocious curses flung at Jonah. Leo nudged him slowly out of the room, closing the door quietly behind them. Jonah started to leave. Still sitting behind his desk, Isa said,

"Let's talk, Jonah. We may have a common interest."

Jonah stared at him.

"Do you know what that means?"

"No."

"Do you have a job?"

Jonah said nothing. Isa waved him back to the chair in front of his desk.

"I didn't think so. I want to suggest something to you."

Jonah took the chair. Isa closed the desk draw with the revolver in it and smiling, leaned forward and rested his arms on the desktop.

"In a way you have created one for yourself."

Jonah kept his empty stare on Isa, but leaned back in his chair, interested.

"Poor Carl. He never was meant for this job. He's big and looks fierce, but...well, as you see. He's an easy take."

"You want me to replace him."

Now, it was Isa's turn to lean back. He connected his fingers across the back of his head and said in a between-us tone,

"He was also timid in some respects. Sometimes the job requires more, let's say, than breaking the arm of a cheater; but sadly, he never seemed up to what was required. I couldn't trust him to...well, to do more than the superficial."

Isa's eyes were x-raying Jonah.

"Do you know what I mean by superficial?"

"I don't know the word."

"I mean he was good doing easy stuff, but not the hard stuff."

"He couldn't kill people."

There it was. Spoken with the clarity of a bell. This is what Isa had sensed earlier in the young man. There was barrenness, vacancy, indifference in his expression and manner. He had seen how effectively and nonchalantly Jonah could maim; now, he believed he could kill with equal indifference.

"Correct, he couldn't kill people."

Isa waited for confirmation.

"I have."

Jonah said it knowing that his own killings were untraceable and that killing was what this man wanted.

Isa's eyes narrowed. His face was as somber as a priest's listening to a repentant sinner.

"I know you have, Jonah. Men like us sense these things." He paused.

"How much do you make a month working the tables?"

Jonah had the street smarts of a seasoned criminal, but he had never bargained for money or needed to. He simply told Isa the truth.

"As much as I need."

"How much over the past year, Jonah?"

That he knew. "One-hundred-and-fifty-thousand dollars."

Isa expected more, but wasn't surprised. Jonah was careful. He spread his talent across many casinos and never spent too much time in one.

"I want you as a dealer at fifteen hundred a week, but that's just to keep you in beer."

"In beer?"

"Pocket money, Jonah. Money for food, drink and women. Your real money will come from the special assignments I give you."

"How often?"

Isa smiled inside himself. "Let's say one a month. The amount will depend on the assignment. Are you interested?"

"I need a place to live."

"I am taking that as a yes. I'll find comfortable rooms for you. Do you have a woman?"

"No."

"That will change, Jonah. That will change."

Isa hit his cell phone.

'Leo, get Carl's arm fixed and tell him to meet me in the Centennial Room at midnight immediately after the last shift. I want to talk to him privately."

Leo gave an okay and clicked off.

Isa straightened up in his chair and looked at Jonah with the intensity of a lion studying a prey.

"Carl presents a possible problem to my businesses, Jonah. He will be angry and resentful when he learns I'm hiring you to do what he thinks he's responsible for. Angry men cannot be trusted. They do or say risky things. They can be manipulated by others. Carl could reveal something that a competitor could use to damage me. He will also want revenge for his broken arm. He's a problem."

Jonah nodded.

Isa drew a diagram on a note pad and handed it to Jonah.

"The room I marked will be empty at midnight except for stripped down tables and chairs and movable curtain racks. The service door I marked comes in from an alley. You can park your car there, behind a large dumpster. Carl will be sitting at one of the tables at midnight, waiting for me. I will be on the casino floor talking with customers. When you return, I'll have your first bonus waiting for you."

No more needed to be said. Jonah memorized the layout and handed the note pad back to Isa. He looked at his new boss and raised the right side of his mouth a half-inch. It was as close to a smile as Jonah could get. To Isa, it was his new guard dog snarling.

I have my man, thought Isa, but I'd better watch him.

It was 11:30 when Jonah nosed his car into the alley and parked in the dark shadow of the dumpster Isa had described. The only light was from a dirty, yellow bulb casting a dull, pallid glow down from its perch over the service door. The narrow alleyway was bordered by the back of the casino on one side and the high, windowless wall of a warehouse used to store highway equipment on the other side. Jonah's car was pointed to the end of the alleyway that opened to a service road which in turn fed into a major highway. He put a roll of duct tape in his pocket and slipped a hammer in his belt.

Inside the building, he flipped a light switch illuminating a section of the Centennial Room that was crowded with barren tables and chairs scrambled into a pile like victims of a flood. He pulled out a table and two chairs and set them apart from the others. Lined up along a wall were seven-foot-high green curtains stretched between metal rods on rollers for use as privacy walls by exhibitors. Jonah slipped in between the two closest to the table he had arranged and waited.

At 12:05 Carl entered from the main door and saw the table and two chairs. But for a ceiling light above the table and chairs the huge room was dark and silent. He took a few steps in, looked and listened, and rubbed the shoulder supporting the sling for his broken arm. He pulled back one of the chairs with his foot and sat, facing the entrance door. His back was to the row of green curtains lined up as neatly as pages in a book. He raised his good arm to check his wristwatch and looked around the vast convention room. Jonah was behind him, standing between the first and second "pages" of the book of green curtains. He squatted and lifted the bottom bar of the outer one and flipped it over Carl like a fish net. Carl's back was pressed forward under the green canvas. He raised his head to shake it off, creating a lump in the otherwise flat surface. Jonah smashed the hammer on it with the full strength of his arm. The man struggling to free himself went limp. A deep red stain started spreading across the green curtain.

Jonah quickly pushed away the table and two chairs, unsnapped the curtain from its rods and double-wrapped the dead man's head in it. He rolled the corpse and hammer into the rest of the curtain and dragged the body out the service door onto the back floor of his car. He went back inside, returned the table and two chairs to the disorganization of the others and took the rods that had held the death trap over Carl's body. He turned off the room's only light and returned the unused duct tape to his trunk. Inside the dark Centennial Room, the remaining privacy curtains remained in their ranks, silent and unconcerned; the bare tables and chairs remained the jumbled mess they were before. The floor was clean.

Jonah drove his car to the service road onto the highway and away from town until he came to an unlit side road. In the off-and-on moonlight the only sign of civilization was a barn and a small house with a split-rail fence around it. He steered out of its sight, lights off, stopped and found a desolate area where he knew the earth was unfit for farming or grazing. He dragged the wrapped body and steel rods to it and dug a grave. It was familiar work. He had dug graves many times after killing a sick or wounded dog or cat or other farm animal that his "mother" insisted should be buried "...to keep the buzzards and night critters from eating on it." This animal just took longer to bury.

CHAPTER 7
(Present)

When I need insight into the upper socio-economic ranks of Manhattan I call my all-knowing New Yorker, Edgar Corton. I was immediately invited to another lunch. I believe my friend is feeling a bit lonely in his new job at Collin Brothers. He misses the power and complexity of the Mayor's office and needs someone to break bread with who reminds him of the good-old days. I begged off.

"Edgar, I need to know about a Gerald and Mona Harris. They're Upper Park Avenue art collectors. That's all I have. Do you know them?"

"I know someone who does."

Edgar's quick connection made me think about that six-degrees-of-separation thing. It claims that if we want to find a total stranger anywhere in the U.S., it takes no more than six intermediaries to locate him or her. First, you call the person you think is most likely to get the game going, then he or she suggests another person who might know and then that person suggests another and so on. Six "knows" and you've landed the person you set out to find. I'm convinced there are no more than *two* degrees of separation in Manhattan's high end. The tighter connections among this small, elite population come from a shared school, charity work, the arts, a club, a similar profession...whatever the nexus the first person you ask will nearly always know a person who knows the person you want to find, as Edgar had just proven. In fact, Edgar often knows the person himself.

"I'm listening."

"Jack Harris. I believe Gerald is his brother."

"And who is Jack Harris and what does he do?"

"He's a real estate developer. He was part of the World Trade Center's rebuilding among other things. I have his office number if you want it."

"He'd probably clam up, if a PI wanted information about his brother. Anyone else?" I wrote it down anyway.

"No."

"Lunch may be hard for me for a while, Edgar. How about dinner?"

"Fine, but not tonight. Call me tomorrow."

Freddie found the Harris's address – 740 Park Avenue between East Seventy-first and East Seventy-second Streets. Very nice. The building is one of Manhattan's "Towers of Power" and has seen celebs and titans flow through its halls since it opened its doors over eighty years ago. It's not for rookies. One of its duplexes sold this year for seventy-one million. Our new client, Hugh Patterson, talked about billionaires pushing up the prices of art. The pushing is Herculean in Manhattan real estate. Billionaires from around the world are using its condos as savings accounts. Forty, fifty, seventy million – one condo went for over a hundred million. These over-the-top purchases are savings accounts they use for sleeping once in a while.

What sounded like a maid answered my call. I took a chance.

"I'd like to speak to Mister or Mrs. Harris. My name is Tower. I'm an insurance adjuster."

"One moment, please."

In a muffled female voice, "Who is it, Jennifer?" followed seconds later by,

"May I help you, Mr. Tower?"

"Is this Mrs. Harris?"

"Yes."

"I am the insurance adjuster for your Picasso painting that was stolen. May I have ten or twenty minutes of your time for some routine questions?"

"Is anything wrong with the claim?"

"No. We're required to ask owners of very valuable items a few questions in person before we can close the file. It's strictly routine. If you're available, I can come now. The sooner we do it the less delay with the payment."

"All right. But I have to leave at two-thirty."

"We should be done before then. Is Mister Harris at home?"

"No, do you need him?"

"Probably not, but if I do, I can use the phone. We are required to meet only one owner in person."

"But Gerald owns it."

"Spouses qualify, Mrs. Harris."

"Okay. We're at 740 Park. But I have to leave at two-thirty."

I hung up and turned to Arnie.

"I'll go from the Harris apartment to my new art studio. Meet me there at three before Holden arrives. We need to scout the area."

"Aye, 'ank. I spoke to the 'ospital. Lydia is getting moved to an Assisted Care place. She said she wants us to come visit 'er as soon as we can."

"Tell her we will. Ask Freddie to do a background on Gerald and Mona Harris. He has their address. And Gerald's brother, Jack Harris. He's in the construction business. Tied to the World Trade Center project."

" 'arris and Jacobs?"

"Do you know them?"

"Aye, a bit. A few years ago one of their scaffolds fell in the West Forties, killing a pedestrian and putting a sergeant friend in the 'ospital. 'e was giving the lady a 'and with something when it fell on both of them. It was a 'arris and Jacobs job."

"Go on."

"The criminal case was dismissed by the prosecutor, but along the way we found that Jacobs is a ghost name. We never discovered who 'e was."

"Some shady dealing? Money laundering? Terrorist money?"

Tracking money suspected for terrorists was my job as a spy.

"We never got to it. Once it went from criminal to civil, the Department moved on."

"Why use a ghost name unless there's a purpose?"

"We just let the case go, 'ank."

"Ask Freddie to track Jack Harris's dealings with the World Trade Center and anything else he can find."

"Ye suspect something?"

"No, but New York is entwined in many ways..."

"I'll tell the lad."

"Three o'clock."

"Aye. I'll be there."

On the way to meet Mona Harris I called Bill Sanchez. Bill was my mentor when I left business school to join a small group of spies who worked for a man we called the Headmaster. None of us knew his real name. The Headmaster lost Bill to the National Security Agency where he now works in a high position. He's done favors for me in the past that might raise an eyebrow in some quarters, like tracing a person's movement by satellite. The last time I tried to finagle a favor somewhat close to that I got a warm and friendly response that went something like this:

"For Christ sake, Hank! Do you read the papers?"

It's possible he was referring to Congress's concern about the NSA eavesdropping on everyone from the German Chancellor to your favorite bartender. Still, the world moves, times change, attitudes soften. Fortunately, one thing was still the same. He still answered my calls immediately.

"Hank. I was afraid you were pouting. I was a bit curt the last time we spoke. Let's see, what was it you wanted? Oh, yeah, it was a wiretap on the Chief Justice. Or was it the Secretary of State? These small things slip from my mind as time goes by."

This wasn't going to be easy.

"I understand, Bill. Things were pretty sticky a while back. Has the temperature moderated? With all that's happening in the world, NSA must have some cred back, maybe not hero buttons, but more slack from the public."

He avoided an opinion.

"How's Carol?"

"Better, much better. Thanks."

"Nora and I would like to have you both to dinner."

"Let me talk to her tonight."

Silence, then,

"I'm waiting."

"It's a small favor, Bill. Nothing like your examples. It could even be a national security matter."

"Of course."

"There's a construction firm called Harris and Jacobs that is involved in the World Trade Center rebuild. Jacobs is a ghost. There is no Jacobs. Curious, don't you think?"

"Two names make a firm seem stronger."

"Then why not three? Can you look into it? You remember how a ruse like that could be used to funnel money. Fake paychecks, bonuses."

Silence, the thoughtful kind. I was getting to him.

"We can't bug…"

"Of course not, but there are so many other ways."

"What's your involvement?"

"Murder, theft, insurance fraud, more murder, theft

and insurance fraud."

"Local matters."

"What you do unto my smallest you do unto me."

"What in hell are you talking about?"

"The quote's a bit botched, but it means even the littlest grievance can upset the world stage and you're in charge of the world stage..."

"All right. I'll see what I can find."

"The Harris part of the name is Jack, Jack Harris. Jack's brother is Gerald. Gerald's wife is Mona. Gerald and Mona live on Park Avenue and collect art."

"Thank you."

"I appreciate whatever you can find. I'll ask Carol to call Nora about dinner."

I got a low mumble and we hung up.

The cab dropped me at Seventy-first and Park a half-block from the entrance to the "Tower of Power." The building's doorway was modest for such a grand nickname and was most likely intentional. It consisted of two doors with curlicue metal designs covered by an ordinary-looking canopy. One of the doors was opened for me by a courteous doorman in a neat gray suit who announced my arrival and politely pointed me to the elevator. Moments later the maid opened Mona's apartment door for me.

"This way, Mr. Tower. Mrs. Harris will be with you in a minute."

Understated elegance, old money sophistication, whatever you wanted to call it, the apartment's large foyer and the high-ceiling living room and all their appointments radiated a subtle, restrained opulence, as if extra care had been taken to avoid appearing *nouveau riche*. I took a seat, gazed around and let the nature of the setting soak in. Damned if it didn't feel like a church. If a red-robed Cardinal had glided in, I wouldn't have been surprised. But rarely is anything what it seems, Freud's observation, I believe, but it doesn't matter who observed it. I know it's true because I've experienced it over and over. Mrs. Harris entered the room. I stood to greet her.

"Mrs. Harris, my name is Hank Tower."

She extended her hand. "Mona Harris, Mr. Tower. How can I help you?"

Her hand was soft, weak. She stepped back from me and sat on the front edge of a dark blue wing chair. I did the same on a matching sofa.

With my most disarming smile,

"Mrs. Harris, I have a confession to make. I hope you aren't alarmed by it. I'm a private detective investigating the murder of the art conservator who was working on your Picasso. I used the disguise because when I identify myself as a private investigator the phone often goes dead."

She gave a weak grin and said, "You mean Gabriel."

"Yes. Did you know him?"

"No, I only spoke to him when he picked up the painting. Gerald arranged for the work."

"You're aware of his death."

"Yes, I am."

Mona Harris was a small, attractive woman somewhere in her low-fifties. She was conservatively dressed in a dark green skirt and jacket and sat erect in a guarded, anxious way. She reminded me of someone who dreaded being called on in school. Her lack of any reaction to Gabriel's unnatural departure seemed a bit off tune for how I read her. She seemed more on the softhearted side of our species, yet there was no "Yes, horrible" or similar condolence for the dead conservator. Maybe there was a hidden toughness or maybe she was simply uneasy with me.

"Do you know if the painting was finished?"

"Yes, it was. Gabriel called Gerald to arrange delivering it."

"Do you remember how long it was ready before Gabriel was killed?"

"I would guess about two weeks. Gerald insisted on seeing it before he delivered it, but was always too busy to go to Gabriel's studio."

"You said your husband owned the painting. Is he an art collector? I see several pieces in this room that appear valuable, but I'm an amateur."

Her facial muscles were tightening up. Whether it was from talking to a PI or some other reason I couldn't tell.

Weakly, "We both love art."

"Mrs. Harris, have the police talked to you about Gabriel?"

"No."

"They will. If you think of me as a dress rehearsal, it may help you relax with them. Don't let my Private Investigator title intimidate you. I'm mostly normal. I eat, drink, laugh, pet dogs and cats, kiss my lovely companion when I get home, go barefoot, that sort of thing. It's a regular life, even boring sometimes."

She managed a genuine smile. I'll have to try the speech on Carol.

"It's possible you know something you feel unimportant, an overheard conversation or something that Gabriel said when he was here that could help prevent another murder. A conservator was killed in Chicago only days ago and the police think more may be killed. It's fairly easy to steal from a freelance restorer."

There was no visible reaction to the Chicago news. Unusual. I kept the Soho murder to myself, for now.

"Mr. Tower, the only conversation Gabriel and I had was my offer to help him handle the painting. It was the first and only time I met him. Perhaps Gerald can help you. I'm afraid I can't."

I was being dismissed. I tried another approach.

"Jack Harris, your husband's brother…"

She flinched as if I had dropped her Ming vase.

"…is he involved in art as well?"

Quickly, "No, no. He's in construction."

Then holding her eyes on mine for the first time,

"Why do you ask?"

"A friend knows him. The firm is Harris and Jacobs, I believe."

She slid back in the chair, as if to say, "Thank goodness. It wasn't the Ming."

"Yes, that's right."

"Actually, I am more interested in Jacobs, but the office is no help. Can you tell me how to reach him?"

"No. I 'm not familiar with Jack's business. Maybe Jacobs doesn't live in New York."

"That might explain it. Do you know where?"

She sensed something.

"Mr. Tower, why don't you speak to my husband or his brother? As I said, I'm not…"

"I understand, Mrs. Harris. Let me go to my main purpose. The police will ask this question. I hope you'll share the answer with me. How much was the Picasso insured for?"

"Fifteen million dollars. Is there anything else, Mr. Tower?"

"No, but if I call again, I hope you'll answer the phone."

With a half-grin, "I'll refer you to my husband."

I gave her a vote-for-me smile and started toward the door. The maid appeared from thin air to open it for me. Mona had vanished into the depths of the apartment.

I met Arnie on the corner in front of the building on the Westside that housed what could be my last Manhattan apartment. It was a typical brownstone about five stories high with a walk-up stoop to the front door and steps beneath the stoop to the basement door. Holden had said I was on the first floor in deference to the killer. If so, he or she would have to ascend the stoop to get in. That didn't seem to accommodate the assassin. He would be on stage, so to speak, and easily spotted by a neighbor or passerby.

Looking at the townhouse from across the street,

"What do you think, Arnie?"

"It makes it easier for you, 'ank, but not the killer. Putting you in the basement would be easier for 'im."

"What do you see for surveillance?"

"The townhouse across the street, first floor window. It covers the area."

"Holden can arrange that for you."

"Back entrance?"

"Not to the basement, to the first floor."

"Okay. We'll let Holden figure out where to put his bait, but I want you in the window across the street."

As I spoke my Captain friend called. He had moved my studio to the basement.

"We decided it was less threatening for the killer," he explained dryly.

CHAPTER 8
(2002-2005)

Twenty-five thousand in cash for only a few hours of work. That amount of money would have taken months for me to accumulate going from town to town, casino to casino, thought Jonah. Two days later there was another reward – a two-bedroom apartment with a large terrace in a new complex only ten minutes from the casino. It was on the top floor and its terrace had a view across a long rolling stretch of cacti, aloe, mesquite and prickly pear to the snowcapped Rockies towering in the distance. The amenities included a tennis court, an indoor and outdoor swimming pool and a par-three golf course. More furnishings were coming which, as Isa said, "will please you."

Jonah was made a Twenty-One dealer with the salary Isa had promised, but that job was only to acclimate him to the rhythm of the casino. Jonah was destined for the craps table after a month or so of simply sliding cards out of a shoe. After the craps table, Isa planned to have him roam the floor during the casino's busiest hours. His photographic mind was ideal for spotting card-counters. After some experience as a stickman, his sharp eyes would detect those attempting to beat the house with dice as well as with cards. And, of course, if a cheater were found, Isa could rely on Jonah's premier talent, if there was no other solution to a disagreement. Isa Hajjar was very pleased with his new employee. He was also careful with him.

Jonah's satisfaction with the new arrangements tended more to contentment than delight. He no longer had to sleep and bathe in grungy motels and dry himself with towels as rough as sandpaper. The fresh air and open space of his new home recalled the wild freedom he had enjoyed on the farm. But even that feeling went only so far, for Jonah's capacity for joy had never developed. When he was left tied to a stranger's barn door by his natural mother any chance for normal development ended. From that moment until he left the farm at sixteen he was a recluse. He sat with no one and talked to no one but his "mother." And those exchanges were limited to discussing the duties necessary to survive on her "God-given" farm. There was no time or energy left for touching or affectionate talk, only the required amount was spoken when Jonah was small. He never had a friend, nor did he know the concept of one. He was a loner unable to feel lonely.

His relationship to the world was also crippled, although that was changing rapidly as he was exposed to men and women of every level of education. His only response to emotion was when Nature's deepest root was stirred. If he were threatened or thought he was, or if he believed he had been ill-treated, his reaction was automatic and soulless. These traits did not go unnoticed among the casino's staff.

After the disappearance of Carl, employees began watching Jonah with an attentive unease, as one might watch a puma that had strayed into their backyard. Isa was quick to explain to the staff that Carl had "...taken another job back East at a salary we couldn't match." It was a plausible explanation, except Carl had never mentioned to any of them that he was looking for another job or that he had accepted one. Speculation spread about what might have happened and with it came an unspoken fear of Jonah. When a male employee saw him ahead, he would take a different route to his destination.

A different dynamic arose among three adventurists

on the female staff. Jonah was danger and danger was excitement and excitement was partly why they worked where they did. On one occasion an attractive twenty-three-year old virtually asked him to go to bed with her and was stared at with such empty eyes that she backed away frightened. She reported to her friends that…"He's spooky. His eyes…they're like looking down a well." This challenged the other two. They offered themselves as a pair to him as persuasively as they could without causing an X-rated scene on the casino floor, but they were simply looked at blankly. The assumption was that he was homosexual, but one of the three young women rejected that. "He's a neuter," she said. Her conclusion prevailed and spread. Jonah, despite his mystery and generally good appearance, was no longer bothered sexually by any of the staff, young or old, male or female.

Five weeks of dealing Twenty-One and Jonah was transferred to the craps table. The difference in play was extraordinary. This was not the studious, formulaic routine of Twenty-One. Here, he had to watch as many as twenty players at once, often with another twenty standing behind them. Here, there were cheers and pleas and pushing and shoving with nearly every throw of the dice. The method of play at the craps table was faster and far more complex than Twenty-One.

Bets were placed before the shooter threw the first dice, as they were in Twenty-One, but bets could also be made or changed while the shooter continued to throw. They could be made on the Pass Line, the Don't Pass Line, the Come and Don't Come, the Field, the Big Six and Big Eight, to mention some. The stickman, Jonah's job, had to watch and track every bet to know who made it and for how much and had it been increased. Then, when a shooter crapped out, he had to pay off the winners accurately, determine the losers and rake in their chips. It had to be done quickly, for the table had to be clear for the next round of betting and players were always in a hurry. The craps table is the heart beat of a casino. It's where the high action and excitement reside. It's what customers run to when the word spreads that a shooter just made his fifth pass. Everyone wants to bet with him or her.

More important, the craps table is where a gambler can get his odds of winning closer to fifty-fifty than anywhere else in a casino. Depending how it's played, craps can favor the house from as high as seventeen percent to as low as less than one percent. Jonah had grasped this immediately. He knew the house's odds on every one of over twenty bets. If a player consistently arranged his bet to secure the most favorable odds, Jonah would notice. It wasn't card counting, but Isa didn't like those bets. "I can't make any money at fifty-fifty odds," he said. He told Jonah to keep a mental list of those who routinely bet so sophisticatedly in case something had to be done.

Weeks passed before an issue arose. Jonah, according to procedure, had given five dice to a man he had seen before. From these the man would choose two to throw against the wall at the other end of the table. The throw must be handled with one hand – no shaking the dice between two. Jonah noticed the man worked his hand in an unusual fashion before he threw the dice, but dismissed it as an infirmity. This time he noticed another man among the fifteen at the table whom he had also seen before. Something clicked. The man was always at the table when the man who had just selected the dice was shooting and he always bet on the Pass Line along with the shooter, as he did now. The shooter rolled a seven. He and the other better won. The shooter kept the dice and the procedure repeated itself. Jonah allowed one more roll before switching the dice. The shooter rolled another seven and the pair won for the third time. Jonah took the two dice with his stick and passed five more to the shooter for selection. The man smiled jovially and said, "I can't press my luck past three passes. I'm going to the roulette table." The down-table player made a cheap bet, lost it and left the casino. Jonah pressed a button and a substitute stickman arrived. It was half-past midnight.

Jonah whispered to the man who had gone to the roulette table for him to join him for a free drink away from the commotion. Jonah's voice, always even, had no threatening tone, but the man wondered why the stickman wanted to buy him a drink. The protocol is for a gambler who wins to give the stickman a tip. He accepted the invitation partly because of the touch of southern in Jonah's speech. It resembled a Georgian accent, the man's home state. He rose from his seat and the two went toward an off-traffic table. Jonah's lean five-foot-eleven made him a couple of inches taller than the short, pudgy man walking next to him.

The two pulled up chairs and Jonah asked a waitress for his usual club soda with a wedge of lime. The man ordered a Jack Daniels on the rocks. Jonah's expressionless look was starting to make the man nervous.

Jonah lifted his glass. "Here's to gambling. I'm new to it. Are you?"

The man felt a slight tremble rising in his hand.

"No. I don't take it seriously though. Just fun. Thank you for the drink." He raised his glass.

"I've seen you at the craps table before, but not anywhere else. Do you ever play Twenty-One or baccarat or the slots?"

"No. Just craps. I like the action."

"You do well."

"So, so, I guess. I have a gut feel when to quit."

"Your partner does well, too."

"Partner? I don't have a partner."

Jonah stopped his glass just under his lips and froze his eyes on the man. The dark, unblinking stare said more than words. Jonah kept staring in silence. The man was scared.

"I...I have to go. I appreciate the drink, but I promised my wife I'd be home by one."

Jonah's eyes remained fixed on him. He set the glass on the table without moving his eyes or head.

"I'll be glad to pay for my drink, but I really have to leave."

He rose and started for the exit. Jonah grabbed his right forearm in a vise grip. Under the fabric of his jacket he felt a long piece of elastic. He followed it up the man's arm. It was fastened to something under his armpit. He moved his grip back down, tightening it as he progressed. Just above the wrist attached to the elastic chord he felt a small thimble large enough to hold two dice.

"How much did you and your partner win?"

"I have no partner. I just came in to pass some time before going home. Let go, man."

Jonah pulled down the thimble into the man's hand and squeezed his own hand around it hard.

"I asked an honest question. Unless you give me an honest answer I will have to make my own estimate."

Jonah's lifeless eyes, his pulseless composure, his everyday tone intensified the danger the man felt. His hand was being crushed.

"I won six hundred dollars."

"Your partner?'

"The same."

"How many nights?"

"Five."

"Before noon tomorrow you will return six thousand dollars to me."

"I can't...I don't have..."

Jonah looked at the man and said passionlessly, "If you want to live."

He ran his hand up under the man's sleeve, ripped out the elastic cord and released his grip. He pocketed the thimble.

"By noon tomorrow," said Jonah.

The man walked away trembling. Jonah's cool, unchanging manner told him to obey him. He would have to draw money from his wife's savings account to cover his previous winnings. He would also have to convince Gil to come up with his share – a task he knew would be difficult. Just before the door he looked back and saw Jonah standing looking at him, his eyes as fixed and chilling as those of the mountain lion he happened upon once while hunting. He felt the same shiver in his spine.

Jonah threw the rudimentary dice-switching device into a trash bin and returned to his job as stickman.

The short, pudgy man immediately called Gil, but Gil was adamant.

"Bullshit. I'm not giving back my three thousand. I don't even have three thousand! I'm out of here at noon tomorrow anyway. Why the panic? Do you think this hood is going to follow you for a lousy three grand? Come on."

"Gil, you didn't see him. He's inhuman."

"Right. Well, I'm keeping mine. You can do what you want."

"He destroyed the switcher."

"We can make another one."

"It's not that easy. You have to match the dice..."

"I'm leaving tomorrow. Next stop Denver. It's a big city. You should do the same, if you're worried. The hood won't find you."

The terrified man hung up and went home to make

his case to his wife. He didn't share Gil's blasé attitude. His primeval need to stay alive was threatened. Gil... he just doesn't understand. Explaining the incident was hard, but it prevailed. His wife saw something new in her husband that convinced her that not returning the three thousand presented a far greater danger than whatever benefit they could derive by keeping it. At ten the next morning the short, pudgy man entered the casino and asked for the stickman at a certain table at a certain time the night before. Jonah appeared. He took the money and said,

"Three thousand is missing."

"My friend refused to give it to me."

"Is he at home?"

"He's leaving for Denver."

"Come with me."

Jonah grabbed his arm and led him through the Centennial Room to the alley behind it.

"Do you have a phone?"

"No."

Jonah handed him his.

"Call him and say that if he doesn't have the money here in two hours you will be buried alive."

The short, pudgy man went white. His hand shook and he nearly dropped the phone as he clumsily punched in Gil's number. Gil answered in his hotel room. Jonah's message was relayed with a voice hardly understood in its fright.

"Gil...Gil..." He gushed out in terror.

"He's bluffing. I need the money," he repeated. But he paused thoughtfully. The two were not close friends. Either could leave the other in a lurch without a feeling of desertion. Still...

"I'll give back part of what I have just to help you out, but I'm not going to the casino. I'll leave what I can at my hotel desk with your name on it. Relax. This isn't a mafia town. Come to Denver with me, if you're that scared."

"God, Gil, please. Don't...don't go...if you don't give it all back..."

"I need it, Henry," he said firmly.

Jonah had listened to the conversation. He took the phone back.

"Where is the hotel?"

The man mumbled it out.

Jonah tied his hands behind his back and slapped duct tape across his mouth. He pushed him toward his car parked on the other side of a large dumpster and shoved him in the trunk. At 11:30 he drove his car with the little, pudgy man in its trunk to the hotel's front parking lot. From there he watched the entrance. At 12:30 the thin, dark-haired man he had seen at the craps table drove up to the entrance, left the motor running and rushed in holding an envelope. He returned to the driver's seat in less than two minutes and pulled away. Jonah followed the car until it stopped for gas. Gil went to the lavatory. When he returned Jonah was sitting in the back seat of his car.

He pushed the cold muzzle of his gun into the back of Gil's neck and said,

"Drive until you come to an off-road."

Gil knew who it was. He said,

"I gave back what I could. It's at my hotel desk with Henry's name on it. I don't have all of it..."

"Drive."

Ten minutes later away from the town they came to a turnoff. Jonah pressed the gun's muzzle harder against Gil's neck. He directed him onto a side dirt road and told him to continue driving. Finally, Jonah saw a deserted field with a deep arroyo running through it. Jonah order a terrified, trembling Gil out of the car to the edge of the dry, overgrown ditch and shot him in the head. He took two thousand dollars from his pockets, cut identifying marks from his clothes and rolled him into the gully.

He drove Gil's car back toward town and parked it unseen behind a stand of thick trees about two miles from the gas station where he had left his own car. He walked back to his own car, drove to the alley behind the casino and parked. He opened the trunk and helped Henry out. He removed the duct tape and untied his hands. The man was shaking uncontrollably.

"Mister, please, please, I have a wife. I'll never cheat again. Please..."

Saliva was drooling from his mouth...the front of his pants was wet.

"Give me some identification."

Shaking like a naked man in a freezer, he handed Jonah his driver's license.

"Okay, you can go."

The man stared at him.

"You did as I asked. Your friend didn't."

The man kept staring, motionless. Jonah looked at him with his dead eyes.

"You saw nothing. You heard nothing. Leave Colorado and you'll be safe."

Still too traumatized to move, Jonah pushed him.

"Get your car and go."

The man walked cautiously to the end of the alley not knowing if he would be shot in the back, turned the corner and dashed to his car in front of the casino. Jonah drove his own car to collect the money at the hotel desk.

First, he handed the six thousand dollars he had recovered to the casino's Cashier, then he drove to a large dumpster behind a Chinese restaurant where he disposed of Gil's personal effects and his license plates. From there he drove to the secluded spot where he had hidden Gil's car. Two bullets into a full tank of gas and it exploded in a ball of flame. Gil's worldly possessions, except one, were gone. From the car's trunk Jonah had taken a shiny acoustic guitar. Before he blew up the car he had strummed the instrument with a childlike curiosity, pressing the strings with his fingers this way and that. At one point his fingers accidentally strummed a G-major chord. Its harmony triggered a sensation he had never felt before.

CHAPTER 9
(Present)

I met Arnie again at the townhouse trap…

"I 'ave the key to the apartment across the street, 'ank."

"Good. I have one to my new office. Check your layout and I'll check mine. Have you seen Holden's man?"

"No."

"That could be good or bad. If he's here and we can't see him, that's good. If he's not here, that's bad."

"The Captain won't let ye down."

"Holden and I agreed my working hours are from ten to seven."

"That's almost two 'ours of dark time."

"If he had his way, it would be dark all day. Arnie, do you know why I'm doing this? I want to get the Captain deep in my pocket for when I need him."

"Aye, 'ank. 'e's a powerful officer to 'ave on our side."

Manhattan townhouses generally have about ten or twelve steps from the sidewalk up to the main entrance. The entrance to my studio was beneath those steps about five or six steps down from the sidewalk. At the end of the descent is a window with bars. Behind the window was a room furnished with a reddish area rug, a worn, faux-leather sofa and a matching chair. The walls were a pale gray. Accoutrements of my new trade were on display. Stretched out on a large table was my art restoration in progress, a three-by-four-foot painting of smiling parents, two adoring children and a cuddly dog with sad eyes. It had a stain in its upper right corner. Next to the work table was a massive easel with a cloth hanging over its contents. At its side was a small table adorned with various bottles – chemicals, I assumed – a quiver of brushes and a large cup holding what looked like a variety of scalpels. Two wooden stretchers to hold an art piece tight, a collection of empty frames and shipping tubes of various sizes leaned against the wall. But the *piece de resistance* dominating the assemblage was a device that looked like a cross between a dentist's x-ray machine and a microscope. To see through a painting's canvas, I supposed. The room's last touch was hanging from a wall peg – a white jacket, the kind doctors wear over their regular clothing. Here was my lab, my trap, my grave, if the catch got loose.

I lifted the cloth covering the easel and saw the bait. It was a painting of a mother holding her small daughter's hands while they smiled and danced. I'm not versed in art, but it had a vague recognition for me. I Googled Renoir on my iPhone and there it was. The master's real painting of the same two women was titled "Two Sisters on a Terrace." This painting had the same two women dressed in the same period clothes, but dancing instead of sitting. To my untrained eye, it was an exquisite work. I phoned Tom Holden.

"Tom, I'm in my cage. Do you have a glossary for all these contraptions? I might need to prove my trade."

"I doubt it. The killer only wants to snatch the painting and get rid of you."

"I wish you would phrase things differently. Where in hell is your man? Arnie and I couldn't see him."

"You're not supposed to."

"Right. Well, the bait is absolutely beautiful. I want it when this is over. How did you pull off such a masterpiece? I know you didn't do it."

"Our police artist used an existing painting and changed it around. It's supposed to be an unknown work."

"Your guy could make a fortune forging. Who'd suspect a police artist was a crook on the side?"

"There's a back entrance to the upstairs. Be aware of it. You saw the window with bars next to the entrance."

"Yes, I saw the window. Any news on additional killings?"

"No. Corton has dropped the word into the art world that an unknown Renoir is being repaired by a top-of-the-line conservator."

"And my address as well."

"Yes. We want this over as soon as possible."

"A noble objective. Why waste time?"

"You have your .38?"

"Damn right I do. Arnie is across the street watching the front of the place from a first floor window."

"You'll be fine. There's no reason for the killer to suspect a trap. Only a few people in the art world know about the painting."

"Tom, I'm out of here in two weeks, if he doesn't show."

"Agreed."

"What do you know about Gabriel, the murdered conservator?"

"No leads. It was a pro. That's why we wanted you."

"I'm flattered."

"You'll be okay."

"You keep saying that. Do you know there's an inverse correlation between the number of 'You'll be okays" and actually not being okay?"

"Never heard of such a thing."

"Well, there probably is."

We hung up and I called my new, blond, Mohawk employee, Freddie, for any information he had on my real-money client, Hugh Patterson.

"Yes, I have, Mr....Hank. I found him in an article on

an art theft ten years ago."

He stopped. I waited and finally said,

"And what was in the article, Freddie?"

"The article says three paintings worth over five million each disappeared from Mr. Patterson's studio on Madison Avenue. All were insured. The police questioned Mr. Patterson about the robbery, but didn't go any further with it. Mr. Patterson blamed the theft on the person he bought them from. The article says he was never found."

"Seller's name?"

"John Smith."

"John Smith?"

"The article quotes Mr. Patterson as saying that he bought the paintings from John Smith, but doesn't say for how much."

"Address, anything on John Smith?"

"Nothing in the article. Shall I look into it?"

"No. You'll get a blind trail. John Smith, for Christ's sake."

"Does it say what the paintings were?"

"One was an Andy Warhol. He died in nineteen-eighty-seven. They're worth a lot of money today."

"The other two?"

"It only says they were contemporary artists."

"Anything else?"

"Not on Mr. Patterson."

"Who else?"

"Mr. Jack Harris."

"What, Freddie?"

"He runs a construction company called Harris and Jacobs. There was a scaffolding accident…"

"I got that. Anything on Jacobs?"

"No. Jack Harris's brother, Gerald – the one who lives on Park Avenue – is an art collector. I found an article about his contributions to various museums, mostly in New York, but also in Los Angeles and Chicago. One article has a picture of him at a reception in Chicago with a big smile, holding a drink. There are two attractive women with him, one on each side. I found that he's the Senior Partner at a law firm that advises international companies."

I was surprised Corton didn't know Attorney Gerald. He seemed a player. He only knew his brother Jack in construction. I filed it for a future needle. I thought of Mona's jumpy reaction when I brought up her brother-in-law Jack's name and the two beautiful women at husband Gerald's side. Brother-in-law Jack and a neglected Mona? Interesting, but not very exciting, except for the fifteen million insurance claim in the mix.

"Freddie, is there any way to check on Gerald Harris's finances, brokerage account, say?"

"Brokerage accounts are too protected, but I can check on real estate holdings and mortgages."

"Do it. Do it on construction Jack, too. You found nothing on this Jacobs person?"

"No. He's like a ghost."

"That's what Arnie called him."

"How can you find if he's exists? It's damn hard to hide today."

"I can try for Harris and Jacob's payroll."

"Sharpen your cyber sword and go for it, and anything else you can think of."

"Okay."

He was silent. I was about to sign off when he said apprehensively,

"Hank...am I doing all right?"

"Yes, Freddie. Stay with it. We're going to work well together. Call your aunt and tell her so. I will too, but she'd love to hear from both of us."

"My hair. I think it bothers you and Arnie. I saw you

look at each other..."

"Your hair is your own affair. But I will say this. I can see my own is receding. If there's a healthy crop hiding underneath that bare scalp of yours, I'd let it loose while you have it."

"I never thought of that."

"Let me know what you find on the Harris brothers."

I clicked off and called my NSA friend Bill Sanchez. He might be giving me a hard time lately on my requests, reasonable as they are, but he's staying with me on answering my calls. Before I could speak,

"Gerald and Mona Harris live in one of Manhattan's towers on Park Avenue. Gerald is the senior lawyer in a law firm working for international corporations. His brother Jack heads a construction company with contracts tied to the rebuilding of the World Trade Center. I was unable to get any data on his titular partner, Jacobs."

"That's it? That's what the great and powerful wizard comes up with. The omniscient NSA with headquarters the size of Manhattan Island and satellites spying about in space?"

"Hank..."

"My twenty-seven-year-old assistant with headquarters smaller than a Ping-Pong table and a desktop computer got that."

Coolly, "Hank, there's more."

"Oh."

I let it go, uncomfortable about my editorial. I not only needed him. He's a close friend.

"We have an open file on Jacobs, but all that's in it so far is three payments from Harris and Jacobs, large payments. They went to a numbered account in Bermuda where the trail ended."

"How much?"

"A total of seventy-one million. We picked up the transfers thinking they might be for terrorists groups like Al Qaeda affiliates or ISIS. Once they reach Bermuda we lose contact."

"I apologize for the sarcasm. It appears Jacobs' ghost has been discovered."

"Eh?'

"The nickname Arnie and Freddie gave him."

"There's more."

"Now I really feel bad."

"It won't last. We matched some of the payment amounts to this Jacobs with a series of art thefts and their likely value in the private market."

"Somebody's stealing art, selling it on the private market and sending the money to Bermuda."

"Maybe Jacobs is the thief."

"I'd bet someone is stealing for him."

"Possible. It's not a perfect match, Hank. Don't go too far with it."

"Thanks, Bill."

His spy nose smelled something.

"If you have information, your country would appreciate your sharing it. If that money is going to the wrong people, we have to know."

"I will share whatever I know. Thanks again."

But not right away, I said to myself.

"What about that dinner?"

"I'll speak to Carol tonight."

We rung off and I called Freddie.

"Freddie, see what you can do tracing news reports of stolen art. Put a time line on what you find and the most likely price each piece might bring on the private market. I can have our art-dealer client, Patterson, help on the last part."

"Okay."

It was a bit after 5:00. Arnie was set to start his watch

tomorrow at 9:30 and I was set to enter my studio thirty minutes later. Counting the day ending, which I intended to do, I had to live thirteen more days sitting from 10:00 to 7:00 in a fake art-restoration studio behind a barred window in the bottom of an Upper Westside townhouse. I've talked to enough combat veterans to know that waiting tensely for something possibly fatal to happen can be worse than the fight itself. My own experience bears that out. I did not look forward to the next thirteen days.

When I returned to my office Freddie was hunched forward toward his computer as anxiously as if he were matching numbers to a lottery ticket.

"Save some brain power for tomorrow, Freddie."

He gave me a faraway look then a weak grin.

"Just a little more on this site and I'll call it a day."

"Okay. The door will lock after you. I'm going across the street for a drink."

"Aye," he said with a big smile. I grinned back.

The Thirsty Tongue, a bar-restaurant across from my office on East Fifty-sixth Street, is where I met my large Scottish Associate. He was bartending to support his wife, two young daughters and a mortgage. The downgrade in status started on a dark night when he confronted a black teenager who had just robbed a convenience store. The youth was standing facing Arnie with a knife in one hand and a black pipe in the other. He raised the pipe. Arnie thought it was a gun and shot him. He was dismissed from the force and lost his sergeant's salary and pension. My opening salary was more than he made bartending, but what he really wanted was to get back in the action. If I was offering a desk job, he wasn't interested. The firm earned a huge bonus in a case a while back and I gave him a share of it large enough to pay off his mortgage. Arnie has saved my life twice.

"A glass of pinot, Jake. Your best."

"Haven't seen you for a while, Hank."

"My fault."

"Ever since that guy came in who looks like you..."

He went on.

"Extraordinary resemblance. A little older, I'd say. But he even walked like you. Didn't stay. Just in and out, like he was checking on something."

He handed me the pinot, a David Bruce, Sonoma, California. I took a healthy sip and let him chatter on while I half-listened. He had opened a recent memory some intervening events had buried. The look-alike he was talking about was a half-brother who came into my life about a year ago. Neither of us knew about the other. We share the same mother, now in an Alzheimer's home in Hartsdale, New York. One might say he saved my life or at least helped me save my life. He's a cool character, too cool, about ten years older than I am. His modus operandi, best I could tell, was deal-making whenever he saw a promising opportunity, regardless of the moral aspects accompanying the opportunity. He's wealthy, I'm certain of that. We parted sensibly and knowingly, like friends who could think of no reason to see each other again. He had his way of life; I had mine. He grew up with a sister. I grew up with neither sister nor brother. He has a father who was an Earl before he deserted England and took his fortune with him. My father was a problemed policeman who died drink-by-drink, leaving debts and his .38 as his son's inheritance. The three of them, the Earl, my half-brother and his sister, live happily, I imagine, in Bermuda, probably with an ocean-going yacht.

Bermuda...Bermuda. My god, Ronald. I hope you

aren't mixed up in the transfers…

I quaffed down the rest of the David Bruce.

CHAPTER 10
(2005)

Even if Jonah had cared about his age, he would have had a difficult time determining it. On the hardscrabble farm where he and his "mother" slaved for daily survival the idea of age was not among their thoughts. One got older not by the calendar, but by feeling a sudden pain in the back or a hip or a knee and noticing each passing week and month that it was growing a bit more painful. Then one day, as his "mother" knew, one day the strain of hard labor would overcome a person, perhaps while sleeping or while milking a cow, and the pains would end. His forged driver's license, long expired, offered no help. The seller simply assigned an age he thought matched his looks. Jonah didn't know – or care – that in the year 2005 he was twenty-five.

But he cared about being stopped with an expired driver's license. He was meticulously careful never to exceed the speed limit and always to stop before a yellow light turned red. Isa, however, was concerned. He could lose his enforcer, if he were stopped for simply making a wrong turn. So he arranged for a forged Colorado license good for five years. A picture was required so the forger gave Jonah long, bushy hair and a matching mustache that he could say he had removed should a question of a match come up. If he lost the license, he couldn't be identified by it. For now, his name on the license would remain the one he had created in Nevada from his "mother's" religious musings.

Isa planned to take one hundred percent ownership of a large riverboat casino resting on the east side of the

Mississippi River at St. Louis. It was a far bigger establishment than the one in Colorado and there were few restrictions on its bets; yet it was making less money than the one in Colorado. Isa was convinced cash was being skimmed by his half-owner partner and he wanted Jonah's talents at his side when the subject came up. Isa would take an airplane to St. Louis, but Jonah insisted on driving the thousand miles across eastern Colorado, Kansas and Missouri. His car was his bank and that bank still had two-hundred thousand dollars in hundred dollar bills in its underbelly. Isa didn't know that was why he wanted to drive, but he didn't argue with him. He never argued with Jonah.

Jonah planned to overnight in a motel near Abilene, Kansas, on U.S. 70, about halfway to the riverboat casino. He had looked forward to driving his new BMW across the Kansas flats even though others had told him that it was dull and boring. Isa had disposed of his killer's apartment and its furnishings. All that Jonah owned was either underneath the BMW or in its trunk, except one special item. The shiny acoustic guitar he had taken from the departed Gil was positioned regally on the back seat wrapped in a soft, protective blanket. Over many months Jonah had learned how to arrange his fingers on its strings to find the sounds he wanted. His instructor was an iPod loaded with uncomplicated folk music that he could match on the guitar when his ear caught a sound he wanted. Once he had a chord fixed in his head, his photographic memory locked it in. Months of this had advanced him to a level of some competence. The handsome young man's humanity would always be a lifeless desert, but in that desert there was now a small oasis from which he could drink and, if necessary, deceive.

It was 9:00 p.m. when Jonah pulled into a comfortable motel alongside U.S. 70 just west of Abilene. But for two short stops, he had been behind the wheel for twelve hours. He was hungry, but not tired.

He prepaid one night, faked his registration information and stepped outside. Thick black clouds had formed across the Kansas sky. The air was still and tense, as if it sensed a danger unseen to others. He strolled toward a barn-shaped, roadside inn about a hundred yards away. Pellets of rain had started falling and a westerly puffs were bending a line of tall, windbreaking poplars. Lightning flashed in the distance sending rumbles of thunder and briefly exposing the endless fields of shaven crops on both sides of U.S. 70.

Inside the inn, a country band with an attractive young woman was performing. She was eye-stopping in a bare-shouldered white blouse, a short, plaid skirt and leather boots snugged tightly to her shapely calves. She had a microphone at her lips and was moaning an eyes-closed story of a love painfully lost. People were slow-dancing to the sorrowful tale, moving their bodies in rhythm with its steady, unhurried beat. A few were so close to each other they seemed sewn together. Some of the expressions were faraway and dreamy, some appeared sad and some were lost in ecstasy. The deliberate, grinding movements of a few were so sexual only clothing stood between dancing and intercourse.

Jonah stood at the empty end of the bar and ordered a hamburger, fries and a Coke. Through a window behind the bar flashes of lightning let him watch his BMW parked near the motel's office. He decided it was safe. He turned and stared at the singer. She was titling her head back and forth, closing and opening her eyes as if she were the doleful woman suffering in the song. On one of her turns she saw him alone, looking at her.

Jonah was acceptably handsome and kept himself well-groomed. Perhaps it was his standing away from the others at that bar that drew her attention. Or maybe it was his stance and the curious unsmiling stare he gave her. She turned and with her eyes fixed on him sang the last words of the song's pain in a low, pleading voice "...the storm in my heart will rain its tears until you're in my arms again."

The band ended on a long, blue note and she announced "A short break. We'll be back." A few dancers clapped, but most looked as if they had been awakened from a coma. She took a graceful jump off the raised platform and walked to Jonah. Within a few feet of him, she said,

"I get so caught up in that song I want to cry. Can you help a suffering girl with a drink?"

She was twenty-one-or-two, blonde and perky. Her eyes had not moved from him since she left the stage. His were fixed defensively on her movements as he tracked her coming toward him. He gave no sign of welcome. A husky young man further down the bar started toward her and stopped.

With a big smile she said, "Please...just a Coke."

Jonah turned to the bartender who poured one from the bar hose.

"See, I'm cheap." She grinned and peered over the glass at him.

"Are you alone?"

"Yes. I'm staying at the motel next door."

"Just tonight?"

"Yes."

A waitress set his order on the bar.

"Would you rather sit at a table?"

"Yeah, I would."

She led him from the bar and away from the man who had started for her. The waitress delivered their food and drinks. She sat facing Jonah, crossed her legs and arranged her skirt to show a tantalizing amount of thigh. She freed her hair from a tie and let it fall over her bare shoulders.

It's somewhat known that women who know they're attractive are attracted to men who show no interest in their attractiveness. Some men exploit that fact, but Jonah wasn't exploiting. He was truly uninterested and it challenged her pride.

"Are you staying for our last set?"

"Probably not. I've been driving all day. I need sleep."

With a slight waver in her voice, for human nature abhors rejection, she said,

"I'll be free in forty-five minutes."

Jonah showed no interest in the invitation. She felt a flash of anger at the apparent "No thanks," but her need for acceptance prevailed. She stayed, looking at him. Jonah remained unmoved and ate as if she weren't there. She stood up and touched a hip against his shoulder. In a low, intimate voice she said,

"Not much new ever happens around here. If you are free…"

She stopped. The husky man had arrived and yanked her away from Jonah.

"Knock it off, Hetty. You better leave, mister."

Jonah looked up at him, blank-faced and said,

"It's raining."

"Then you'll get wet. Hetty, you get out of here." The man scowled down at Jonah.

Jonah continued his meal as if he weren't there.

"You got ears, mister?"

He reached out for Jonah's throat. Jonah lowered his powerful arm and rammed his fist up into the man's crotch. He screamed.

"You son of a bitch!"

But he couldn't straighten up. Two other men came hurrying toward Jonah. He remained seated. One of them sensed danger and paused. The other continued.

Jonah stood to meet him, hiding a fork in his hand, waited and jammed it into the fleshy part of the man's shoulder. He fell back in pain.

"Goddam it! You bastard!"

He looked at the man behind him for re-enforcement, but he stood still. Blood was spreading on the man's shirt. He pressed his hand over it. The first man was still hunched over holding his crotch, his face contorted in agony. Jonah sat back in his chair and dipped a French fry into a cup of catsup. From behind the stage a large, portly man hurried toward the confrontation, red-faced and wielding a baseball bat.

"All right. Stop it! Go back to the bar or get out of here you two! Hetty, get up on the stage."

It was the owner who had used the bat before. The two backed away toward the third man.

"You're welcome to stay, stranger," said the owner, "but these two and that one are hot heads and she's a flirt. I've called the State Troopers on them before and I will again. I'll call them now, if you want me to."

"It's not necessary. I'm leaving in the morning."

"Suit yourself."

The owner gave a fierce look at the three now huddled at the bar and walked slowly back to his office. Hetty was frozen. A surge of sexual power had her in its grasp. She had seen Billy's jealousy before, even provoked it, but it had never turned out like this. The men she flirted with always left when Billy confronted them, filling her with a sense of power and superiority. Billy's anger would make him want her more afterwards. But this time Billy was not on her mind…this time she wanted the man who had beaten him, this new man.

Jonah finished his meal, paid and walked past the three without a hint of notice.

Outside, the rain was falling in sheets whitened by the bursts of light above. The thunder was more frequent now and breaking closer. Jonah dashed for his room and shut the door. He dried himself, pulled up the Venetian blinds on a window to check his car and slipped into bed. He was awakened shortly after midnight by a light tapping on the door. He checked the car. Clear. He wasn't going to be patient anymore with the three locals. With his gun behind him he opened the door slowly. Hetty was there soaking wet. To a normal man, it would have been hard to envision a more desirable woman. Her wet blouse clung to her breasts, outlining every curve; her hair was hanging in a wild, primordial way. Her skirt was tight against her thighs.

"Can I come in?"

He opened the door. She looked at his naked chest and muscles.

"I can't go home. He'll beat me."

Jonah closed the door and slipped in the lock chain.

"There are towels in the bathroom."

She went in, stripped, dried herself and emerged holding a long towel across her breasts. Jonah waved his hand at the one bed. She dropped the towel and slid in under the sheet. Across from her, resting on the side table, she saw his gun. It sent the same current bristling through her that she had felt watching him dispatch the three men. He kept his shorts on and slipped under the sheet next to her. She waited. Nothing. She rolled over to face him. Nothing. She ran her hand gently over his shoulder and down his side. Nothing. She touched his outer thigh then moved her hand inside it. Nothing. She raised herself on her shoulder and looked at his face. He was asleep. She rolled away from him, still too excited to sleep. She squeezed her eyes shut, but sleep wouldn't come. In the dark of her eyes she saw his blank, dead face when Billy threatened him and the lack of anger when he stabbed Ted with the fork. Ted seemed no more than a bothersome fly. The desire for sex was fading. Fear and awe were mixing with it, creating a new kind of electricity, one that blended desire, respect, anxiety, need and protection. She wanted him sexually, but he also made her feel safe, safe from the storm, safe from Billy. The sex would come. She was sure of that. The thought helped her sleep. An hour later she heard Billy at the door. He was drunk and screaming hot with anger.

"Open the door, Hetty! I want that son of a bitch. I'm going to beat the shit out of both of you."

Terrified, she reached over to wake Jonah. He was gone. A whisper.

"Say 'I'm coming'."

He was standing flat against the wall next to the door. He motioned for her to stay in bed. She rose up and said,

"I'm coming, Billy."

Jonah removed the chain lock and turned the doorknob slowly. Billy came crashing in, paused when he saw her in bed and fell face first to the floor. Jonah had slammed the butt of his gun into the back of his head. In Billy's right hand was a lug wrench. Jonah started to dress and said calmly,

"Get dressed."

Without thinking, "My clothes are all wet."

He gave her a don't-be-stupid look.

"Stuff them in a pillow case and wrap yourself in a sheet."

She obeyed quickly.

"He's out for two hours."

He put a hundred dollar bill on the bed table.

"Follow me to the car."

The rain had eased, but the wind was fierce. Hetty looked like a specter out of the grave, trying to keep her burial gown from blowing away. Jonah went to the pickup truck and jammed a small pebble into the intake valves on both back tires. The air began hissing out. Hetty was in the back seat wrapped in her sheet as Jonah drove the BMW onto U.S. 70.

"Move the guitar carefully away from you. Don't touch its blanket. Hold your clothes next to an open window. Let the air dry them out."

Once again, she obeyed. Ten, twenty minutes passed.

"Where are we going?"

"I'm going to St. Louis. You can get out whenever you wish. Your boyfriend will be discovered in the morning. He won't call the police. He would have to answer questions about that lug iron. The owner has more than enough to replace his sheet and pillow case."

She absorbed the logic. Fifteen minutes later.

"Do you play the guitar?"

"Yes."

Another ten minutes went by.

"I want to go with you."

Jonah tapped in the phone number of a hotel in St. Louis. In a flat tone he said,

"Isa, I have a girl with me. She's a singer. Needs a job."

A girl, thought Isa. Well, I'll be. Jonah and a girl. The incongruity of it was considerable. He almost immediately said, "Of course," curious about what she might look like. But Isa was a careful man. He always processed several outcomes before making a decision. This time, one of those outcomes was what to do with the girl if she were a helpless waif or, worse, a nosy bitch? But there was another possibility that trumped all the others, the risk of angering Jonah. He had never denied Jonah a request and didn't want to start now. He'd make it work, even if the girl was a nosy shrew.

"Bring her along, Jonah. I'll find a job for her."

CHAPTER 11
(Present)

As always, the soft, mellow taste of the pinot noir warmed my temporal soul and eased the major concerns of Life, in this case, Carol's coolness and the possibility of being shot, garroted or knifed by a professional killer. The first concern was hurtful, but seemed to be healing and even if the coolness changed to ice, the result was survivable. The second one, however, would put a permanent end to my earthly tour.

I paid the bill and walked to the Fifty-ninth Street Express station. The subway is the *sine qua non* of New York. Without its daily movement of people the City would crash. It's why the police and other agencies protect it sedulously. Fifteen minutes later it had me at home in our Greenwich Village apartment. I hung my .38 in the hall closet, flipped off my shoes and flopped on the living room couch. Carol was most likely a half hour away.

Hugh Patterson's hundred thousand dollars was many times bigger than Captain Tom Holden's rate card fee. That's where my energy should be; instead, I was grounded in an artist warren waiting for the Grim Reaper to wield its scythe. To earn the hundred, I needed to talk to Gerald Harris, the art collector lawyer, and his brother Jack, the real estate developer with the ghost partner, Jacobs. I needed to know more about Gerald's wife Mona and her Ming-vase flinch when I mentioned her brother-in-law, Jack. And the meaning of the two beauties at her smiling husband's side. And the money transfers to Bermuda. The deal with Tom Holden was clearly not good business, but neither was asking out of it. Tomorrow morning at 10:00 I'd be doing my duty, working my phone and twiddling my thumbs instead of doing face-to-face interviews for a hundred thousand large ones. Arnie would be twiddling his thumbs across the street. Another waste.

For two weeks.

I called Freddie.

"I have information on the art thefts and the transfers to Bermuda."

I waited.

"Freddie..."

In a rushed voice,

"The news reports I can find say three thefts and three murders all within a week, one in Chicago, two here in New York – Gabriel and, according to *The Times*, a man named Richard Kern in Soho. I guess you knew that, but I also have the names of the artwork that was stolen from them. I can research their value, but you said you had someone who could do that."

"I do. Our client, Hugh Patterson is an art dealer. Email me the list."

"I'm sending it now."

"Your aunt. You said she's settled in her new home."

"Yes."

"Find out where and send a bouquet of flowers from Hank, Arnie and you, say, fifty, sixty dollars. Red roses."

"Okay."

"I'll be in tomorrow about eight-thirty, gone before ten. Anything else?"

"I have this list of art conservators."

"Hold on to it. I'll see you tomorrow."

I re-flopped and re-drifted. Art thefts, murders, private sales, proceeds to Bermuda, end of trail. Whether he was involved or not in this game, it made me think of my Bermudian half-brother, Ronald Mason. It was his kind of deal, except I didn't read him for murder. Killing seemed outside an otherwise broad criminal range; but maybe it wasn't and maybe I didn't want to think he was capable of it. I had no doubts about his willingness to sell stolen art, even arrange for its theft. And it wouldn't be a hard scam for him. He was a world traveler who knew people who could steal and who could pay well to buy a rare piece of art. An unscrupulous middleman was closer to my reading of brother-Ronald. Still, three people are dead because of the thefts. He had to know that. Would he care? I had to admit that he probably wouldn't. Still he helped save my life. He was a blend of straight-up ruthlessness with a splash of charity. I could see him kicking a dog and petting a puppy at the same time. Fortunately, a sizable number of people live in tiny Bermuda, seventy thousand, to be exact. It made me feel better.

"Hank, I need help."

She was balancing three bags of groceries at the front door. I grabbed two of them.

Breathlessly on her way to the kitchen with me following,

"I saw my therapist this afternoon. He feels I'm 'cured' – that's my word. He phrased it differently. He said we should meet again only if I think we should."

I started unloading my bags.

"He had some words about you."

I looked up.

"Compliments, of course."

Opening the refrigerator, "Sort of."

"He thinks I'm a bit off doing what I do."

Putting things in the refrigerator, "Well…"

"I'm sure he understands that I'm helping society."

Closing the refrigerator door,

"He was vague on that point."

"Well, he should, if he's bright. He's bright, I assume."

"Oh, very. Awards and degrees all over his walls."

"Well, if he's helped you, that's all I care."

"Uh, uh."

But it wasn't all I cared. I wanted to know what the s.o.b. said about me. And she knew I did. I pretended disinterest and finished unloading the bags.

"Do we have some red wine?" she asked.

"Uh? Oh, yeah. I'll open a bottle. How about a Chianti Classico?"

"Perfect. I bought some meat ravioli. I'd open the wine and let it breathe."

She moved around the kitchen doing this and that, avoiding eye contact, knowing damn well I was searching for a nonchalant way to get back to what he said about me.

"How was your day?" she asked perfunctorily.

"The usual. I tracked down nine murderers and six thieves."

"That's nice."

"I also rescued two cats from trees."

"No dogs?"

"Since you ask, I snatched a poodle from in front of a bus."

She stopped doing this and that and smiled that wonderful smile at me.

"He said I was lucky to have a hero in love with me."

He didn't say that, of course, but it didn't matter. She said it and I knew the black memories were near their end. She came around the table, kissed me softly and said,

"Let's eat, drink and make love."

"Why in that order?"

"It's more romantic."

And so it was.

My cell rang at 6:30 a.m.

"Hank, I need the man assigned to your watch. Some Mideast king is arriving at the U.N..."

"Tom..."

"But just 'till five. He'll be on station by five-thirty when it's getting dark."

"I feel better."

"It's highly unlikely the killer will try to kill you in daylight. Relax, we're on it, and very appreciative."

I had gone into the bathroom and closed the door.

"Tom, this thing I'm doing cannot get back to Carol. Don't let anyone leave any messages with our new man, Freddie Larson. No one but Arnie."

"Heard and agreed."

"And I'd appreciate a different reason for diverting your man, like 'It's unlikely he will try to steal the Renoir in daylight' instead of '...try to kill you in daylight.' It's easier on my ear."

We logged off. The news wasn't as disturbing as it sounded. I was thinking of doing the same with Arnie. Having him sit idle from 9:30 until dark was wasteful.

I freshened up and outside of her sight I slipped my .38 into the holster in the small of my back. Suited up, I begged off breakfast.

"I'll get a muffin and coffee near the office. Aren't you due for another meeting with your beast – boss Grover – about the quarterly bonus?"

"Tomorrow."

"Any idea?"

"I'm hoping for something in the ten thousand range. The ads on the site have been good, but the Cretan won't let me in on the daily accounting."

This oversight had come up before and usually led to an even more unflattering description of boss-

Grover. She was heating up, another good sign things were returning to normal.

"I'm a major stockholder, damn it. Twenty-five percent. I should see the books as often as he does."

"Absolutely."

"It's not fair. It's not capitalism!"

"Clearly."

"I'll have to face him down on this. It's been two years – two years I've been asking for this!"

"Highly recommended."

I kissed her on the cheek before she could launch more injustices and departed for the subway. Freddie was already in the office, fixed on his laptop. Without looking up,

"I took care of the flowers. Hank."

"Good. Anything on the ghost half of Harris and Jacobs?"

"I tried to break into the payroll."

"No luck?"

"Not yet, but I know someone who can..." He stopped and looked at me.

"I hear no evil and see no evil. Try him."

"It will take a while."

"As soon as possible. I'll be available by phone all day. Let me know what you find."

He nodded okay as Arnie walked in.

I've always admired my friend and ex-sergeant's serenity. I attributed it to a sort of blasé attitude acquired from his nearly twenty years of "seeing it all" on the streets of New York. Not much that happens in the world doesn't happen within the City's five boroughs. I believed that over his career Arnie simply grew an immunity to the wide variety of human behavior he experienced. That's what I thought at first. But after a few personal conversations I realized the equanimity came from something deep inside him. He has a loving wife and two young daughters he adores and who adore him; in other words, he has a happy, fulfilling home life. The realization had me recall a scene from an old movie I happened on late one night called "Save the Tiger" with Jack Lemon. Lemon owned a garment company that was going broke and had an unloving wife who spent all his money. At the end of a particularly stressful day he found himself alone, one-on-one with one of his tailors who said he felt sorry for Lemon. Lemon was startled and asked the man, an elderly Jew who had survived the Holocaust, how, after all he'd been through, he always seemed to be at ease with himself. He stroked his sewing machine and said, "I have my craft and my woman." And that's what Arnie has, plus two lovely daughters for icing. I have a craft and, hopefully, a woman, but for complicated reasons unknown to me I still lacked what my Scottish associate had.

I explained the call from Holden.

"It makes sense for you, too, Arnie. Sitting on your thumbs during daylight hours is a waste. Why don't you see what you can find out about the missing half of Harris and Jacobs, old friends on the force, contacts, anything."

"Aye, 'ank I'll see what I can do. But I'll be across the street at five-thirty."

I nodded and said,

"These thefts are a double score. The owner gets his insurance money and the thief gets his money from a sale to a private collector. Everybody's happy, except the conservator. Bill Sanchez senses some of the money might be going to ISIS or some other terrorist group. NSA has tracked some of it to Bermuda then lost it. Not a good sign."

I paused and said a bit despairingly,

"I'll be in the studio sitting on my ass, as contracted,

but there's no need for you to sit idle."

"Ye 'ave yer phone."

"Right."

He smiled mischievously. "Did ye ask the Captain for a lunch break, 'ank?"

I grinned. "No."

"I'd say ye probably didn't ask because it's a normal thing."

"Right, and I know who to have it with."

"Mona Harris."

"Right. Let's put a tail on Jack Harris. I'd like to confirm a hunch."

"Aye. I know just the man. 'e just retired from the Seventeenth."

I started walking toward Third Avenue to catch a cab to my Upper Westside studio.

The prior evening in a small French restaurant in the East Eighties two people sat at a table for two. A small candle in a short, round glass waved its tiny flame valiantly against gusts of wind when the front door opened for a customer. The checkered table cloth had stains from the liquid wax some strong gusts had lifted out of the glass. The silverware rested on red, cloth napkins underneath small menus. Edith Piaf crooned from an old recording of "*La Vie en Rose*" in the background. One of the people waved off the waiter and said softly to the other,

"I'm uneasy about it."

"Why?"

"Instinct, gut, too easy."

The listener shifted uncomfortably, waved for the waiter to come back, ordered a bottle of Cote de Rhone and said,

"We'll have the wine first."

The two remained quiet, waiting.

"Too easy? What the hell does that mean?"

"It means you're stretching the rubber band by moving again so soon."

The other person shifted again, struggling against anger.

"A missing Renoir. That's good for a hundred million!"

"Probably."

The dissenter leaned back, calming. The waiter pulled the cork, poured and got an approving nod. The two watched as he filled their glasses.

"In a minute," said the agitated one to the waiter, pointing to the menu. They sipped without clicking their glasses. It was 6:30. The tiny room was half full.

The uneasy one asked, "Have you spoken to your associate about it?"

"No."

"Why not…"

No answer.

"Because you think he will feel as I do."

"I'll speak to him when I feel the time is right."

"When you do, I suspect you will get a similar opinion. And suspicion of your judgment."

"What about the old adage striking while the iron is hot? While we have an edge?"

"Do we?"

"Of course, we do. Three successes. A theft in Chicago and two in New York. Not an error. Millions of dollars."

"So speak to him."

Again, the hidden dare.

"If you want to use aphorisms, think about this one. The cautious seldom err. Confucius."

The aggressor leaned back resigned to the situation. The waiter arrived with menus and the two ordered. A customer came in followed by a puff of air that attacked the small candle. Its flame fluttered dangerously over the melted wax, but bravely straightened itself.

On the west side of Central Park, Hank Tower clicked off his cell phone and paced around the ersatz studio like a lion looking for a way out of his cage. It was 10:30 a.m., two hours more of suffering before meeting Mona Harris at the Yale Club near Grand Central Terminal. Tower and Mona's lawyer-husband, Gerald, were both members which, unknown to Tower, made her feel more secure about lunch. Tower had told her that he had a way to speed up the fifteen-million-dollar insurance payment on her stolen painting. It was a lie, but it cinched the lunch.

CHAPTER 12
(2005-2008)

The BMW rolled along at a smooth sixty mph over U.S. 70 through Kansas City, skirting the meandering Missouri River to its north, carrying Jonah and Hetty eastward to the Mississippi riverboat. Taken as one, the Missouri and Mississippi are exceeded only by the Nile and Amazon in length. The two rivers carry an outsized proportion of America's commerce and a gargantuan amount of its mud, as the three million acre delta stretching into the Gulf of Mexico attests. But there was little attention given to rivers or the other aspects of America's vast landscape that the two travelers encountered along their thousand-mile trip. Jonah's eyes were fixed on the road and Hetty's total being was focused on her situation. She was concerned about her livelihood – she had no money and only the clothes she wore on the stage – but a larger worry was her attraction to Jonah. His fearless, quiet self-assurance, his cool, maddening disinterest in her considerable feminine assets and the strange allure of the gun he carried. It all challenged her vanity and excited her sexually. She wanted to be with him, to have him in bed with her, despite a nagging voice trying to warn her of unknown consequences. His distant silence means something you should fear, it said. He's not a lover. He's a disengaged, disinterested, human island riddled with peril. He said she could leave whenever she wished, but she remained with him, admiringly, as they drove farther and farther away from Abilene, Billy and her job. She wanted the adventure, despite the whispering voice.

Jonah pulled into the parking lot in front of a diner

just west of Columbia, Missouri.

"Jonah, I can't go in there. Look at me. I'm half naked. My shoes are still wet. My hair's tangled and stringy. I look terrible."

"What do you want? I'll bring it to you."

"Anything. I'm starving."

"Okay."

She started to say what she would like, but he was already on the stairs to the entrance. A car arrived. She snuggled her near-nakedness under the sheet she had taken from the motel. A tall, burly man, well-dressed with a blond mustache saw her wiggling under the cover as he walked by to the diner. He stopped outside her window.

With a wide grin, "My gosh, lady, you still in bed?"

She looked at him suspiciously.

"No harm. Just ain't seen a young woman pretty as you dressed in a sheet in many a year. You got someone with you?"

Hetty nodded quickly. Inside the diner, Jonah was watching from a booth.

"You look like a starved kitten. Can I get you something?"

She shook her head. The man looked up and saw Jonah looking at him from a window booth.

"That must be your fella, eh?"

She nodded again.

"Well, tell him to get ya some clothes. A lady pretty as you can't go around in a sheet. No telling what will happen."

She smiled weakly and the man went into the diner. He went to Jonah.

"Lad, you need to take care of that lady out there before something happens to her. I've traveled these parts from St. Louis to the Colorado for years and ain't seen something like her before. You married?"

Jonah studied the man. "…traveled these parts…" Would it cause him a problem?

"We ran into a bad storm at our house. We're on our way to a store after we eat."

The man handed Jonah his card.

"Gilbert's, about ten miles down the highway. I've sold to them for fifteen years. Fine store. Top quality. I'll swear to the Almighty on that. Give the owner my name – Manny's his name, short for Manchester. He'll take good care of you."

The waitress handed Jonah a white bag of hot hamburgers and fries and two cans of Coke.

"Don't forget. Tell Manny Big Sam sent ya."

He walked away to the counter. Jonah followed him with his eyes then looked outside to the man's car. A red, crossover Chevy with a Missouri license plate. Boxes were stacked in the back seat. He heard Big Sam at the counter talking to the waitress and anyone else in earshot.

"Ever seen a woman in a sheet in a BMW? Well, ya got one in your parking lot. A beauty. On their way to Gilbert's to dress up. Look like nice people."

Shaking his head and smiling, "America. Damned if ya can't find just about anything in it."

Jonah left for the car and wordlessly handed Hetty the food bag. Big Sam couldn't have known it, but his blaring that the "nice people" were going to Gilbert's might have saved his life. It allowed Jonah to take a different route. Jonah required anonymity which he felt the gregarious salesman had jeopardized. Seeing Hetty dressed in a sheet was a story he would love to tell. Announcing to the diner that Jonah and Hetty were a couple in a BMW going to Gilbert's made Jonah far too easy to identify. So he left U.S. 70 and drove south on Route 63 to U.S. 44. From there, he drove northeast into the southern part of St. Louis while Hetty devoured her sandwiches, not knowing that she, too, as the lady in the sheet was momentarily in danger.

The highway took them to St. Louis's waterfront and past the park beneath the huge arch on the St. Louis side of the river. Watching the signs, he wove his way onto the Eads Bridge, the first to cross the Mississippi, toward East St. Louis, Illinois. From the bridge, Jonah could see the huge casino floating on the Illinois side of the river below. He phoned Isa.

"I'm entering Illinois. I need a place to take the girl. She's not dressed."

Not dressed! Isa loved it. The girl's naked in his car. Damn! If I were only his age...

"Get off at the first exit and pull over. I'll give you directions to a small apartment we've set up for you and the lady. Drop her and come to the casino. You can see the boat from the apartment."

Jonah hung up without a farewell. Fifteen minutes later he pulled up to a three story, brick-faced building with a small parking lot. He got the keys to 3C from the superintendent and walked his sheet-covered companion to their new residence. She was ecstatic.

"Jonah, it's just right! How did you...I don't care. Is it mine, ours?"

"Yes."

Standing at the large bay window she could see the river and on its other side a shining, stainless steel, six-hundred-and thirty-foot arch proclaiming St. Louis as the Gateway to the West. To her right was a modern kitchen stocked with plates, flatware and other essentials. Behind her was a large bedroom with an *en suite* bath and two white robes hanging in it. There was a king-size bed decorated by a luxurious gold-colored bedspread and four colorful throw pillows. On a side table, two flute glasses stood next to an ice bucket with a bottle of champagne dripping rivulets of moisture down its sides. She pulled back the spread and, looking at Jonah, ran her hand over the satin sheets. It was a love nest and a far, far more comfortable home than the one she had shared with Billy. Whoever did it, Jonah or someone else, its intended use was not lost on Hetty.

"Jonah, let me shower and do something with my hair. Please have a glass of champagne and wait for me."

He nodded and gazed out the window, fascinated by the gleaming arch and the powerful tugs pushing quarter miles of barges filled with coal, steel, sand, grain and gravel, some moving effortlessly down river and others straining against the current upriver. He went to the champagne bottle and poured a glass for Hetty. Moments later she emerged from the bathroom, her hair somehow neatened and spread over her shoulders in a show of blonde femininity. Her robe was cinched tightly around her waist with a V that showed her skin flush from the shower down to her navel. She went to the glass, raised it and set it down untouched. She looked at him and started undoing the robe's tie. He stepped forward quickly.

"I want to hear you sing."

She would have flown, if that was what it took to get him in bed with her. But he made no move in that direction. He just stood, looking into her eyes, waiting. She twirled around, holding the open robe close to her body. In a melody of her childhood she started to sing.

"Wait."

He rushed out of the room and returned minutes later with his guitar.

"Again, Hetty."

She started her song on a G note.

"Hold it."

He found the chord and asked her to follow him as he tried all the chords he had learned. The simple duet was childlike to Hetty, but for the first time since meeting him she detected a softening around the mouth and a glow in his eyes. She knelt next to him and responded to his changing chords. With fear in her heart, she moved her hand slowly up the inside of his thigh. The tight muscle seemed to relax. He continued changing chords and she followed with her voice. She rose, letting the robe fall open and was leaning forward to kiss him when Jonah's cell phone rang, instantly changing his mood. It was Isa.

"I need you, Jonah. Whatever you're doing can wait. An important meeting is starting in ten minutes."

He stood abruptly, wrapped his guitar in its blanket and was out the door. Hetty fell on the bed, shaking, caught in a whirlpool of anger and frustration. My god, what do I have to do, she thought? What do I have to do? She dug her fingers into a reddish throw pillow so violently they perforated its thin cover.

A round poker table with six chairs occupied the middle of the room. A long bar packed with an array of whiskies, gins, vodkas, rums and mixers dominated an entire wall. Across from the bar was a large, disorganized desk with file cabinets on either side of it. Above the cabinets were pictures of nineteenth-century, two-stack, stern wheelers navigating the river near the levee on the St. Louis side of the river. The magnificent Gateway arch with smaller buildings behind it was framed in a large rectangular window on the west side of the room. Isa entered followed by Jonah. Three men were seated at the round table. One of them rose, smiling, with his hand out to greet Isa; another smiled at him from his chair; the third remained hard-faced with his eyes trained on Jonah.

"Isa, welcome. We haven't seen each other for, what,

five years? Far too long. Please have a seat. This is my CFO, Eddie Garth and our Security Chief, Johnny Marino."

Isa scanned the two carefully and said,

"This is my associate, Jonah Flood. I want him privy to whatever we discuss. I did some memory work on the way here, Victor. It's six years. As you say, far too long. The place has expanded. I even smell fresh paint." Smiling,

"Is that for me?"

Victor ignored the question. "We have doubled the number of slots and added baccarat and some wheel games. We have three restaurants now and a nightclub. We're open twenty-two hours a day."

Isa laid his briefcase on the table. "Business is good?"

"It can always be better, but we're doing well. I've sent you reports."

"Yes, I've seen them. They're thorough. One of them even had the cost of bathroom cleaning broken out."

"We have eighteen of them."

Isa removed a manila folder from the briefcase.

"Including your private one?"

Suspiciously, "Yes."

"Victor, I have a proposition for you I think you'll like. I have grown tired of the mountains and deserts. I'm getting older, I guess. I need more civilization around me. You, however, you're fifteen years younger than I am. You have a young man's ambition. Me, I want to coast, relax, spend some of my money, enjoy some travel. You'll see what I mean when you reach your sixties."

Victor was listening with suspicious eyes. Eddie Garth was shifting positions in his chair expectantly. Jerry Marino was fixed on Jonah.

"So I propose you take over the Colorado and Nevada casinos and I take over this one."

Victor looked blankly at Isa.

"Now, I know this business is bigger than those I'm offering, but with the cash I'm prepared to include you can do with them what you have done here. It's the American way. The old giving the young an opportunity to grow."

A cynical smile flashed across Victor's face.

"Isa, you haven't changed. How much cash?"

"Twenty million."

"I handle that much in a month. Why would I want to do what you propose?"

"Opportunity, Victor. The West is where the growth is. There's room for expansion. With your talents you could double, triple the handle in a couple of years."

"We're fifty-fifty here, right?"

Isa nodded.

"With only a modest growth rate, I can make more money staying here enlarging my half."

The moment had come.

"The handle, yes, but your profits are subpar. It's better for you to have one-hundred percent control of an operation, so you can watch your profits more carefully."

Victor's face was reddening.

Isa turned to the CFO sitting next to Victor.

"Eddie, you know the percentages. Why is the Golden Swan not meeting the averages?"

Eddie looked at Victor for guidance.

Victor was fixed on Isa with gritted teeth. He said,

"My sixty-something-year old friend I have no intention of selling my half. And that mountain-and-desert routine is a silo full of bullshit. The Swan does well, that's why you want it..."

"But, Victor, your profit is miserable."

Isa turned to Johnny Marino. "Is someone stealing from the Swan, Johnny?"

Johnny did not turn to Victor for direction. He simply said no without a change of expression.

"Jonah and I will stay until you realize the size of the opportunity I'm offering you. Think of it. A fresh start, full control of an existing, very profitable business, release from an unprofitable business and twenty million dollars in working capital. I'm staying nearby. Here's my cell phone number. Call me tomorrow after you and Eddie and Johnny have a chance to think it over."

He got up and looked around. "What a shitty room. It'll be my first renovation."

He looked at a seething Victor and put the manila envelope with blank sheets of paper in it back in his briefcase.

"Call me, Victor. Let's not let this get out of hand."

He went to the door. Jonah followed, watching Johnny Marino carefully.

Outside in a rare act of questioning his boss, Jonah asked,

"Is it worth twenty million and the other casinos?"

"Barely, but I have no intention of making the deal, even if he agrees to it, which he won't. The next step, Jonah, is yours. First the Marino hood then Victor, if necessary, but after Marino I think he'll agree to whatever I finally offer. He's smart and he cheats, but he has no real balls. Once this is done, I have a five-year plan to make this boat the showcase of the Midwest, then we're off on another adventure."

They were walking the wide gangplank from the boat to shore. The river was rushing dangerously beneath it. Isa asked,

"What about the girl?"

"She should stay here and sing."

"Good. I'll make sure it's taken care of." He paused.

"It will take Victor minutes to find out that I'm staying in a hotel across the river." Smiling, "Ready to defend your boss?"

Looking down at the Mississippi's fast current,

"I'm already on the job."

CHAPTER 13
(Present)

"'ank, I'm drawing a zero on Jacobs. I've talked to three sergeants I know who were on the scaffolding case, but once it went civil they were reassigned."

"Is there a way to get the transcript of the civil case?"

"Aye, there might be."

"Give it a go. I'm buried in this tomb staring at walls. If it weren't for the tie in with Patterson and his hundred thousand, I'd beg out of the deal with Holden. I'm seeing Mona Harris at the Yale Club at twelve-thirty. Her husband and brother-in-law are next."

'She may 'ave an idea about Jacobs."

"I'll find out. I'm surprised at the anonymity. Hiding today is damn near impossible."

"Maybe 'e doesn't exist."

"He probably doesn't. The name could be code for disbursing money from the sale of the stolen art. That's why Sanchez is interested. But I don't think he's our best route to Gabriel's killer."

"Who do ye think is, 'ank?"

"My gut? Mona Harris. She blanched when I brought up her brother-in-law during our talk."

"Let's go for the brother-in-law."

"I will, but he'll clam up. So will her husband, Gerald. She'll be easier to work, especially if she has something in play with brother-in law Jack."

"Do ye think she's involved in the murders?"

"No, but her husband Gerald or her brother-in-law, Jack, could be. Jack's in construction. That's an up and down business. In New York it's also rough and tumble."

"And the husband, the lawyer?"

"Gerald? I can't say. He may like women, but that doesn't make him a murderer. Still, he could be having money troubles. People do desperate things sometimes to maintain their lifestyle."

"Do ye 'ave an idea 'ow much the three pieces could get?"

"According to our client the Picasso could go for twenty million. Freddie has the names of the Chicago and Soho pieces. I'll get their value from Patterson."

" 'ow many people know about your set up, 'ank?"

"Holden said four, but I know from our Venice case that word spreads like pollen in the art world. By now, there could be many times four."

"That's good and bad."

I chuckled. "I know. See if you can get a transcript and let me know. Any good stuff on Jacobs will get us points with Sanchez and NSA."

"Be careful, 'ank."

"I'm all right, just bored and restless. Twelve more days to go, unless I renegotiate with Holden."

At noon I caught a cab for the Yale Club.

Vanderbilt Avenue, a short street that runs between the Yale Club and the MetLife Building, was at present a mess of construction barriers surrounding large holes that exposed part of the maze of pipes and cables and tunnels that make up the City under the City. The driver found a way through it all and dropped me at the front door. Mona Harris was sitting in the foyer waiting for me.

"Mrs. Harris, thank you for meeting with me once again."

She rose and said, "I hope I can thank you, Mr. Tower. If you can speed up the insurance payment, Gerald and I will be the grateful ones."

"Let's go to the Grill Room. It's been fancied up, if

you haven't seen it for a while."

We rode the elevator in silence and were led to a window table for two. Mona Harris wasn't a half-inch over five-foot-two, but that five-foot-two sported a firm and shapely figure, an observation my trained eye missed when we met in her apartment. I blame her rather bland attire at the time. This time, she was far more striking in a red jacket over a tight beige sweater and black pants with a tiny, multi-colored scarf wrapped around her neck. She wasn't a stunning woman, but there was definitely sexual appeal. An eager male could easily imagine an enjoyable romp.

With a glint of playfulness in her eyes,

"Am I about to hear another confession, Mr. Tower?"

"Maybe, but before I declare let's order. Would you like a drink?"

"Yes, a vodka martini with a lemon peel."

That surprised me. I ordered a glass of pinot noir, slightly chilled.

"Did you go to Yale, Mr. Tower?"

"No. I used to work for the government. My expense account included several clubs. I was able to remain a member in a few of them at my own expense after I left."

"What kind of work did you do?"

"Various."

"That's so vague it must mean spy. Spies can lie very effectively."

Our drinks arrived. We sipped and looked at each other. She said,

"So what is the real reason for this lunch?"

Little Ms. Romp was perceptive, which saved me from making another confession.

"The Jacobs half of your brother-in-law's firm. He's a mystery I hope you can help me with."

"That's easy. Jack wanted another name on his letterhead. Harris Construction was not weighty enough for him."

"Jacobs doesn't exist?"

"No."

"Thank you. Do many people know that?"

"I doubt it. Jack refers to him as an inactive investor in the firm. Now, Mr. Tower, I want a favor from you."

I looked up surprised.

"I know you know important people. Not that long ago I was a research analyst for a criminal law firm, if you want to know how I know that. I want you to do what you lied about to get me here – speed up the insurance payment."

"The fifteen million."

"Yes."

"Has the company given you a time frame?"

"Six to nine months."

"That's not so long. Time flies."

"I need – want – it before the end of the year. That's weeks away."

I smiled nicely. "Are you hiring me, Mrs. Harris?"

She cocked her head coquettishly, "Catching you as a spy isn't enough to get your cooperation?"

"Spy is your conclusion."

"Okay, I'm hiring you. How much?"

To choose a flat fee or a percentage of the fifteen million was going through my mind. I decided that a percentage has a softer feel than a flat fee.

"Five percent.

Without hesitation, "One percent."

It was still a bonanza, if I pulled it off. All I had to do, all I could do, was get to the right person at the insurance company. Corton the Omniscient could help me there.

"Okay, it's a deal. I'll have a contract delivered to you. What's the name of the insurance company?"

Raising her eyebrows, "You don't trust me?"

"Of course, but things happen in today's busy life. If you were hit by a bus, your husband, Gerald, could tell me to take a walk."

"I see. The company is Indemnity Assurance. They're headquartered in Manhattan. Deliver it to my doorman. He'll get it to me."

She went quiet and her face assumed a serious look. She turned to face the window, drifting away.

"Are you ready to order," asked the waiter? I said we were.

She grabbed the menu, as if it were a welcome diversion from more conversation. She had what she came for and there was no reason for her to stay any longer, except for politeness. She ordered soup and a half sandwich. I did the same.

"Mrs. Harris, do you expect Gerald home soon? I'd like to meet him."

Innocently, "Why?"

"A man has been murdered and your husband was one of the last to see him alive. He could help me find the killer."

"I see."

I paused and said, "Are you aware another art conservator was murdered in Soho?"

It brought her back from the drift. "No, I…"

"And a valuable painting he was restoring was stolen?"

She was shaking her head slowly.

"Or the murder of another art restorer in Chicago a short time before Gabriel was killed?"

"No, I…I…"

She was wide awake now.

"All three killings were necessary to prevent the thief's identification. The real motive was to steal the art and sell it on the private market. I suspect the other two pieces were worth as much as yours, perhaps more. I'm finding out, but it's not unreasonable to assume all three could have sold for close to a hundred million dollars in today's market."

"Mr. Tower, I'm not aware, I had no idea…do you think Jack's in danger?"

"You mean Gerald."

She flushed. "Yes, of course, Gerald."

"Mrs. Harris, my office has a picture of your husband at an art show reception in Chicago. I'm told that he looks very happy, bubbly happy. He has a drink in his hand and there are two beautiful women at his side."

She stiffened and jutted her chin toward the window. The muscles in her cheek tightened. I had hit a dander button. Now, if I could work that…but there was no need to. She jerked her head back to me.

"Gerald is a philanderer, Mr. Tower. I stay with him for appearances. If what you say is true, he's making it very hard for me to play the good wife."

"It's true, Mrs. Harris."

I waited. The gentle, soft-hearted Park Avenue lady I had originally opined was descending into the criminal researcher she said she once was.

"You're good. I saw you note my reaction when you brought up Jack. I wasn't prepared for it. Jack and I have had some encounters over the last year. I could say Gerald's behavior drove me to it and that's certainly part of it. I wanted an affair and Jack was handy and willing."

She paused. "This is between client and detective, Mr. Tower."

"Of course. I have no interest in private lives unless they have a bearing on a case I'm on. My interest is catching the person who killed Gabriel...and getting the insurance money for you before the end of the year."

She stared at me silently.

"You said Gerald owned the Picasso. That means the insurance money will go to him."

"And then to me."

I gave her a questioning look.

"Through a divorce. Gerald should have remembered my past. I have a drawer full of evidence on him despite his juvenile attempts at concealment. I only need to date and file the complaint."

"Can you help me with Gabriel's murder?"

She smiled sardonically at the implication. "Gerald's a womanizer, but he's not a murderer. No I can't."

The soups and half-sandwiches arrived and we went silent. A womanizer but not a murderer. Lover-Jack was also a womanizer, at least a one-woman womanizer. I wondered if he had a dark side, but her soft spot for her brother-in-law had to be considered. I had enough information from her for one sitting. I'd work her for lover-Jack at another time, after I knew more about him – and Gerald.

Fifteen million to Gerald then to Mona through divorce. Was Jack counting on the fifteen after Mona had it? Was his construction business solvent? Lots of financial leveraging in the world of real estate. If rents or sales don't meet the Pro Formas, the pain is severe.

The doorman signaled for a cab hiding inside the construction mess which I gave to Mona. I walked across Vanderbilt into Grand Central and took the subway shuttle to Times Square. From there I took the Seventh Avenue line uptown to my phony studio on the west side of Central Park. In the crushing quiet inside, I phoned Freddie the contract info and told him to take it personally to the doorman at 740 Park, then called my New York guru, Edgar Corton.

"Edgar, I'm calling to remind you that my days are numbered. A killer stalks me as I speak. He could be aiming a rifle at me this very moment."

"Hank, I didn't know you were involved..."

"I know, but I want you to feel guilty so I can get a favor from you."

"That's honest."

"Sometimes honesty works, but you have to be careful with it."

"What can I do?"

"The Harris's of Park Avenue, the ones who had the Picasso stolen, are seeking the fifteen million in insurance on it. The company's Indemnity Assurance. I'll get a good fee if I can have the proceeds to Gerald Harris before the end of the year. I need a name."

Silence. Unusual.

"Think of the guilt this tiny favor will free you from. You'll enjoy your five-star meals with a clearer conscience knowing my heirs are provided for. Are you there?"

"I'm in my computer."

"Splendid."

"Harold Bullard."

"What's his position?"

"Executive Vice President."

"Splendid again. Can I use your name?"

"Yes. He's an old timer and a bit cranky, but smart. He's been with Indemnity since he was twenty something. I'd say he was seventy now. We had lunch about a month ago."

"Where?"

"The Gotham Bar and Grill."

"That's near where I live in Greenwich Village. I didn't know you ventured that far south."

"He suggested it. It's not bad."

A high compliment from my gourmet friend.

"Thanks, Edgar. As soon as I'm out of this rat hole we have to have dinner. How's Collin Brothers treating you?"

"Excellently. I've brought in above my salary so far."

"With more to come. Thanks again."

I phoned Arnie.

"Aye, 'ank, is everything all right?"

"All except my Type A nervous system. I had lunch with Mona Harris. Scratch hunting for Jacobs and the court transcript. He's nonexistent. It may be a code name for illegal money transfers, however. I'll see what Freddie found out from his friend. If he's got something meaningful, I'll pass it to Sanchez and that will be that. Mona and her brother-in-law Jack Harris have a thing going. Keep the tail on him. He may have more going on."

"I got a call from Patterson."

"I'll call him when we're through."

"I feel we're nibbling at the edges, 'ank. Gabriel's murderer is no closer to us than when we started. If it's a pro, we may never find him."

"The only way to the killer that I can see is to find the person behind these thefts."

"Even then, 'ank, we may not get to the killer."

"I know. This trap Holden set up with me, I don't think it's going to work."

" 'ow do you see it?"

"The brain behind the enterprise won't want to press it, not after three murders so close together. He or she will let it cool. My sitting here in this cave for another twelve days seems pointless."

"Aye, 'ank. I would talk to the Captain. We could set up a camera. The address is out there."

Arnie is salt-of-the-earth practical. I called Captain Tom Holden.

In a private lounge area in the lobby of a midtown

hotel the same two people who had met in the small French restaurant earlier are taking their seats.

"Did you try your strike-when-the-iron's-hot theory?" asked one of them.

"Yeah. Confucius won. Everything is on hold until further notice."

Signaling a waiter for drinks,

"People should pay more attention to the wisdom of the past. I venture there would be much less disappointment in the world."

"I still think I'm right. In fact, I know where the lost Renoir is being restored right now."

"Do you? And you want to go for it."

"Yeah."

"That means that you don't think the police have connected any dots, they're busy with other things."

"Not exactly..."

"And that they're not aware of the Renoir."

"I don't see how. It came to me confidentially."

"Did it? Then I'm sure the police don't know about it. Your source is obviously the only one who knows."

"Well, I don't know for..."

"You think it's possible someone else may know about it?"

"Well, the restorer would..."

"Three murders in a week; but then you don't believe the restorer reads the papers, and none of his friends do either."

"Well, there's the possibility that a friend called him..."

"Yes, there's a possibility."

The waiter arrived. Each ordered a drink.

"Now, do you see why you're not running things?"

Stiffening, "Okay. That's enough."

The speaker leaned back and said,

"It's an obvious trap and even if it isn't, caution is always the wiser course. We will wait until the trap tires and something else is in the news before we resume. You agree?"

The chastised one nodded slightly, but said nothing.

"Stay with what we love best, beautiful women," said the cautious one, smiling.

CHAPTER 14
(2008)

Isa handed Jonah the name and room number of the hotel where he was staying across the Mississippi in St. Louis. They had just walked off the wide gangway that connects the Golden Swan to Illinois.

"Victor's hot as hellfire. He'll have the Security guy, Marino, after me as soon as it's dark. He may have help with him."

Jonah was reading the note Isa had given him. He nodded and looked up at the Eads Bridge above them. "Will he cross this bridge?"

"Yes, it has a walkway. A car would be a liability, if he had to disappear. The walkway is about a mile long and narrow. There's no place to hide on it."

"It looks like there's construction on the road alongside it. I can see the cars are passing a distance from the edge of the bridge."

Isa agreed and pointed out how Jonah could ambush Marino in the walkway from the construction lane. How Jonah would get there without being discovered was a problem Isa didn't want to think about, nor did he want to question Jonah's talents. Instead, he acted as if there weren't any possibility of a problem, that Jonah would find a way and handle Marino effectively. He would not question how. Nor would he repeat the possibility that Marino may have a helper or two. All he said to his killer-employee was,

"There's a better-than-average bonus waiting for you when Marino's gone, Jonah."

Jonah nodded silently, still studying the bridge, and said,

"It's four-thirty. I'll be back when it's time."

Isa said, "I have a gun in my hotel room," then smiling at Jonah,

"But I won't need it. Phone me when you have something."

Isa walked to his car in a nearby parking lot and Jonah drove his the few hundred yards to the apartment. Hetty was in her robe, asleep on the bed with her shapely legs spread bare across a satin sheet. Jonah half-noticed her and uncovered his guitar. He began strumming a country song he had heard on the radio while he and Hetty drove across Missouri. The melody brought her to an upright position against the headboard. She knew the song he was playing and started to sing when he came to the melancholy lyric,

"My Lord above, I need the sweetness of Heaven, so the pain on my heart will hurt no more."

Jonah glanced up at her and quickly returned his eyes to the guitar's strings. She dropped her legs over the side of the bed and continued to sing until Jonah had finished the song. He looked at her briefly unsmiling and caught her looking at him with an expression half pleading for him to take her and half dreading that he wouldn't. She held her eyes longingly on him, her body partially exposed, waiting. He set the guitar aside, covered it tenderly and walked to her. He stopped two feet in front of her. She gazed up at him hopefully, but it wasn't meant to be. He said dryly,

"I'm taking a shower and leaving. I'm not sure when I'll be back. Isa has a singing job for you."

He started for the bathroom.

"Jonah."

"Yeah?"

"I...I..." She dropped her head. "Nothing...nothing."

He closed the bathroom door and turned on the

shower. Moments later he returned to the room wrapped in a towel and opened his suitcase. From it he took a pair of black tapered pants, a black turtleneck sweater, a pair of black socks and black shoes with soft rubber soles, black gloves and a black ski mask. Hetty watched him dress, fascination replacing her aching libido. He strapped a knife to his leg and holding his gun wrapped black tape around its butt and barrel. He shoved it inside his belt.

She knew. Before it was suspicion; now, it was fact. The man she wanted more than any other man she had known, the man who had let her in, protected her, when a drunken Billy would have beaten her, the man who was giving her a new job, a new life, she now knew was a professional killer. But it didn't frighten her. Instead, the danger, the excitement from such a forbidden knowledge made her wish for him even stronger. He was power, the ultimate power, the power to take human life. Who was he going to kill? The man named Isa? No, she was certain that he worked for him, that he was the person responsible for the apartment. It was someone at the huge casino on the river she could see from a window. That's why they were here. That's where Isa got her the job. But who? The owner, of course. Jonah was going to kill the owner for his boss, Isa. A warm tingle went through her. She wanted to go with him. She wanted to see him kill. The hideous thought shook her imagination awake. What's happening to me? How could I even think such a thing?

The last shade of sunlight hung heavily behind downtown St. Louis, silhouetting its high rises, giving the towering arch a stunning copper glow and bouncing dim ripples of light off the undulating current of the river. In a few minutes it would be dark.

"I'll be back late. I would stay away from the casino. We'll go there later when I meet Isa."

She nodded. "Later." Will he be alive later? What happens to me, if he isn't, she thought?

Jonah slipped on an old brown suit coat to hide his blackness and closed the door quietly behind him. Hetty cinched the robe around her and went to the window. A few minutes later she saw Jonah's car leave the parking lot and drive toward the river. He turned and she lost sight of him.

He pulled into a small parking lot behind the casino's main lot, put his brown suit coat in the back seat and faded into the night's shadows. There was a long series of steps up to the walkway on the bridge. A short way up a locked gate barred further advance with a sign stating the walkway was closed after dark. "Violators will be prosecuted" it said, and substantiated the warning with the number of State of Illinois statutes. This is good, he thought, for me and for Johnny Marino. It will let him pass unseen to the St. Louis side. It will also lock out bystanders.

Jonah jumped the gate and like a shadow inside a shadow walked slowly up the rest of the steps. At its top, the bridge was night-lighted and oncoming headlights were passing frequently. If he were caught in the lights of one his disguise would certainly arouse suspicion. Given the prevalence of car phones and today's fear of terrorists, he could easily be reported to 911 and trapped once the police arrived. He wondered if Marino had thought of that, if he were also disguised and thought of the terrorist possibility. It was a worry. He couldn't allow Marino to be caught or shot by the police. The plan was for Victor to know that Isa had killed Marino, and would kill him, if he didn't sell out.

On the road side of the walkway was the construction paraphernalia he thought he saw from below. A lane was being repaved. Inside the work lane, spaced about fifteen feet apart, were the orange and white rubber drums used to warn traffic. Jonah advanced along the walkway hunched over inside its wall to avoid the oncoming lights. He was now above the first of two massive stone caissons dug deep into the river bed, supporting the long, hundred-and-forty-year-old span. His goal was a point halfway between these caissons and the next one, a point that would put him dead center above the Mississippi. He kept his head low and waited for a break in the traffic then slipped over the railing of the walkway into the construction lane. During other breaks in the traffic coming toward him he slowly moved one then another of the drums closer together to form a barrier against the oncoming lights. He waited for another break and tightened their proximity until he was confident they protected him from discovery. His black attire camouflaged him from drivers traveling west toward St. Louis in the far lane; now he was hidden from the eastward traffic. He was ready. All he needed was his prey.

Marino and a companion were now approaching Jonah's position in the middle of the bridge. What ensued might have been more difficult, but for the fortuitous rumble of the St. Louis MetroLink passing on the tracks below the roadbed. The noise of the train diverted the two men's attention and buried the sounds he made sliding over the railing onto the walkway. He was now behind the two would-be Isa killers. Jonah was prepared for two men. Three would have been difficult. Johnny Marino and his assistant were now only feet ahead of him. He could hear them speaking.

"When we're done with Isa, I want the other one," said the Security Chief killer.

"He's yours, Johnny. I'm out as soon as Isa's dead."

"Afraid?"

"Cautious. He looks different. Sort of supernatural. Something like that."

Now, they were only six feet ahead of Jonah. The cautious one was walking behind Marino. He didn't have a chance. Jonah was holding his knife in his right hand. He caught the killer around the neck, held him in the crook of his left arm, pulled back his head and pushed the knife into his kidney. The man uttered a groan and fell to the platform. Marino heard the noise, turned, saw Jonah standing over his cohort with his knife out. He reached for his gun. Jonah lowered his arm and underhanded the knife into Marino's stomach. He bent forward, still holding his gun. He started to raise it, but it was too late. Jonah kicked him under the chin with his heavy shoe, flipping his head back violently, took hold of the knife's handle and shoved it up into Marino's heart. He fell forward, blood running from his mouth. Jonah pulled his body on top of the other man's to keep the blood off the walkway. He took both of their wallets and soaked them in Marino's blood. Hunched as low as possible, he peered over the inside railing. The cars were moving normally both ways. The walkway was dark and empty to the east and west.

Below, tugs were pushing long lines of connected barges north and south between the two massive caissons supporting the center of the bridge. Jonah folded Marino's assistant over the outer railing of the walkway and waited for an oncoming tug to move its powerful searchlight to one of the caissons and dropped the body into one of the four long barges being pushed north against the river's current. He hunched down again and waited until there were no tugs, only black water below. He raised Marino to the railing and dropped him. The river's flow would take the body several miles south before it would finally snag on a branch hanging over the river's edge like a witch's hand. He unfolded a large Ziploc bag and put the two wallets in it. Finally, hunched below the railing of the walkway, he moved quickly back toward the Illinois side, climbed over the "Violators Will Be Prosecuted" gate and, hidden by the darkness, walked to his car. He called Isa.

"It's done. There were two."

"The bodies?"

"One is going north on a gravel barge; the other is floating south."

"Which one's Marino?"

"The floater."

"Good. The body will be discovered eventually, convincing Victor, if he needs any more convincing. You have the wallets?"

"Yes."

"Have them delivered FedEx tomorrow as early as possible. Don't touch anything in them."

"I didn't."

"Good."

Isa paused. Jonah waited.

"I need you for another week, then you can do what you wish. Your bonus is a hundred thousand dollars. Take some of it and your girl for a vacation."

Jonah was silent. Isa knew his quiet had nothing to do with the money – it was his attitude toward women.

"Jonah, I've seen and done everything a man can do in my lifetime and can say with authority. The best of all pleasures is a beautiful woman. Don't let it escape you."

Dispassionately, "I'll have the wallets delivered tomorrow."

Jonah found a row of garbage cans and shoved his bloodied gloves midway into one of them. An inspection of the rest of his cloths revealed only a streak of dark red on the front of his left trouser leg. His sweater, the dark, pullover hat, shoes and socks were clean. He wiped his knife on some grass intending to wash it thoroughly in the apartment. He went to his car in the small parking lot, slid underneath it and extracted five hundred dollars from its safe. From there, he drove the few hundred yards back to the apartment building.

Hetty was still in her robe when he entered. She had no other choice. Her only clothes were her Abilene attire. He passed by her without a word and went directly to the bathroom. Behind the closed door, he washed the knife clean, stripped and removed the leg holster. He slipped on the clothes he had previously worn and put the Ziploc bag in a drawer in the sink's cabinet. Hetty's eyes were fixed in wild curiosity when he emerged. Before she could say anything, he said in a matter-of-fact tone,

"You need clothes. Tomorrow morning we'll go to a store. I have some money for you."

He held out the five hundred dollar bills taken from his car safe. She took them respectfully, staring back and forth from the bills to him. She had seen a hundred dollar bill only once before when the donor offered her one for a few minutes in his car with him. She'd never seen five of them at once. They held her gaze for a few seconds before she looked back at Jonah to thank him. He said quickly,

"We'll stay here tonight. Tomorrow, I have an errand then I'll take you to some stores."

Hetty was still lost in a swirl of where-have-you-been, what-have-you-done, but her chance to shop with five hundred dollars was blurring her focus. And so was something else. Jonah's gift carried more than the promise of new clothes. It let her fantasize him as her provider and protector, her lover. Such a gift would never have come from Billy. Even if he could have afforded it, he would not have thought of it.

It was 11:30 and she and Jonah were here for the night in one bed, as they were when Billy broke into their motel room. Jonah was tired then. Will he be tonight? If he plays the guitar and I sing, will that help? She decided it wouldn't. They had done it before and it didn't change him. She tried another approach.

"Jonah, you must be tired. If you take off your clothes I'll give you a massage."

He looked upbeat. "I would like that."

He stripped down to his Jockey shorts and lay face down on the bed. She straddled his back with her knees and began moving her fingers into his neck and shoulder muscles. They were firm, but not tight. Whatever he did tonight, it didn't tense him. She dug her fingers deeper into his smooth, nearly flawless skin then moved her hands to his sides and up under his arms. The effect was to excite herself. She wanted to roll him over and kiss him deeply and...

A snore, slight and soft, but a snore. She rolled over onto her side of the bed and looked away from him. Her pillow was damp from tears before she fell asleep.

CHAPTER 15
(Present)

I decided to leave this hellhole today and make my case to Captain Holden tomorrow. The argument I made to Arnie about the killer cooling it until the media had its guns trained on some other event seemed convincing, given the brilliance of its source. So I took my advice and locked the cell door behind me at 6:05 p.m. It was dark – daylight savings time had ended weeks ago – and there wasn't a discernible creature, good or evil, stirring on the street. At 6:50 I removed my jacket, shoes and .38 and spread myself out on the living room sofa to plot how I would present my case to Holden. Remaining on his payroll was better than not remaining on it. He was rate card – no bonus – but rate card paid the bills and getting Hugh Patterson's hundred-thousand dollars or one percent of the Picasso's fifteen million insurance payment might not prove out. The next steps in those more important pursuits were seeing Mona's lover and brother-in-law, Jack Harris, and Harold Bullard at Indemnity Assurance. At 7:05 Carol came in struggling with her computer case and what looked like a hat box from an old movie.

"Set it on the dining table, carefully."

I felt something shift inside it.

"Is there something alive in here? Carol, you haven't bought a cat…"

"No, but I might."

I shuddered and delivered the box as directed.

"Should I get my gun before I open it?"

"Hank, don't open it."

The mild panic in her voice held me off. A while ago she mentioned a fellow News Corp employee who maintained a menagerie of exotic pets – snakes, parrots, ferrets, that sort of thing. Was she pet-sitting one of them? I flicked my finger on the side of the box and it moved a bit. I had disturbed something.

"Carol, I'm not turning off the lights tonight until I know what's in the box."

"I'll be there in a minute."

I waited and watched. She came into the room.

"Well, big brave detective, are you ready to open the box?"

"It's something from that weird person at your office."

"Yes, but just for tonight. She's on a trip and asked me to pick up her new pet. It goes back to her tomorrow morning."

"What the hell is it?"

With a smiling challenge, "Why not see for yourself, carefully."

"Carefully?"

"Recommended."

I undid the tie and started to lift the lid.

"Wait. Let me do it. If he gets out we'll never find him."

She raised it, reached in and lifted out a bull frog on a leash. He rotated his huge eyes around the room and apparently satisfied that we were the only two living things to worry about, gazed intently at me, puffing his chin.

"Isn't he cute? His name is Ovid."

"Ovid?"

She had Ovid's belly cupped in her hand with his legs dangling in the air. A red string around his neck with a finger-wide loop at its end hung alongside his long legs. He was looking fondly at her.

"I think we should get one."

I avoided that. "It seems to me that this woman's other pets might take a liking to Ovid. She has a snake, I understand, and a ferret"

No answer. Sill looking into Ovid's eyes,

"Do you feel safer now, my brave protector?"

I avoided that, too. She returned Ovid caringly to his hat box, shook a small tube of what looked like dead flies into it and tied the top shut.

"Won't he suffocate?'

Why I asked is a mystery. I didn't give a damn if he suffocated.

"There are small air holes in the sides."

"I suggest we go out to dinner and leave Ovid here to contemplate his poetry."

"Okay. Let me freshen up."

Minutes later we were at a table in a restaurant called 'good' a short walk from our apartment. I ordered a bottle of Chianti Classico, anticipating a pasta dinner.

"Now that Ovid is fed and reviewing his *Metamorphoses*, tell me, did you get the bonus?"

"I did."

"And?"

The waiter arrived and poured a taste for me. I nodded. We watched while he filled our glasses. I said we would order in a few minutes. I asked again,

"And?"

"You don't want to guess?"

"Ten thousand."

"You say ten thousand?"

"I say ten thousand."

"Twenty-five thousand."

"Carol, that's terrific. That's a total of fifty this year."

"Add in my salary and I guess I'm not doing too badly."

"Not at all! And you have your own thing, well, except for the fiendish Grover."

"He's not so bad..."

"You're softening. Ah, the power of money. Like music it soothes the savage beast, only better. In your last report you placed him among one of Nature's lower life forms."

"Yes, I did. Let's order."

I waved over the waiter and we both ordered the fall special, acorn squash ravioli. Delicious. Our table was against a window that paralleled Greenwich Avenue. We were silent for a few minutes while we looked around the small restaurant, one of our favorites. During that quiet moment a tiny bell rang in my lower brain. In my business you develop a sense of a foreign presence. I feel it when I'm being followed. Perhaps it comes from a peripheral glance of the person following you that's too fleeting to reach consciousness, or from an unusual noise or a new smell or a familiar one that's out of place. The feeling enters your lower radar screen like an enemy aircraft. I once compared the feeling to the change in air pressure, unfelt by us, that warns animals of a coming storm. Whatever its origin, the little bell told me someone was watching me. I moved my eyes casually around the room then to the partially opened Venetian blinds alongside our table. Two eyes were looking at me. They disappeared immediately when I made contact with them.

"Excuse me a minute, Carol."

I moved quickly out the door to the sidewalk, but not quickly enough. The only pedestrians near the window were too short for their eyes to reach the level my viewer reqired. Whoever it was, he or she was gone. I went back to my seat.

"Are you all right, Hank?"

"Yes. I thought I saw an old friend."

I needed a thought diversion. The dinner date with

my old friend and mentor, Bill Sanchez, and his wife came to mind.

"Speaking of that, have you and Nora set a dinner date for us?"

"Tomorrow night at their apartment. Seven-thirty. Okay?"

"Fine."

My mind was wandering. How could I be known as the art restorer who's working the Renoir? Only Corton and Holden knew about the set up. Who else would be tailing me? Mona's husband, Gerald? Her lover-in-law, Jack? Mona could have mentioned me to both of them, but why would they tail me or have me tailed? Then a familiar cold shiver went through me. Carol. If it was the man who had killed in Chicago and twice in New York, he had seen Carol as well as me. Were we followed from our apartment? Maybe. My mind was caught up in frogs and cats. I looked at her. She had seen through my weak lie about an old friend. I hoped fervently she hadn't sensed my worry about her safety. Shit! How can I keep her insulated from my business?

We finished our meal and wine and walked home hand-in-hand while I glanced back nonchalantly and used the windows we passed as mirrors.

"Carol, do you really want a pet frog?"

She grinned that wonderful grin at me.

"No, but since you brought it up, I would like a cat."

My guilt had led me into that one.

"How would you take care of it?"

"Just me?"

'Well, I could pour some milk off and on..."

Tightening her hand to mine,

"It can be worked out. Let me think about it."

She rested her head on my shoulder for the rest of the walk home.

At 8:30 a.m. I called Tom Holden from my office.

"Tom, I believe the Renoir trap is a bad idea."

I went on to give him my rationale and Arnie's idea about a camera.

"So in your view when do you think the killer will be back in business?"

"Certainly not immediately. Reason it yourself. You've committed two murders here and one in Chicago, all three art conservators in one week. If whoever is behind it is as smart as we are, then he knows we'll be protecting those still alive or setting him up by using a fake one. I'd say he's on leave for at least two months before he strikes again, maybe longer."

"You want out of the arrangement."

"No, just the freedom to help solve it. If I sit in that art hole waiting for my nemesis, I'll go mad and you'll lose access to my wisdom."

"Eh, well, you may be right, about going mad, not the wisdom."

"Let me loose and I can help. I have a client who wants the Gabriel murderer imprisoned. If I can tie that and other pieces together, you'll get your murderer and the brain or brains behind him. Every art restorer in the West will bring myrrh and incense to your door. Life will resume."

"I can't keep you on contract for two or three months."

"I know. The two-week agreement is fine."

Thoughtful quiet.

"All right. We already have a camera focused on the door…"

"I'd do more than that. He'll case the entire area, looking for a trap. Get three cameras and hide them well. We want someone who strolls by more than once, who fakes an interest in the townhouses, trees, sidewalks, talks to dog owners, anything."

A little testy, "I understand."

"Tom, when did Corton put out the word on the Renoir?"

"Last Wednesday. We set up the apartment the same day."

"And the address of the art restorer was released at the same time?"

"Yes."

"Okay. I'll stay in touch."

I pocketed my cell phone with a breath of relief about the fee. Overhead. If you don't fence it in, it will consume the garden like a hungry weed. The money from Holden's two-week arrangement would cover it nicely for about eight weeks.

Arnie came in at 8:45.

"Am I on again today, 'ank?"

"No." I explained my call to Holden.

"Aye, it makes sense. It might be more than a couple of months before 'e strikes again. The major papers will 'ave it in the middle pages in a week or so. The tabloids even sooner. 'e'll know the police will pay attention longer. It will take quite a while for art conservators to relax in their work."

"Yes."

I explained the one percent bonus to him.

"I'll 'ave Freddie fill in the contract. Do ye want to sign it before it's delivered?"

"No. Have Mrs. Harris, Mona, sign both and return one. I'm going to see the insurance guy behind the fifteen million then call on Mona's brother-in-law, Jack Harris. His name's Harold Bullard, Indemnity Resources. Low seventies and cranky, according to Corton. He's in the Seagram Building. Check with Freddie about the Harris and Jacobs transfers..."

Our mid-twenties, student-of-ancient-philosophers came in the outer door on cue. I called from my inner office,

"Freddie, let me know about your digging into Harris and Jacobs' payroll."

"I will. Let me boot up first."

"Arnie, while I was having dinner at a restaurant last night with Carol…"

I explained the incident.

"Would ye say 'e was your height, 'ank?"

"He had to be at least six-feet. He couldn't have got his eyes to the level he needed otherwise."

"We moved ye into the art studio last Thursday. You told me to leave early Friday. Did ye stay long or go in over the weekend?"

"I went to lunch with Mona Harris on Friday and left the townhouse at six. No, I didn't go in over the weekend."

Arnie asked, "Did you see anything before ye left Friday?"

"No. I assume you didn't either."

"Nae, I didn't."

"By the way, you can forget the camera set up. The police are taking care of it."

Freddie entered with a manila folder, looking like a person who had rehearsed asking for a raise. He took the black chair in front of my desk and opened the folder.

"My friend has given me..." He looked at me. "I had to promise not to reveal his name to anyone."

'That's fine, Freddie."

The tenseness subsided. He leaned back and said,

"He found a way into Harris and Jacobs' accounting. I have a long list of wire transfers from them to an account in the name of Myer Jacob at a bank in Florida called First Sunrise Savings. I looked at twenty stock exchanges, including foreign ones, and couldn't find it. It's either too small to list or privately owned. From there the money went to an account in the name of John Smith in Bermuda. The payments are marked either Salary or Reimbursement. They range from a million to two million and go back four years. This year there were three very large transfers, one for twenty million, one for twenty-five million and one for twenty-six million, seventy-one million in total. The three large transfers occurred after the Chicago, Soho and Gabriel murders. All the transfers over four years add up to a hundred-and-ten million."

He stopped, looked at me with a mix of apprehension and pride.

Rather than congratulate Freddie I was deciding whether to phone this information to Sanchez now or wait for a moment when I needed something he would be reluctant to provide otherwise. I decided to wait for the something.

"Freddie, this is very helpful. Can we pay your friend for his or her help?"

"Well..."

"Freddie, he or she has provided us valuable information. I don't want to take it for nothing."

"Well, I was hesitating because..."

He stiffened up.

"He'd like two tickets to the Knicks game next weekend."

I almost chuckled, then caught myself. This was not as easy as it sounded and they would not be cheap, unless I parked the guy in the upper reaches of Madison Square Garden. The work was worth more than that.

"Tell him he'll have two of them for this Friday or Saturday night."

Freddie smiled and remained seated, looking like a student waiting for a grade.

"And thank you, Freddie. Are you a Knicks fan, too?"

"No." Pause.

"I just wanted to know if…"

"If you did well? You did very well. Stay in touch with your friend and…and Freddie, we don't forget jobs well done."

"Thank you, Mr.…Hank." He swelled a bit, handed me the folder and returned to his world.

"Well, Arnie?"

"It seems simple, 'ank. Murder, steal something valuable, sell it and pass the money to…"

"Right, pass the money to whom? ISIS? Al Qaeda? Or someone's personal savings account? And what about the insurance money? Three murders, Arnie, three murders. And if it's that simple, why stop at three?"

I reached for the phone to call the grumpy septuagenarian Executive VP of Indemnity Assurance, Harold Bullard.

CHAPTER 16
(2008)

Jonah slipped out of bed early, washed and dressed silently not to disturb Hetty. She was curled up with her arms caressing her pillow as if it were a lover. She was also naked and a good part of her nakedness was open to view. Most men would have slipped in beside her, but Jonah was not among most men. He simply wanted to be sure he hadn't awakened her. He returned to the bathroom, retrieved the Ziploc bag with the two wallets in it from the cabinet drawer and went to his BMW. At a UPS Store he bought a box for the Ziploc bag, sealed it and addressed it to "Victor, Golden Swan." He wrote "Personal" in capital large letters next to the address. He gave the young man behind the counter a fifty dollar bill to have it delivered to the Golden Swan this morning. He left a message on Isa's voice mail.

Back in the apartment's bedroom Hetty was yawning and stretching herself. Jonah watched the awakening for a few moments then with the flourish of a toreador spun the cover off of her.

"Time to shop."

She rolled over wide-eyed, momentarily frightened and pulled her bare legs tight against her chest. Was that a smile, she thought? For a half second she thought it was. If I'm right, it's the first time he's come near one. Whatever it was it was fleeting. His face quickly returned to its usual detachment.

"Jonah, I'll have to wear my stage clothes..."

His face said, "So?"

"I'll look strange in a store. Maybe you could buy a

long coat…"

"You'll look fine. Pick something out you know you want and wear it. I would keep your stage clothes for your new job."

She picked up her white, off-shoulder blouse, short plaid skirt and half-calf boots and went into the bathroom. Jonah's cell phone rang.

"I got the message, Jonah."

"Hold it."

Jonah stepped out into the hallway and closed the door.

"What do you want me to do?"

"Watch the Swan and call me when you see the wallets delivered. I'm close by, but I don't want to be seen. As soon as the package is inside, I'll meet you at the entrance. We'll wait a few minutes and drop in on my friend, Victor."

With a lightness in his voice, Isa said,

"It's time for a little drama, Jonah. A hundred dollars says he's out of Dodge by sundown, just like the movies."

"No bet."

"A wise man. Call me when the wallets are in."

"I will."

Back inside the apartment, he turned to the bathroom door.

"I saw a woman's clothes store this morning. I'll drive you there as soon as you're dressed, but then I have to leave. Buy what you need and take a taxi back here. I can't say when I'll be back."

Hetty called out a disappointed okay. She was hoping to have a male opinion during her shopping spree; but, then, Jonah would not be a meaningful critic. Besides, today she planned to shop for everyday wear and save for another day buying a more flamboyant wardrobe for the stage. Would he be helpful in that, she thought? She had to concede he wouldn't. No matter how sexy she dressed, I can't be as sexy as in a bath towel and when I wore that he showed no interest. Another flash of that sadness hit her, but the thought of shopping overcame it. The ego bruise would return, but for the next hour or two she would be free from it. Now…now, she thought, I will enjoy myself and shop and shop and dress myself ready for whatever Life has awaiting me, on stage and off. She slipped on her Abilene outfit and looked in the mirror. I'm going to get some eyes in this, she thought. Then gave a tiny grin.

Jonah stopped in front of the women's clothing store he had seen on the way to the UPS Store and looked at her. She waited for him to say something, "Good luck or have fun," perhaps. Something. But he just moved his eyes up and down her. Finally, he reached inside his pocket and handed her another five hundred dollars.

"You'll need more for your singing clothes."

She thanked him. It was one of those rare and damnable moments that she thought he might care for her. Then it occurred to her that he did care for her, but not as a woman, more as a man cares for a vintage car. He wanted her to look good, but in all human matters she was inanimate to him, a chattel to polish and service and protect. She took the money and went inside the store.

Jonah drove to the same small lot he had used before the slaughter on the bridge and locked his car. He walked to a small food store that stood in a direct line of sight to the gangway onto the Golden Swan. He ordered a coffee and went to the window. It was 10:00 a.m. At 11:00 a young boy with a package parked his bike and strode up the gangway to a security guard. The guard held out his hand to stop him, listened to his speech, took the package and handed it to another guard who carried it into the casino. Jonah phoned Isa.

"It's in. I'm about fifty yards away in a coffee shop."

"I see it. Order me a decaf."

Three minutes later Isa entered the shop and took a small container of decaf from Jonah. They both stood at the window watching the only way in and out of the Golden Swan. Fifteen minutes passed.

"Let's go," said Isa.

They waked up the gangway. Isa said to the guard,

"We're here to see Victor Santel and Eddie Garth."

"Top deck, St. Louis side." said the guard, tired of having to explain port and starboard. Five minutes later they were at the door to Victor's office. Isa knocked. A young man opened it.

"We're here to see Victor."

"Names?"

"Isa Hajjar and Jonah Flood."

The man started to announce the names when Victor bellowed from his desk,

"It's okay, Fred. Let them in."

They advanced toward two chairs facing Victor sitting behind his desk. Eddie Garth, the Golden Swan's Chief Financial Officer, had a chair pulled up to the right side of the desk. In his lap was the package the boy on the bike had delivered a half hour ago. It was unopened. Isa and Jonah saw it and said nothing.

With a sincere, half-pleading expression, Isa said,

"Victor, we're back to see if you have reconsidered your position on selling your share of the Swan. We've all had a good night's sleep to wash away the unpleasantness of our last meeting. We're all fair and open-minded men. I'm sure we can come to a solution."

Eddie Garth, the CFO, set the package on Victor's desk, leaned forward alert and ready to participate in whatever followed.

"I told you my position, Isa. I haven't changed it. Why should I? Give me a reason why I should."

It was curtain time. Isa said,

"Eddie, open the package for Victor. I see it has his name on it."

Eddie looked at his boss. Victor, suddenly suspicious, nodded. A tenseness crept across Victor's face. He shifted in his chair while Eddie opened it and kept his eyes trained on Isa. Eddie blurted out,

"There's two wallets soaked in what looks like..."

Eddie's face froze. He pushed the package in front of Victor. Victor saw the contents and immediately knew their meaning. The wallets were covered in dark, dried blood. Now, he knew why Johnny Marino and his sidekick had not shown up this morning. He turned his stare from Isa and saw Jonah's eyes fixed on him with the bored, uncaring expression of a professional executioner. Victor's stomach started churning in the way it does before vomiting. Eddie the accountant had now grasped the full meaning. His face was white in fear. He stood up.

"Victor, I have to go to my office. This is not what I thought when I…"

He didn't finish. He picked up a folder from the desk with a shaking hand and left the room. Isa's eyes had never left Victor. He waited. Finally, Victor said in a weak, defeated voice,

'Where are they?"

"One's in a gravel barge going up river; the other's floating down river."

Victor glanced back at Jonah's stone face, dropped his chin to his chest and said,

"Make me an offer."

Isa handed him a folder. "A few signatures and you own the casinos I just left, but there's no cash bonus."

Victor flipped through the papers without reading them and signed where the stickies indicated he should. Isa took the folder and with a steady hand carefully separated the copies, laying one set on Victor's desk and keeping another for himself.

"You'll leave tonight, of course," he said to Victor.

Victor nodded, his eyes still looking down at his desk.

"Good. I'm sure you'll find the books in proper order and a welcoming and competent staff. I will inform them later today. I would appreciate you're telling the staff here that a new owner is taking over who has big plans to expand the Golden Swan and that their jobs are secure."

Victor nodded again, his chin still inches above his chest.

"So we're done. Life goes on. You'll love Colorado, Victor. Absolutely beautiful. Snow-capped mountains, clean mountain air. New horizons and a business to grow. What do you say?"

Isa rose from his chair and extended his hand across the desk. Jonah stood, watching Victor carefully. With a hand as limp as a mitten and without standing, he accepted Isa's handshake.

"There's a direct flight from St. Louis to Denver at six this evening. I recommend you and your financial assistant take it, if he wants to go with you. I will have all your personal things boxed and sent to whatever address you prefer."

Victor raised his head to him.

With a tone of voice filled with irony, Isa said,

"I believe you know where I'm staying in St. Louis. Your two employees did. If you have any questions before you leave, I'll be glad to answer them, if I can. Jonah won't be far away."

Isa kept his eyes on Victor and with a tone fraught with warning said,

"I recommend highly that this end our business."

Jonah reached across the desk and took the package

with the bloody wallets in it.

Firmly, "Let me hear you say yes, Victor."

Victor simply looked at him.

Forcefully, "Say it."

"It ends our business."

"Good."

The two left. Victor buzzed Eddie, his CFO. In a shaky voice before Victor could say anything, Eddie said,

"Victor, I'm resigning effective immediately."

Outside.

"Jonah, I'm going back to my hotel. I'm ninety percent sure he's beaten, but that ten percent can cause trouble. Watch this place and call me if there's anything suspicious."

He paused. "Tell your girl to come in tomorrow at ten. I'll set her up." With a grin,

"If she's got a great figure and face, she can sing off tune and still wow the hungry ones. How old are you, Jonah?"

"I don't know."

With a burst of laughter, "Wonderful, absolutely wonderful. What a blessing to be young."

They both wandered into the Swan's large parking lot and Isa drove his car toward the Eads Bridge. Jonah retrieved his BMW from the smaller lot and parked it where Isa's had been. He had a clear view of the entrance to the Golden Swan. Would Victor leave from the river side to avoid being seen? No. Jonah had seen the river up close and from the bridge above. Its banks were high and its current was fast and treacherous. If Victor or someone else was going for Isa, he would leave from the gangway Jonah was watching.

Hetty was not bashful or shy nor hesitant in her

ways. She had been on the stage in front of some tough crowds for six years – since nineteen – and under fire from boys and men since sixteen. She was so good at handling hecklers they were often mocked by the crowd after she fired back a sharp riposte. Her defense against Life was strong and sharply honed from her years on the stage. Yet, she froze at the front door of the women's clothing store. The manikins in the windows were dressed far more elegantly than she had ever been and made what she had on now – a short skirt, a white, off-the-shoulder blouse and calf boots – look like the stuff of a prostitute. There were no shops like this one in Abilene or in any of the other small, Midwest towns where she performed her country songs. One of the manikins grabbed her attention. It had blonde hair like hers and was dressed in a light, soft blue jacket with a matching pullover blouse beneath it and black pants. It had a subtle whisper of sex. What she had on was not subtle or whispering. The model next to it had on a deep red, long-sleeved, vertically-ribbed turtleneck sweater over black pants. Both ensembles exuded a world of dress she had never seen. It was intimidating, but not overpowering. She went in with her head high ready for the hecklers. A saleswoman approached her.

"I need your help getting out of these while I shop. Can you help me? I'm not what you think."

It was fresh and sincere and unaffected and it rang true for the lady. She found a rain coat in the back and let her wear it while she walked the store. Hetty had a thousand dollars in the tiny pocket of her skirt. She planned to spend half of it here and half where she could find sexier and cheaper clothes to wear on stage. She drifted from one rack to another, holding dresses up to her chin, cocking her head, bundling her hair, letting it fall over her shoulders while examining the effects in a full-length mirror. The saleslady watched her innocence with a smiling admiration. In the right clothes this young woman would be a force, she thought.

Finally, Hetty decided on the red-ribbed turtle neck and another outfit equally stunning. Four hundred and fifty dollars for two ensembles did not leave much for at least six different stage attires, but she didn't care. The clothes were so intoxicatingly different from her past she had to have them. Where she would wear them appropriately never entered her thoughts.

"You look beautiful in both outfits, madam, especially in the red and black. Your blonde hair sets off the colors, and your figure…well, I shouldn't say it, but it would look good in anything. May I recommend a large necklace? It would be a *piece de resistance* over the red. You have selected two excellent choices."

Madam! She had never been called madam. Bitch, teaser and sometimes worse, but never madam. Now, in her new clothes she was suddenly madam!

She bought a comb and some makeup, paid the woman and took a cab to the apartment. Tomorrow, she would look for her stage clothes.

She bathed, combed her hair, applied light make up and put on her tight-fitting, red-ribbed turtleneck sweater and black pants outfit. Yes, she needed a large necklace. Standing in front of a full-length mirror she wondered what Jonah would say when he saw her dressed so elegantly. He won't say anything. Do I care? Yes. But…but…I really look different. She turned this way and that, looked at herself in profile, arranged her hair different ways and made the most of the moment. I've never seen myself like this. I'm different. I finally look like a real grown up…I'm…I'm…She said it out loud with a smile, "Yes, madam, you're beautiful."

Victor exited the Golden Swan at 3:30 carrying two brief cases. A cab was waiting for him. Jonah fell in behind the car as it crossed the Eads Bridge into St. Louis and turned onto U.S. 70 north. Twenty minutes later the driver deposited him at the Lambert-St. Louis Airport. Jonah watched the airport exits for thirty minutes after the Denver flight had left to be sure Victor wasn't faking a departure. He called Isa.

"He's gone. He had two briefcases."

"One was probably filled with cash. Let him have it. Tomorrow, Jonah, we start building the Golden Swan into a real enterprise. I intend to take out a sizable loan and redo the entire ship. Better entertainment, better tables, better food. It will take a four or five years to get it where I want it and running on its own, then we'll find a new enterprise."

CHAPTER 17
(Present)

Harold Bullard, the grumpy Executive VP of Indemnity Assurance, took my call after I mentioned Edgar Corton's name to his Assistant. His first words were short, pointed and hoarse, probably from a throat that for decades has had high-proof bourbon running down it.

"What do you want?"

"I'd like to speak with you for a brief time about a claim Indemnity is processing."

"What claim?"

"Can we discuss it in your office?"

"No."

When you speak to people like this you must listen closely. Often the tone of their toughness suggests you are being tested for your staying power, rather than summarily dismissed. If you waiver or show alarm in your response, you may be deemed not worthy of further consideration. I detected more challenge in Harold's "No" than dismissal.

"What I will propose may take some give and take, but in the end it will serve Indemnity well."

A little less edgy.

"How?"

"Probably in more ways than I know. That's why I need your input."

"Edgar said you're a PI. Used to work for the government."

"That's correct."

"A spy."

"Analysis."

"Huh. A spy. I need to know the claim."

"An art piece stolen from Gerald and Mona Harris."

A more businesslike pause.

"All right, I've got thirty minutes at eleven."

"I'll be there."

I called Hugh Patterson, my client, high-end art dealer and boyfriend of Gabriel, the murdered art restorer.

"Hugh, are you free for lunch?"

"Yes, if it's early. Do you have something?"

"Meet me at Bull and Bear in the Waldorf at noon. I'll make a reservation."

"What do you have?"

"Let's talk about it at lunch."

Reluctantly, "All right."

We clicked off.

Arnie was standing in my doorway.

" 'ank, the tail has something on Jack Harris."

"Let's hear it."

"After your lunch with Mona Harris at the Yale Club she took a cab, right?"

"Yeah, I took a subway."

"She went one block in the cab to the Roosevelt Hotel on Madison and Forty-fifth. Brother-in-law Jack was waiting in the lobby under watch by the tail. 'e flashed a room keycard with a smile and they went to the elevator. Two hours later they emerged. She left in a cab and 'arris went to 'is office."

"Well, that answers that. Let's remove the tail."

"There seems to be a circle 'ere, 'ank. Theft, murder, insurance, resell…theft, murder, insurance, resell."

"Yes. I'm seeing the insurance part of it at eleven. Harold Bullard."

"Could 'e been in on it?"

"Unlikely, Well, I shouldn't say that. I don't know."

I called out to the outer office.

"Freddie, do a file on Indemnity Assurance, what they insure, etc. Try for their financial status. Phone me if you find anything."

I got back an "Okay."

"Arnie, I think he's growing his hair. I noticed some blond stubble where it was skin."

Smiling, "Aye, 'ank. I saw it, too. 'e's got a way to go to catch up with the fence 'e's got down the middle of 'is scalp."

"Maybe he'll cut it down – or create a new style. I'm off to see Bullard. He's a gruff old boy. Corton says he's seventy. I thought insurance people were pleasant people, eager to protect their clients from Life's slings and arrows."

"Aye. It's my experience."

I stopped at my office door and looked back at Arnie.

"What if the super brain behind this killing scheme is a *nouveau riche* billionaire building a collection?"

"That would make the case more dangerous, 'ank. A billionaire can buy a lot of killers."

I decided against a cab and walked west across Second Avenue then Third then Lexington. At Park I was only three city blocks north of Harold's office in the strikingly handsome Seagram Building. The building is over five hundred feet straight up with a façade of tinted bronze glass. Its front yard is close to a half acre of a raised plaza with steps to the adjoining sidewalks along Park Avenue, Fifty-third and Fifty-second. It was built in the late fifties and is as striking now as it must have been the day it opened. Indemnity's offices were on the thirtieth floor.

"Hank Tower to see Mr. Bullard."

She picked up a phone from the nineties and announced me. Were the old boy and his elderly assistant resisting the new world?

"You may go in, Mr. Tower."

A large desk, a floor-to-ceiling window facing Park Avenue, large, comfortable chairs, a four-cushion sofa, a picture of himself with President Carter and others, a couple of awards, no sign of a computer or tablet.

Without rising from the high-back leather chair behind his desk,

"Ah, the spy. Have a seat."

"Thank you."

My love of old movies was nagging me. But for the missing cigar, he could have been Edward G. Robinson, the insurance guy in *Double Indemnity*. He appeared as short as Robinson in the large chair and had dark hair and a squished face like the actor's. Even his sandpaper voice was similar. He stared at me and said,

"They want fifteen million dollars."

"Isn't that the policy?"

"Yes."

"So why do I detect a reservation in your voice?"

"I hate to pay out money."

I ignored the answer.

"What do you want? A faster payout?"

That threw me for a second.

"Yes. I get a bonus, if I can speed it up."

"Honesty. That's rare. How could that help Indemnity?"

I explained the steal, kill, get the insurance money and sell the stolen piece to the private market that I thought was in play. I told him that two other art conservators had been murdered in addition to Gabriel, one in Chicago and another in New York, all three in a week. I also said the proceeds from a private sale could be going to terrorists, but I didn't reveal how I arrived at that possibility. He listened intently, but was poker-faced. He said,

"How could paying early help the firm?"

"We could trace the money. If what I suspect is true,

an early payout could help a lot of people…"

"Including Mr. and Mrs. Harris."

"Frankly, I don't know why they want a faster one – we're only talking about five or six months, right?"

He nodded.

"Let me ask you this. Would a shorter period hurt the firm?"

He shook his head almost unperceptively.

"Then do it and let us follow the money."

"Us?"

"Yes, but I can't reveal any more than that."

"Terrorists."

"Maybe. It could also be a brand new billionaire building himself an art collection and murdering to get it. Do you have any other expensive paintings insured?"

With a one-upping smile, "I can't reveal any more than that."

"If you do, then the sooner we catch the brains behind this the less likely you will have another claim."

He studied me. Hubbard was clearly an experienced hand at looking into people and unleashing his instincts. As the old saying goes, "I don't want to hear what you say, I want to feel what you mean." He was letting his years of experience determine if I meant what I said or if I was deceiving him for some unknown purpose. He decided on the former.

"I'll okay it for payment tomorrow. We can wire the funds. Have Mona Harris give me her bank numbers. In return, I want to be kept aware of what you find. Deal?"

"Deal."

With a glint in his eye, "Should I withhold, say, two percent?"

"It's one percent. No, I'll handle that."

He was grinning. "Damned, if you aren't a spy. You

used just enough honesty with me to get what you wanted and no more."

"I did analysis for the government."

"Un huh."

"Mona gets the money. I guess I just assumed Gerald owned the painting. Now, a good spy wouldn't make that mistake."

"She owns it." Then suddenly he burst out...

"By god, you really didn't think she owned it, did you? Now you know she does. You got me."

He came around the desk with a reluctant grin and his hand out. He wasn't quite as short as Edward G. Robinson.

"You'd better go before I reveal all of Indemnity's secrets."

I shook the old codger's hand.

"Before leaving I want a view from that window."

"Be my guest."

It was floor-to-ceiling glass which let you put your toes only an inch away from a straight drop to the concrete plaza thirty floors below. It's not for vertigo sufferers. The view up and down Park Avenue was stunning in its breath. I could see from the MetLife Building on my left up through the long, sheer canyon of high rises to my right. Hidden from view beneath Park Avenue were the trains that bring workers and visitors into Grand Central Terminal from suburban New York and Connecticut. What a City!

I returned to the matter at hand while descending thirty floors on the elevator. Mona, why did you lie to me? To divert me from something you don't want me to know? Didn't you realize I would learn you owned the painting when you hired me to hurry the insurance payment? Whatever your reason, you don't need a divorce to claim the fifteen million. And where is your lawyer-husband, Gerald? Hiding? Shacked up with another woman? Dead? I called her from the lobby.

"Mona, the fifteen million will be wire transferred tomorrow. All they need are the proper bank numbers. Call Indemnity and ask for Harold Bullard."

"Hank, that's wonderful! I'll give you a check after the transfer."

"I'll pick it up tomorrow afternoon."

"Let me give it to you at lunch tomorrow. Jean Georges. One o'clock. All right? My treat."

"I'll meet you there."

"You're a very capable man. Frankly, I didn't think... Gerald will be ecstatic."

"See you at Jean Georges."

Ecstatic? Not if he knows you're sleeping with his brother. But then...

Like Harold Bullard, I let my instincts run free. They groaned and stretched and wandered about and finally whispered,

"Husband Gerald's dead."

Hugh Patterson, my harder client, was at the bar when at noon I entered the already crowded Bull and Bear restaurant on the Lexington Avenue side of the Waldorf Astoria. He had a wide-rimmed martini filled to the edge in front of him. There was a time when I drank that mind-numbing elixir, but around year thirty-five or six I quit, along with scotch on the rocks. They were aging my face. Vanity? Yeah, but along with retaining a normal face came a clearer mind. Now, it's wine and an occasional cognac.

I shouldered my way in between Hugh and another martini man.

"Hank, good to see you. Should we sit?"

"Absolutely."

I waved to the *maître'd* and he took us to our table.

Hugh sipped down his overflowing nectar before starting the short journey. I ordered a club soda with a twist. The good stuff would come later in the day.

Anxiously, "What have you found? Do you have a lead on Gabriel's killer?"

"No. The police are trying to draw him out."

"The Renoir?"

I did a stomach jerk. How in hell did he know about that? Had I said too much?

"Art dealers live in a small world," he said. "I heard a privately-held one is being restored from a hurricane Sandy accident by a private conservator."

"Where?"

"In New York somewhere."

"Do you know where or by whom?"

"No. Just New York. I need to order. Do you mind?"

I signaled for a waiter. We both ordered the special, thinking it would be faster.

I changed the subject from the Renoir.

"It's going to be difficult to track Gabriel's killer. The police and I both believe it was a professional. They murder then disappear into the world's billions. We need to ferret out the person who hired him, or her. Do you have any idea who might be capable of it? Think of the end user, the person who would like to own a Picasso. Someone with new money, for instance, who wants to build a private collection."

"I can think of a lot of people who would like a private collection."

"That's not what I asked."

"Right. No, except..."

"Jesus man. Out with it, if you have something."

"A man who called himself John Smith."

"The man who sold you the Warhol, van Kooning and Norman Rockwell."

It was his turn for a stomach jerk.

"How do you know that? It was ten years ago."

"Paintings similar to the last two just sold for about seventy million. Did you know that?"

"Yes, I heard."

"That's big money, Hugh."

Silence.

"And you bought the name John Smith."

"Yes and no. I knew it was phony, but didn't care. He had the pieces and I wanted them."

"No questions asked?"

"No."

Our specials arrived. We nibbled for a few minutes.

"How many art dealers do you think know about the Renoir?"

He exhaled a sharp huh!

"By now, all of them."

"How about the location of the conservator? How many know that?"

"There's no way to know."

"Guess."

"Really, there's no way to know."

"From what I've learned there aren't many secrets in the industry."

"True, except when a valuable piece is involved. If anyone I know is aware of where the Renoir is being restored, he or she would never reveal it."

"They'd find the owner, make a deal and inform a high-rolling client."

"Yes."

"Back to question A. Who do you think might be capable of hiring a professional killer to secure a valuable piece of art?"

"Hank, you're asking me to…to make a big mistake. I…"

"What would Gabriel want you to do?"

He dropped his head.

"The man's dangerous."

I stared at him "Who?"

"He doesn't live in the U.S."

"Hugh…"

"I could be wrong. There's no way I can be sure. It's just a feeling…"

"Is it John Smith? If you don't open up I'll ram this fork in your feeling."

"His real name is Ronald Mason."

My hand froze. The Ronald Mason I know lives in Bermuda, is smart, sophisticated and can be dangerous. He's also my half-brother.

CHAPTER 18
(2008-Present)

Hetty already had her Abilene outfit for performing country western songs. Now, after careful shopping, she had one for throaty love songs and another more conservative one for pleasing the senior crowd with some old favorites. But she applied her deepest attention to finding one for what she hoped would become her signature performance: a repertoire of songs from *Showboat*, a musical story of the days when large stern-wheelers plied the Upper and Lower Mississippi with St. Louis a key port. She expected to do two sets a night and hoped four costumes would be adequate. If they weren't, she was in trouble. She was down to her last thirty dollars.

It was the form-fitting, deep red, long-sleeved, vertically-ribbed turtleneck sweater with black pants that she would wear to meet Isa. With the help of the saleslady who sold her the ensemble, the two had fashioned her blonde hair tastefully over the red and added a large-ring necklace that fell between her breasts. "Madam, you are stunning" was the woman's assessment as Hetty stood in front of the full length mirror. It buoyed the girl from Kansas immensely, for Hetty had stepped out of her league dressed as she was. She needed reassurance from someone who knew fashion.

Hetty hid her new personae under a light gray raincoat taken from Jonah's closet. She might be new to these clothes, but not to stagecraft. She wanted a full-orchestra effect when she took off the coat in front of her new boss. Jonah drove her to the Golden Swan, waved to the guard to assist her and left to perform some vague errand.

"Mr. Hajjar is on the top floor, madam. The elevator is straight ahead on your right," said the guard.

"Madam" from another person. Another flash of new pride rushed through her. She smiled, straightened her shoulders and went to the elevator.

A pleasant-looking, young man opened Isa's office door, hesitated a moment and stepped aside.

"Come in, come in, Miss Hetty," roared the handsome Lebanese man sitting behind a large desk. "Welcome to the Golden Swan."

Hetty walked up to the desk and stood next to a chair. She removed the plain-colored coat, held it out for the doorman to take and shook her hair over her shoulders. The man froze for a second then stepped backwards toward the window, oblivious to the coat hanging over his arm. Isa stood up, impressed but practical, and said,

"My god, if you can sing, you'll add ten percent to the gross. Where's Jonah?"

He was holding out his hand to her. She took it.

"Sit, please, sit."

She obeyed.

"He said he had an errand."

With a lascivious grin, "The lucky s. o. b. If he weren't so jealous, I'd move in on him."

His eyes were fixed on her, looking for a confirmation of what he suspected about their relationship, but her street smarts dodged him. The last thing she wanted in her life was a boss running a hand up her leg.

"Jonah and I get along very well, Mr. Hajjar."

"Mr. Hajjar. There goes my fantasy down the toilet. Call me Isa, please."

"I can sing very well, Isa. I've been on stage since I was nineteen. I can also handle different styles, country, blues, show tunes…"

"No need to go any further. You're hired. You could caw like a crow and the audience would come. How are you fixed for stage clothes? You're dressed for a cheese-and-wine art show in some museum. Ever been to New York?"

"No. I have four different outfits, but I'll need more. I want to create a series of shows that play to the Mississippi. *Showboat*, for instance, and some Memphis songs like…"

"Say no more. I love it. I want you to start as soon as possible in our nightclub room. Jerry here will show the layout to you. You start at a thousand a week. If the show goes well, that could double in months."

He stopped and looked down at her black pants. "Make sure some of your outfits show leg."

"They do. Cleavage, too."

"Splendid. Do some *Showboat* shopping in St. Louis…here's a thousand dollars. Tell Jonah the three of us will dine in the Swan's main restaurant tonight. Eight o'clock."

"I'll tell him."

"And wear what you have on. I want to watch some of these Midwest eyes react. Jerry, show the lady the nightclub and other parts of the boat. Introduce her around."

Isa shook his head. "Two-to-one the staff thinks she's here to buy the place."

Hetty smiled wider than she had for many years. A thousand a week! A wardrobe! A show I can create myself! The ecstasy was still with her as she exited the elevator and saw Jonah coming aboard.

Smiling proudly, "I got the job."

He paused, looked at her with an expressionless face, nodded and walked on with a silent "Of course." It sent the familiar hurt through her. I can't talk to him.

I can't sleep in the same bed with him without frustration. I have no another place to go. I owe him my escape from Billy and my new job. What am I going to do with him? They were thoughts that would slowly conflate to…how can I be free of him?

The dinner with Jonah and Isa included Jerry, the quiet, slender man who met her at Isa's door. Isa did all of the talking. Hetty felt Jerry's eyes scanning her hair and cheek and breasts, each glance undressing her a bit more. She looked occasionally at Jonah to see if he noticed it, but saw the usual disinterested eyes. Other men in the room were casting looks at her as well as Jerry. Isa was in the middle of delivering his grand plan for the Golden Swan when a handsome man in his late thirties interrupted him with…

"Isa, I've seen these two gentlemen with you before, but the lady is new. May I ask you for an introduction?"

Jerry shifted uncomfortably in his chair. Jonah remained in neutral.

"Of course. Hetty, this is Greg Roberts. Greg makes loans from one of St. Louis's largest banks. I intend to relieve it of several million dollars in the next week or two."

With his eyes on Hetty. "And the lady's last name?"

Isa quickly said, "Just Hetty, Greg. She'll be singing in our nightclub in a few days. Better get your reservation in. She wowed the crowds in Las Vegas."

"I will, I will. Thank you for the heads up."

"It's nice to meet you, Hetty."

Without noticing Jonah or Jerry, the man rejoined his male dinner companions.

"You've made a hit with someone who can help fill the club with people. He's well-off and knows everyone. Sing a song to him when we open."

Her eyes were following Greg's departure. "I will, Isa."

The encounter was enough to disturb Jerry's warming blood, but Jonah's remained unaffected. He was studying the room for anyone who might do harm to Isa, the first person since his "mother" he had ever respected.

Months later, Isa's five-year plan to lift the Golden Swan into an elegant dining, entertainment and gambling destination on par with the best hotels in Las Vegas was underway with the help of a twenty-million dollar loan from Greg Roberts's bank. Hetty, under instructions from Isa, had changed her last name from Bancroft to Staar. Her *Showboat* set was now fine-tuned to the delight of audiences. Part of Isa's renovation plan was to enlarge the nightclub at the expense of a small fast-food restaurant adjoining it. Isa had increased her salary to two thousand a week and had her sign a three-year contract. She had waited weeks before finally discussing her own apartment with Jonah. In his terse way he agreed. "I'll be traveling soon," he said, and offered to let her have his. She declined. The exchange brought a few tears to her eyes. He saw them but didn't recognize their meaning. The blankness would always be there, she knew. Perhaps it was required for what she suspected he did.

Jerry made a few attempts to see her, but she backed away. They both worked for the same man and her instincts said don't stress that triangle. The same wasn't true of Greg Roberts. He had called her a week after they met to join him at a Garth Brooks concert in the Scottrade Center in St. Louis. She had checked with Isa before accepting. He was delighted. "Go, for god's sake, go!" He didn't add "Go to bed with him," but she got his undertone. After that, he took her to a St. Louis Blues hockey game and some casual dinners that always ended early. She knew Isa had his motive for her seeing Greg, but she had one, too. He was different, refreshing, easy to be with. She wanted to sleep with him, but not before all their planets were aligned. He was a quality person; at least that was how she saw him. It was an attribute she had never known in men. They all, except Jonah, had one common goal – getting her in bed as fast as they could. Greg seemed at ease with himself and wasn't demanding of her. He could be serious minded and funny. He made her laugh and smile and feel feminine. No other man had ever done that for her, certainly not Billy or Jonah who was neutral on all aspects sexual. She enjoyed the young banker and missed him when days passed without a call.

She was growing professionally. Her talent as a singer had reached the *St. Louis Post-Dispatch* and local TV critics. "There's a new Staar over the Mississippi called Hetty," said one. "Kern and Hammerstein's *Showboat* is shining bright in the Golden Swan, thanks to a new light in the firmament, Hetty Staar. You can't help lovin' dat wo…man. Shows at nine and eleven," said another. She had received calls from agents who wanted to handle her "the minute you're off-contract." A new and exciting life had begun.

Then the break she had hoped for arrived. Isa announced that he and Jonah were going to Chicago for a few days. Jerry would watch the daily routine, but anything out of the ordinary had to be phoned to him.

The two had been gone only one day when Greg Roberts asked her to come with him to New York. She tingled at the idea. They had been seeing each other off and on, but had never slept together. He was always working while she slept and she was always working while he slept. Her second set often went to 1:00 a.m.

The sexual tension between them was near a bursting point and now...now their planets were aligned. The nightclub where she performed would be closed for a week for renovation. She asked Jerry for the week off and he agreed. Two days after Jonah and Isa left for Chicago, Hetty and Greg boarded a plane for New York.

CHAPTER 19

In a private corner of the main lobby of the Peninsula Hotel in Chicago…

"Jonah, tomorrow I'm meeting someone face-to-face for the first time. I believe he's five star, but the money involved requires extra caution. I want you where you can see him and me, but he can't see you. Stay in the shadows unless there's a threat to me. If what I was told is true, the deal can make more money in a couple of years than the Golden Swan can in twenty. All I can say now is that somehow this guy has a window into the movement of certain valuable things. It's the movement of those things that we need to interrupt without leaving a trail."

Isa waited.

"I understand."

"This visit is a one-time-only. If it works, we move on to New York."

Jonah nodded.

Isa smiled at him. "It's only a two-hour flight."

"Okay."

"Will you want to have Hetty with you?"

"No. She has her own apartment now."

"Really? Why am I – the guy who signs the checks – the last one to know these things?"

"We're different. She should be with someone else. I have no interest in what she wants."

It was the most profound sentence Isa had heard his killer utter. Was a seed of humanity blossoming in his brain? The thought woke Isa's natural suspicion of all things affecting him. He wanted Jonah as he was – dead to human caring. Maybe he's not a zombie, maybe he's capable of changing. If so, thought, Isa, that's a problem. He would be no use to me, if such a thing grew. He seriously doubted that it would. Jonah was a true-blue psychopath, the kind he'd been wanting at his side for years. Yes, he had to be watched; but not for turning soft on his job – for turning on him.

"Here's your room key. You're two rooms down the hall from me. Enjoy it. You have a view of part of Chicago's famous skyline and Lake Michigan. Tomorrow morning a UPS box will be delivered to you. There's a weapon inside. Are you hungry?"

"Yeah."

"We can have dinner – the dining room is beautiful, or you can eat in your room."

"I'll eat in my room."

The answer further eased Isa. This man had no interest in people. He'd kill a two-year-old as thoughtlessly as a mosquito, given a reason he understood. The number of people he had killed before coming to Colorado was unknowable; but Isa sensed that each time Jonah killed, he had a purpose, as a farmer does when he slaughters an animal for food. After a few killings, there is no longer revulsion or regret or reflection on the act. It's a part of life.

Yet, despite the man's indifference to life, Isa knew he was safe with Jonah as long as his requirements remained within the boundaries of how Jonah understood the world. That meant his instructions must always have a purpose Jonah could understand and accept, and the more the instructions somehow linked with Jonah's nebulous past, the easier they would be for him to carry out. As long as he was careful with what he asked, he would have Jonah's respect. If something interfered or confused him, something that seemed wrong to Jonah's primal thinking, Isa's life would be in danger. It was the ageless dilemma of the dictator. As long as he was strong, his killers would kill. If he faltered, they would kill him.

Isa leaned toward Jonah. "The meeting's tomorrow morning at eleven. I don't know where yet. It could be on a park bench. You'll have to follow me. If I smell a rat and say no to the deal, I'm in danger."

"I understand. You will not be in danger."

Isa leaned back in the sumptuous lobby chair and smiled. "Good."

While Isa and Jonah were sitting in the lobby of one of Chicago's most luxurious hotels, a ninety-foot yacht of equal opulence was steaming silently underneath the Verrazano Bridge into New York's Upper Harbor. Her destination was the North Cove Marina near the foot of Manhattan on the Hudson River. She glided over the dark water like a ghost, moving so smoothly the bay seemed to spread its water for her. Her white hull was spectral in the reflected moonlight. Her superstructure was dark. Only the necessary running lights were on. On her stern, written in large letters, was White Falcon; in smaller letters beneath it was her home port, Bermuda.

CHAPTER 20

I returned to my office a bit shaken after the jarring news at lunch from Hugh Patterson. I had thought my enigmatic half-brother and I had parted our ways after discovering each other over a year ago. We saw no reason to develop a relationship. Neither Carol nor Arnie knows about him. I was hoping to keep it that way, but now...now that he's mixed up in these thefts and murders Arnie will have to know.

Freddie had his nose inches from the screen on his computer, exposing the top of his head.

"Freddie, the grass is growing. I bet with a pair of tweezers we could stretch them out ..."

He grimaced.

"I agree. It's best to let Nature do her thing. Think of wheat and corn. Do you water often?"

He had a pained look.

"Just kidding, Freddie. In two weeks your hair will be ready to harvest. Do you really want to grow it back? You're not doing this to please Arnie and me, I hope."

"Yes and no. I want to do it. It looks silly now, but..."

"I promise no more ribbing during the growing season."

"Oh, I don't mind."

I smiled. "Still, no more ribs from me, although…"

"What?"

"The Mohawk running fore and aft down your head looks like a tennis net. Maybe you could trim it down, get it down closer to the upcoming crop."

He ran his hand over the top of his head.

"I could do that."

"Just a thought. Have you got anything?"

He narrowed in on the monitor. "Richard Kern, Soho."

"The other conservator who was murdered."

"Yes, in a building just south of West Houston that has a fire escape zigzagging up the face of it. It couldn't be used without notice – it doesn't reach the sidewalk – but if someone got on it from a second or third floor window, he could use it to enter the top floor where Kern had his studio. Here's a picture."

"I see. What was the painting that was stolen?"

"*The Card Players* by Paul Cezanne. Not the real one. That's owned by the government of Qatar. They bought it for two-hundred-and-fifty million dollars during the Great Recession."

"Freddie, painting prices are leaving the atmosphere. These prices are crazy. So what was Kern repairing?"

"A replica and a very good one. It's insured for forty million."

"Who would want to pay forty million for a forgery?"

"Replica is a better word. Horace said art is a poem without words. I suppose if a painting is as perfect as the original, so is the poem."

I looked at him and remembered the Great Philosophers book I saw on his desk. What he said made some sense. If you didn't need the bragging rights of owning the original, why pay two-hundred-and-fifty million for a famous piece of art when you can pay forty or fifty million and get the same poetic enjoyment?

"Who owned it?"

"The insurance records say a woman."

"Address?"

"In Brooklyn near Prospect Park. Nice neighborhood. I run there once in a while. I'll write it down for you."

"Who's the insurer?"

"Indemnity Assurance. They're in Manhattan on Park Avenue."

"I know. Good work, Freddie, very good work. When you're ready to harvest your crop it will be on me."

He grinned and returned to his computer. In a second he was focused on the screen like a scientist waiting for a test tube to bubble.

I went to my desk and punched in a number on my cell phone.

"Indemnity Assurance."

"Harold Bullard, please, Hank Tower calling."

His gravel voice came through without a hello.

"I've authorized the wire transfer. Give it time."

"That's not why I'm calling. How many paintings do you insure?"

"That's proprietary. I told you that."

"I know you insure *The Card Players* by Cezanne. Forty million."

Silence.

"Yes, we do. It's a replica by a less famous artist of the time."

"It was stolen the same way the Picasso was stolen – the conservator was killed."

"That is true."

"Why didn't you tell me you insured more paintings?"

"I didn't say we insured more. I said we insured an extraordinary reproduction of *The Card Players*."

"Why the payment favor? Am I just a nice guy?"

"We have our own investigators, but none has your experience tracing money. You're free help."

"How do you know I have experience tracing money?"

"How did you know we insure *The Card Players*?"

"I didn't. You told me."

"Damned if I didn't! You're a spy all right."

"I did government analysis, Harold."

"Un huh. Remember, you owe me whatever information you find."

"I remember. I'd like more from you."

"Give me something and we'll talk."

My mind saw him leaning back in his chair with one leg on his desk and a cigar in a side of his mouth.

"Okay. I'll be back."

I spun my chair around from the window and saw Arnie standing in the doorway. I waved a note paper at him.

"Here's the name and address of the woman who owns the painting stolen from the conservator in Soho. Freddie has more info. Get an interview with her to see if she has any connection with the downstream part of this scam. The painting is insured for forty million, about a sixth of what the original sold for in the middle of the Recession. After my lunch with Mona we can compare notes."

"Aye, 'ank." He smiled. "Did you see the fuzz on Freddie's scalp?"

"Yeah. I suggested he level the playing field."

"It would be nicer on the eye."

"See what you can find, Arnie."

A cab was unloading a passenger at the corner of Second Avenue and Fifty-sixth. I let out a loud whistle and jumped in the back door before he could pull away.

"One Central Park West."

He turned west then north to Fifty-ninth and west again to Columbus Circle. I got out on the east side of Central Park West and walked across the street to Jean Georges, one of only five restaurants in New York that Michelin has consecrated with three-stars, its highest honor. The restaurant is in the Trump International Tower, a tall hotel/condo building with panoramic views of Central Park. It was 1:00 when I was led by the *maître'd* through a stunningly beautiful dining room to a table for two in a banquette recessed part way into one of the room's walls. The table was set for its occupants to sit side by side and look into the room. It's a romantic little grotto, but a man or woman with a broad center of gravity would not find it so.

A glamorously dressed, petite Mona was already in residence, looking at me with a pleasant smile. I slid my normal center-of-gravity in next to her and the waiter locked us in with the table. We were hip to hip with a tiny hint of a fine perfume filling the space. It's noteworthy that after first classifying Mona as an attractive but dowdy woman, that I no longer saw her that way. Now, a combination of the perfume and knowing that she was having an affair gave her a flamboyance, a new persona, at least in my mischievous mind. I thought of the dull librarian with Coke-bottle reading glasses who slowly takes them off, undoes a few buttons on her blouse, tosses her bundled hair to the wind and morphs into a sexual huntress. That's a bit overstated, but it's in the direction of what I felt sitting next to her.

"Mona, thank you for this treat. My usual lunches somehow overlook Jean Georges."

"Perhaps this will help open its doors for you."

Now, a gentleman would have simply pocketed the envelope she gave me as a gesture to the character of the finer sex. I opened it and studied the contents. It was a check for one–hundred-and-fifty thousand, certified.

"Thank you, Mona. I usually don't get paid so promptly. I hope there's something else I can do for you."

"Maybe. Let's have some wine. I find the pinot noir

grape the finest. Do you, Hank?"

"Yes, I do."

She raised her chin and a waiter materialized immediately.

"A bottle of Chambertin."

Depending on the Chambertin the waiter selected, the price could reach four figures. But what the hell? When you have just fattened your checking account by fifteen million dollars the expense of a four-figure lunch is hardly noticeable. I grinned at her.

"I ask again. What else can I do for you?"

She smiled wistfully and looked around the room.

"This is one of my favorite places in New York. The neighborhood, the building, the restaurant. Have you been in the Time Warner Center next door?"

"Yes."

"This whole area. It's the epicenter of the city."

The white city, I thought. She drifted away. The wine arrived.

"You taste it, Hank."

I did. It was properly chilled and heavenly good.

We clicked without toasting. Her eyes were in a worried, dreamy mode. There was something more than a celebratory lunch on this lady's mind. The waiter handed us menus. She ordered quickly. I took my time. These high-end eateries generally serve small portions of exotic combinations. I deferred to the waiter. "If you were ordering..."

He ran his little finger down three courses. I agreed.

I turned to Mona. "It excuses me from ordering too expensively. Now it's his fault."

Another weak smile.

"What is it, Mona?"

"I...let's wait...no, I need to...I'm not sure."

"Have you heard from Gerald? Does he know about the insurance settlement?"

"No…I…"

"What?"

"I haven't heard from him in a month."

"His law practice. Have they…"

No answer.

"A month is serious, Mona. He could be hurt, in a hospital. Have you called the police…"

"No. I don't want to overdo..."

Overdo? You don't hear from your husband in a month and you don't want to overdo?

"Surely his law partners have information."

"Hank, I've got myself in a situation I..."

The lunch was definitely about more than an early insurance payout.

"My services are available, Mona."

The food interrupted. I was right about the fare. It was a piece of art, small and pretty, centered in a large plate. And delicious. We went through our appetizers in silence. I saw her fork hand was trembling slightly. The waiter took our empty plates.

"He was on a trip, right? Where?"

"Chicago."

"Law firm business?"

"I don't know. I shouldn't have…"

The second course arrived. Bigger and equally beautiful, but still looking rather lonely on the huge plate. I let her mull over her apparent conflict and went for the food. Delicious, and when finished far more satisfying that the amount would suggest. The waiter refilled our wine glasses and took our plates. I went for the fence.

"Mona, I'm working on finding who killed Gabriel, but there are two other murders of art conservators that tie in to his. One was here in Soho; the first one was in Chicago. All three were in a week. I need to know how deep Gerald is in the art world."

"You don't think…"

"I don't think anything until I have facts."

Our final course arrived, a light puffy, silo-shaped thing that looked like a whiff of air might carry it away. She welcomed the diversion. So did I, but for a different reason. The light puffy thing exploded with a rainbow of flavor in my mouth. I finished it, took a sip of the Chambertin and watched her fork hand. The tremor was still there.

"Mona, over my youthful years I have heard what most hundred-year olds have never heard. Whatever is on your mind will not surprise me."

She pushed away the dessert and leaned back against the banquette's cushion.

"Gerald and I have been sleeping in different bedrooms for three years. I insisted on it when I learned he was bedding whatever came his way, or he could afford. I've thought of divorce at least once a week, but... but..."

"But the living was good."

"Yes."

"But now you have fifteen million dollars. It won't buy where you live, but it's a hell of a lot of money. Does it change your mind?"

"Yes, but..."

"But what?"

"What if he's dead?"

My theory.

"That would change things considerably, unless there's a pre-nup."

"There isn't. We were married before there was a need for one."

"Where does your brother-in-law Jack fit into this?"

She did the Ming vase thing.

"He...he..."

"I know you and he were alone in a Roosevelt Hotel room for two hours."

Her face went white. "How do you know…?"

"Mona, the three murders I mentioned are part of a scam that finds a vulnerable art conservator working on a valuable piece, steals it, murders him, the owner gets the insurance money for the stolen art and the thief gets its price on the private market. A double score. I'm investigating the Gabriel part of the three. Jack was being tailed as part of that investigation. Jack runs a construction business in New York. That's a tough crowd. It would not be hard to find a killer for hire in it. All he would need is a source to tell him who and where valuable pieces were being restored. Once he had that…"

Looking horrified, "Oh, no, Hank, you've got it all wrong! It's…"

She froze.

"It's who, Mona?"

Nothing.

"Mona, if you have knowledge of a murder, you could be in danger."

She was about to answer when the waiter asked if we would like coffee, espresso, etc. I needed more time.

"An espresso for me. Straight."

Mona asked for the same.

"I had better hire you before we talk. Isn't there confidentiality between private investigators and clients?"

"Yes, but its worth depends on the private investigator."

She studied me. "I want you to find Gerald, Hank. I'll pay your fee whatever it is. Will you do that?"

"Yes, but only if you realize I have another client who wants me to find Gabriel's murderer. If a conflict arises, I have to honor the first client's contract."

"I can't imagine a conflict. Give me another contract. I'll sign it."

"All right. I'll need more information about Gerald's

trip to Chicago, when he left, where he stayed, his purpose, when he said he'd be back..."

She signaled the waiter for the check.

"Of course. But not here. Come to my apartment tomorrow mid-morning and we can talk. Bring the contract with you."

"You don't want to know my fee first?"

"No."

The waiter returned with a small, handsome folder. She took an American Express Card from a small purse and laid it on top without looking at the amount of the check inside. We sipped our espressos while we waited for him to return. The tremor was gone. Am I that comforting? A flattering thought, but a risky one. Something else had transpired to quiet her nervousness. Just having someone on your side can sometimes do that, but that thought was also potentially dangerous. I tried to run my thoughts over our conversation, but only one statement stood out –

"Oh, no, Hank, you've got it all wrong! It's..."

Tomorrow, I would press for who "It's..." is.

CHAPTER 21

It was the first time Hetty had been on an airplane. She had never needed or thought of one. Her early gigs were always within a two-hundred mile radius from Abilene, Kansas. Cars and buses were her transportation. Her current gig kept her tied to the Golden Swan. Greg made her first experience in the air a comfortable one with business class seats for the two-and-a-half-hour flight from St. Louis to La Guardia. It was a treat, but her real treat was yet to come. Greg had reserved a high-floor suite in the Four Seasons Hotel on Fifty-seventh Street in the heart of Manhattan. Hetty was awed by the expanse of the city and the confusion of its throughways while the cab maneuvered its way from the airport into Manhattan. But her eyes nearly exploded when the two of them reached the hotel, saw its grand lobby and entered a magnificent room high above most of the City. Their one-bedroom suite had a panoramic view over Central Park and its furnishings were fit for a Duchess. There was an all-marble bathroom with a large glassed-in rain shower, a wide, deep tub and oils and lotions and sweet smelling soaps and two luxurious robes hanging on the wall. She started to melt. It was more than a dream, for she had no knowledge of anything like this for a dream to form. Their hotel escort pointed out various room controls to Greg and placed their bags for easy access. Greg tipped him and turned to Hetty.

"Greg…I don't know what to say? I've never seen anything like this…"

"And they haven't seen anything like you. While you were standing in the lobby I was watching faces.

When you removed your coat, every male eyeball locked in on you."

He walked over to her and kissed her. She closed her eyes and gave back the most sincere kiss of her life. She dropped her head on his shoulder.

"Greg, can we…"

"Yes…"

They kissed again, pulling themselves tightly to each other to release the tension of the last few months. It broke like a dam. They stumbled against a small table in their rush to the bedroom. Had it been a coiled python they wouldn't have noticed.

That same day Isa and Jonah left their rooms in the Ritz Carlton Hotel in Chicago's Loop for a cab. Isa told the driver to go south on State Street to Fifty-eighth Street. There Jonah and Isa would separate. Isa was told by his contact to walk east into the southern end of Washington Park. Isa told Jonah to follow him clandestinely. It was the rendezvous Isa had jokingly predicted – a park bench hidden from sight under the dome of a spreading oak tree near a small lake. Weather in Chicago in September is usually beautiful, but today the morning sky was covered with dark clouds, the wind was brisk and tiny raindrops were stinging their faces. Isa pulled up his collar, shivered and grumbled about the idiocy of such a meeting place. Jonah wandered out of sight impervious to the wind or rain.

Isa crossed a small drive and walked deeper into the park. Ahead was the rendezvous bench, a weathered creation with green paint peeling off its slats. It was about twenty feet from a shallow lake. A man came toward him from the east, pointed to the bench and the two sat next to each other. Isa saw Jonah crouched on the wet grass hidden by a tree and well within eye and ear shot. The man spoke before Isa could welcome him.

"I have only moments. I know you're a fast study, so listen."

The man went on to explain the vulnerability of many art conservators, the value of some of the pieces they work on, the insurance, the resale and then he stopped, as if he didn't want to include the missing ingredient.

"You want me because you need a thief that leaves no witnesses."

The man nodded.

The lily-livered idiot, thought Isa, can't even say it. Isa asked two key questions.

"How do you know who is working on what and who sells the paintings?"

"I can't reveal that."

"Then we don't have a deal."

Isa started to get up. Jonah saw it and rose like a racer before the gun.

"Why?"

"If what you say is true, this is very big and very risky. I can't go in half blind."

The man leaned back thoughtfully and said,

"The one who sells the art would have me killed, if I ever revealed his name."

Isa stared at him.

"I can give you the pointer's name."

"Write it down."

Isa pulled a scrap of paper from his pocket. The man scribbled on it and handed it back to Isa. Isa read it and nodded.

Sarcastically, "If you're too frightened to give me the seller's name, then give me a way I can contact him myself ..."

Isa said it with the grin of an usher at Hell's door.

"...in case you get hit by a bus."

The man took back the paper and wrote two words on it.

"That's all I'm giving you."

Isa looked at it and said nothing. The man continued.

"My cut for organizing this is fifteen percent. The pointer gets another fifteen and the seller demands half."

"That leaves twenty percent for the person taking the greatest risk."

Isa said it with genuine contempt.

"I suggest you speak to your two partners. What you need I can provide, but my share has to be higher."

"That's impossible! I can't..."

Isa dropped his arm behind the bench and with a waving motion signaled Jonah to stay hidden. Isa raised his chin, thought for a moment then turned to the man and said,

"I know. These things are difficult. Understanding and give and take are important when starting a venture. This one certainly calls for all that."

He took a stage pause and continued, warming to his subject,

"In addition to trust and cooperation there must also be proof of performance. Each partner has to show he can do what he promises. Don't you agree?"

The man nodded his head uneasily, not sure where Isa was going.

"So I propose this, my good man. Let's do a test. Give me the first, let's call it an assignment, to prove my worth to the partnership, maybe another one or two will be necessary to satisfy you and your partner that I can do as I promise. I will watch how the rest of our little team plays out. If a check in the proper amount reaches me for my services on a timely basis, then we go forward as you outlined, perhaps tweaking the arrangement a bit more in my favor. If the checks don't reach me promptly and in the accurate amount, then that will be that. We all return to our own devices. Is this satisfactory?"

"Yes, perfectly. I will inform the other two."

"Good. Now, let me have what the pointer, as you call him, has in mind for the first, eh, assignment."

The man handed Isa a folded piece of paper.

"I see it's in Chicago. Very good. And the delivery is in New York. Also good. Now, let's get out of the rain."

Isa rose and extended his hand. The man stood, accepted it with an unknown suspicion and said again,

"I will inform the other two."

He departed to the east. When he was out of sight, Isa signaled Jonah and the two caught a cab on the west side of the park. On their way back to the Ritz Carlton,

"I have the name of the pointer, Jonah. For the seller, all I could get was some sort of code, but we know the drop point is in New York. We can start there to find the seller."

Isa leaned back, holding the scrap of paper, and mused.

"It always amazes me how people overstate their importance in a deal. Here's this guy claiming he's entitled to fifteen percent of the gross for simply bringing people together. Fifteen percent for having an idea and making a few phone calls and assuming virtually no risk! It makes my blood boil. Stupid and greedy. The idiot is out of his league. Fifteen percent. Ridiculous.

"Then you have the guy who fingers the target. He wants fifteen percent. Another greedy idiot. Fifteen percent for one phone call to you or me. How do these people think? Five percent is closer. If we saw it as a finder's fee, it would be two percent. We're being generous with the s.o.b. We'll address both of these imbalances when the time comes.

"Then you have the seller. An absolutely critical role. But fifty percent? High-end galleries take forty percent of a sale, some take less. We'll address that, too, when the time comes."

He returned his attention to the scribbling on the paper in his hand and said in a low voice,

"It's some goddam code. White Falcon. What could that mean?"

Greg woke first from the dreamy ecstasy he and Hetty had fallen into. It was 7:00 p.m. and the autumn sun had set, changing the view from their room into a rectangle of lights bordering a dark Central Park. He pushed himself up against the bed's headboard and gently ran his hand down her cheek, neck and bare shoulder. She rolled over to him.

"Look at all the diamonds I've ordered for you."

She rose to look out the window and gasped. "Greg…it's beautiful. I've never seen anything like it."

"There probably isn't anything like it. New York is unique. I'm thinking of moving here…"

She jumped.

"Not right away. I've been talking to one of the big banks here."

"Then I have to move, too."

He smiled. "Isa might not like that. You're bringing hundreds of flies into his web."

"I signed a contract with him."

"Are there many months to go?"

"I don't want to count them."

"Well, if I take the job, I'll have to commute to St. Louis on weekends. It's not unusual."

She gave him a worried look. "When will you decide?"

"I'm committed for at least six months. There are

large loan applications pending…"

"I could buy my way out of the contract for two hundred thousand dollars."

"Do you have that much money?"

"No. I'd take out a loan." With a grin. "...from your bank."

"Let's not think about it now. It's seven. Let's freshen up and have dinner in the hotel's restaurant. Hungry?"

She pulled herself tight to his bare chest. "Yes."

He looked at her knowingly. "Eight-thirty is as good as seven-thirty."

She kissed his neck and cheek and forehead. "It's much better."

The White Falcon had a crew of eight. Six were rotated purposely at least once a year for security reasons; more often, if their competence faltered. The remaining two were brothers from Australia. They were permanent and were reliably discrete when asked to perform chores outside their maritime duties. The Captain was nicknamed Cain; the First Mate, Abel. The names were often ridiculed when the two were ashore, but never twice by the same crowd. The ship's owner had given the non-permanent crew, except the chef, leave as soon as the Falcon was secured in North Cove Marina in Lower Manhattan.

The yacht's owner is a woman in her early fifties, bright, educated, sophisticated, a graduate of the best schools and a continuous world traveler. She's a beauty by any man's standard and, like her half-brother, amoral in nearly all respects. Her friends and family call her the Countess. She and her half-brother share an English Earl as their father. Years ago the Earl, in deference to a severe imbalance between his debts and assets, moved the latter and his wife to Bermuda where the Countess and her half-brother were born. He gave up an earldom granted by Charles II in the late sixteen hundreds when he forfeited his English citizenship; but he succeeded in protecting his assets from "the rabble creditors." The Countess's half-brother's name is Ronald Mason, Hank Tower's look-alike and, thanks to the handsome and persuasive Earl, the first son of Tower's mother. The Countess was anxiously readying a dinner.

"Henri, he'll be here at seven for cocktails. The dinner must be ready by eight. I know we arrived late, but you have to do it. I won't hear any excuses."

He started to answer affirmatively, but she had already turned her attention to Abel.

"I want an '85 Lynch Bages with dinner and a Chardonnay for cocktails. A California will do. And do something with these flowers. They look like they've been gassed. Henri, we should have some strawberries in the freezer. Defrost them and add, what...?"

"Some cream and *petit fours*, madam?'

"Yes. That will do. And the lamb is defrosting?"

"I've had it out for two hours, madam."

"Good, good. Now, what else?"

She looked around the paneled dining room.

"A table cloth. Get a fresh one with brighter colors and, Abel, test the lamps over the mantle. Do you have something to wear besides those baggy pants?"

He smiled. "Yes, Countess, I do. We are also anxious to see Mr. Mason. Henri and I will make it a proper occasion."

"Good, good. Now, what else. Abel, see if we still have some of that fifty-year-old rum. Bring the bottle to the bar. Ronald may want some of it. I'll be back at six-thirty to look things over."

Henri bowed his head and went to the galley a bit ruffled; Abel grinned as one who had seen this before.

He waited until she left and tested the lights over the mantle.

At 6:30, earlier than expected, Ronald Mason stepped from the pier onto the White Falcon. He was impeccably dressed in gray trousers, a double-breasted blue blazer and an open neck white shirt. He was in his usual good spirits as the Captain addressed him.

"Welcome aboard, Mr. Mason."

"Thank you, Cain. It's been awhile. How was the sail from Bermuda?"

"Smooth mostly until about a hundred miles out. The sea gave us a kicking, but we're here and all is well. Shall I tell the Countess you're here?"

"Yes, please. Ask her to meet me in the den. I need to talk to her privately. Bring a small rum for me. Do you still have that fifty year old?'

"Yes, we do. I'll ask Abel to pour some for you."

"You'd better ask the Countess what she wants. I can't predict her."

Understandingly, "I will."

The Captain disappeared into the ship and Ronald went to the small library just aft of the dining room. She entered moments later, smiling at her younger half-brother.

"Ronald, you look as dashing as ever." She pressed a cheek to his, then to his other. Pulling back,

"Every woman worthy of the name was asking for you in Bermuda. It's cruel of you to desert such adoring creatures for so long."

"And you look beautiful. I'm sure there was anguish among your admirers when you sailed off."

Abel entered with a small glass of rum and a glass of ice water on a tray.

"Would you like something, Countess?"

"No, I'll wait for cocktails."

Mason signaled for privacy and the second-in-command left the room. He took one of the two leather chairs and motioned his hand for the Countess to take the other one. She sat and stared at him for a moment.

"You have something."

"Yes, I do. With your help it can be worth at least fifty million before we close it down."

"You have it."

"The art world is going crazy. Supply is limited and demand is absurdly high. Match that with the sea of money floating around the world and it's clear why prices are astronomical."

He paused and continued.

"I talked recently to a man with whom I have done a few business deals in the past. We made small amounts. The more profitable side of our acquaintance was his seemingly unlimited access to the other gender."

The Countess smiled.

"The chap went fallow for some time. I thought he had had a conscience fit and decided to forgo life's more interesting ways or was dead. I was wrong on both counts. He surfaced a month ago with an interesting program that required someone of my – and your – talents. I had just arrived in New York when I got his call."

"And the call was lush enough for you to be here as soon as we docked."

"Yes. He says he has a way to acquire expensive art, but he needs a way to sell it on the private market as quietly as possible. You know that world well, I recall, dearest sister."

"Yes, I do, Ronald; yes I do."

CHAPTER 22

I got home at 7:00 to find Carol already in residence. I was shedding my sport coat when from down the hallway that leads to the bedroom came…

"We're due at the Sanchez's at eight. I hope you haven't forgotten."

"No, of course not."

I had, of course, despite an earlier reminder from Carol. These kinds of events get out of the corral sometimes when you're busy keeping other parts of the ranch in the black.

"I'll be ready. I'll take that bottle of pinot I bought a few days ago."

"You mean the one you brought home Monday."

"Well, yeah. I don't remember exactly when I bought…"

"We drank it two days ago, super-detective."

"It was quite good, wasn't it?"

Without a pause,

"You forgot about tonight, didn't you?" It had a touch of reproach.

"You'd better get another bottle in a hurry."

"I'm on my way."

I walked quickly to the nearby wine store, selected an equally fine pinot noir and was back in fifteen minutes. She was still in the bedroom.

"It will take twenty minutes to get to Tudor City at this hour. Do you have the wine?"

I mumbled a yes and went to the bathroom to freshen up.

Bill and I are old friends; his wife Nora and Carol are new friends. Bill was my mentor when, just out of business school, I joined the Headmaster's coterie of fifty spies. Nora and Carol met two-plus years ago and hit it off at the start. They talk often the way women do. Bill is happily married and has been marketing the merits of married life to me in subtle ways. "Why don't you retire your thrill-seeking ass, get a normal job and marry Carol?" for instance. He would no doubt resume his campaign this evening, but this time it was Carol who needed persuading. I had bought in…then the incident.

It was right for her to rethink marriage to me. I've always been a long shot for an extended life, but she was willing to endure it. Then I foolishly endangered her life in one of my cases.

So we wait and see. Bill might know these facts via conversation between Nora and Carol, but I intended to dodge them if the subject came up. I wanted to use the occasion to find out what more he knew about the money transfers from Harris and Jacobs to Bermuda. He had told me that the three latest and largest coincided with the timing of the murders in Chicago, Soho and my client's boyfriend, Gabriel.

"It's twenty of. We need to go."

She was dressed beautifully. What a figure! She could wear a sack and it would still shine through.

"*Si, si. Je suis pret.*"

chap"What are you, Spanish or French?"

"I am neither. I am a thoroughly homogenized American, a mix of Northern European with strains of Lord knows what else."

"Well, so am I, but that's not going to get us a cab."

"I'll go to the corner and find one."

Twenty minutes later we were at the entrance to Tudor City, a massive complex at the far eastern end of Forty-second Street. Bill owns a second floor, three bedroom co-op that he bought when the Tudor City and other Manhattan real estate was sanely priced. The "City" consists of fifteen, high-rise buildings, five thousand residents and sufficient parks and stores and other amenities for a resident to be born, grow up and die there. Nora answered the door, smiling.

"Come in, come in. Carol, dear, you look beautiful. You look handsome, too, Hank. Don't just stand there like a statue. Come in."

Bill was also looking statuesque, standing about six feet behind Nora. We entered, Nora and Carol hugged; Bill and I shook hands in silence and gave each other's lady a light hug. After that, the two women immediately disappeared into some other universe. Bill and I went into the living room, sat and waited for the other to speak. He wanted to know what I knew about the transfers to Bermuda and I wanted to know what he knew. The standoff quickly became apparent and led him to one of his favorite subjects, marriage and its application to me.

"I hear the wedding date was cancelled."

"Yes. We decided to wait a few months."

"Cold feet?"

"No, your repeated wisdom regarding the virtues of married life finally reached my inner self. There was another reason."

"Carol?"

"Yes. She needs some time to work something out."

He nodded and said,

"Once dinner gets underway we won't have time to talk, so let me ask now what you know about the wire transfers to Bermuda."

"I was going to ask you."

He had his professional face on. Steady eyes, frozen face. His pulse was probably at the minimum needed to sustain life. I knew if I didn't give first I would get nothing.

"I'm meeting tomorrow morning with the owner of the Picasso that was stolen. It was insured for fifteen million. With some help from me, she got the money early. I may have something meaningful after we meet."

The same stare, then…

"Okay. I mentioned that before the three big ones there were a series of smaller transfers from the Harris and Jacobs to Bermuda. We have some information on those."

"Okay."

"The money went to the Palestinians."

"Un huh."

"To a charity account."

"Why hide charity behind Bermuda?"

"The charity has links to Hamas."

"What about the three recent transfers, the ones that link to the art thefts?"

"They went into a Bermuda account with a number. From there most of the money went to three other accounts, one in Switzerland, one in Luxemburg and one in Monte Carlo."

"Private money spreading itself."

"Most likely."

"Anything else?"

"No."

"Do you have any more interest in Harris and Jacobs?"

"Low priority. There have been no transfers since those we discovered. Whoever was behind the Hamas money is either afraid of getting caught or dead. There haven't been any more."

Nora rang out ebulliently, "Dinner's ready. I chilled your pinot, Hank. Thank you."

We gathered at a beautifully set table and ate leisurely. Both of our hosts were interested in Carol's job. Nora said that Bill had been offered a job in Washington with the NSA, but after talking it over they decided to stay in New York. There was no mention of the cancelled wedding which meant Nora and Carol had exhausted the subject in the other universe. Nora and Carol discussed a shopping excursion, Bill gave me occasional "You're not telling me everything" stares and I forced myself into the innocent, small talk of my spy days. It was an effort to appear "up" because something large was churning in me. Before, it was only a distant suspicion, but the Bermuda to Switzerland to Luxemburg to Monte Carlo transfers had my half-brother's prints all over it. The day we parted Ronald had helped save my life. I owed him. If he was behind the triple murders, would I turn him in?

The bottle of pinot was emptied as well as, in Bill's and my case, an ounce each of a good Remy Martin XO cognac. Parting words were exchanged. Carol and I were about fifteen feet from the door when Bill said,

"Hank, I forgot to tell you something."

I stepped back. Quietly, "I want to hear about your meeting tomorrow."

"I thought you were off the case."

"I'm never off a case."

"Right. I'll phone you."

"I'd appreciate it."

With the unsaid "...if you ever want help from me again" still in my ear, I hailed a cab for home. We were silent to Forty-second and Lexington when I took her hand.

"Did you and Nora discuss anything about what happened?"

"No details, just that I was very scared."

"Did she offer any...any advice?"

She snuggled up to me and laid her head on my shoulder.

"I guess. The understanding kind. She's a kind person. She saw I was still…not quite settled."

"Anything else?"

"Nothing important."

"Oh."

"Just…" She looked up at me with that ice-melting smile,

"She just said 'You love him, don't you?'"

"Just! What did you say?"

She ran her hand onto my inner thigh.

"I said 'I guess so. He's bright and handsome.'"

"You guess so?"

"You are handsome."

"What about smart?"

"Yes, I suppose so."

"You said I was smart – to Nora."

"Did I? Oh, yes. I forgot."

I pouted a bit, purposely.

She moved her hand up an inch or two and with a different smile said,

"Yes, I love you."

She kissed me under my left ear and whispered,

"Let me tell you how much in bed."

I squeezed her hand.

When I entered my office I found messages from Harold Bullard of Indemnity Assurance and my client, Hugh Patterson. I called Patterson first.

"Hank, where are you on Gabriel's murder?"

It was a strong voice for such a mild man.

"Hugh, I'm working on it. The insurance has been paid to Mona Harris. I'm meeting with her this morning. There may be something there. As I said, Gabriel's killer was a professional, not a riled up lover. It's the hardest kind of case. I've got a lot of high-powered help on it for me. It just takes time."

"What about the police. You said you had connections."

"I will contact them today to see if they have anything new."

"I'm sorry. It's just that I..."

"I know. You want justice. So does everyone else. Stay in touch. You can call me or Arnie anytime."

"Okay. But call me as soon as you have..."

"Hugh, we will. It's a tough one."

I heard a gush of "I know" air and we parted.

My next call was to Harold Bullard. I waited to be connected, then in the crusty voice of my Edward G. Robinson fantasy ...

"Talk to me."

I saw an unlit cigar in his mouth.

"Harold, I'm on it. I'm seeing Mona Harris this morning. I need to know about her husband, Gerald. He's been incommunicado for too long. Something's happened and she wants me to find out what. That's all I have now."

"You owe me a favor."

"I keep my promises, but that's all I know."

"I don't believe you."

Smart bastard. Laconic, but smart.

"The Picasso theft was done by a hired killer."

"How do you know?"

"Trust me, Harold. I've been doing this..."

"This nose smells very well. It says you're holding back."

"I appreciate what you did for me. I won't let you down. Did you insure the painting stolen in Soho?"

"Policies are confidential."

"Okay, but think about it. If I knew, it could help my investigation."

Freddie said he did insure it. I could also ask Captain

Holden to have a judge subpoena the information, but I held back.

Before hanging up, "Call me tomorrow."

I called my Captain friend.

"Tom, do you have anything new on the Soho or Gabriel murders, fingerprints, anything?"

"There was one fingerprint at the Gabriel scene where the Picasso was stolen.

"Where did you find it?"

"On the toilet bowl lever. None were found in Soho or in Chicago."

"Any spilled urine for DNA?"

"No."

"The guy shot Gabriel and took the time to pee before leaving with the painting."

"Yes."

"What a cool bastard."

"You sound admiring."

"No, well, in a way... no, of course not."

"So who owns the print?"

"It's a first for me. Not a match in any database we probed – local, FBI, SEC, military, immigration. He's non-existing."

"An illegal refugee?"

"Possibly, but he's not a one-man band. He needs someone to ID where the paintings are and someone to cash them out."

"Right. What about the cameras you set up in front of my studio?"

"Nothing, except you. I thought you were staying away from it."

My stomach started to churn again.

"When did you see me?"

"Thursday, walking down the other side of the street looking for my cameras. Did you see them?"

"No."

"Good. Stay in touch."

My answer was true. I didn't see the cameras because it wasn't me they saw searching for them. It was my look-alike, half-brother, Ronald Mason, checking out the studio with the expensive Renoir and restorer inside. Jesus!

I slipped my sport coat over the .38 tucked in my back and handed a note to Freddie.

"Check this out. I'll be at Mona Harris's apartment on Park Avenue."

"Okay. Anything else? I have time."

'Use it on what I gave you. I need a standard contract."

He fished one out of his desk drawer. "What should I put in it?"

"Nothing. It's a straight fee."

"Arnie has something on Jack Harris."

'Good. Tell him we'll go over it later today."

I was politely directed by the doorman to the elevator inside 740 Park Avenue. Moments later a maid opened the door and took me to Mona Harris standing in the grand old apartment's understated living room. She was dressed as a multi-millionaire lady should be. Perfectly tailored and coiffured. She's an attractive woman, actually. Not quite sexy, but in the right garb…

She walked to me with her hand out.

"Hank, thank you for coming. What can I get for you, coffee, water, a drink?"

"I'm fine."

"Please take a seat. Did you bring a contract?"

I handed it to her.

"Where do I sign?"

"There's a yellow sticky on page…"

"Oh, I see it." She signed without looking further

and handed it back to me. I signed and put her copy on a side table.

"You said it's been a month since you've heard from Gerald."

"Yes. As I said, he had to go to Chicago for some legal meeting, at least that's what he said."

"Any idea who would be with him?"

"Yes, a woman."

"Name?"

"A temporary woman."

"I see."

"No one else?"

"His partner said he went alone. He said he had no idea what the trip was about."

"What about the firm financially? Is it sound?"

"I have no idea."

"At lunch when I suggested Jack traveled in a tough crowd you blanched and said I had it all wrong. What did I have wrong?"

"You implied Jack might be behind the three murders."

"Yes, I did. Your slip suggested you knew who is behind them. Gerald, someone else?"

"I reacted to the thought of Jack being involved. Gerald? Three or four years ago I would have said no, but now? He's drifted from me and I from him. When he's here, he leaves before I'm up and comes home after I'm in bed. Sound strange?"

"No. Many couples are together on the surface only."

"Are you married, Hank?"

"No."

"A partner?"

"Yes."

"That's good. Yes, that's good."

"Mona, I need something to go on. You must have something I can get into. What about a letter, email, phone call..."

"Phone call." She looked away into space.

"What? You said you hadn't heard from him in a month."

"I was wrong. I forgot he called about a week ago. I assumed he was in Chicago. He said he was all right. We made some small talk for a minute or two and hung up. He probably thought I might have the police looking for him, if he didn't check in."

"Did he call your cell phone?"

"Yes. I was getting in a cab."

"Please get it."

I asked her to search her incoming calls.

"Are there any calls with an area code you don't recognize?"

She scrolled the calls.

"Yes, this one. Area code 314. Do you know it?"

"Yes, it's St. Louis, Missouri, where my fiancé was born."

CHAPTER 23

Hetty and Greg returned to St. Louis after an idyllic three-days in New York. Hetty saw an opera, a Broadway show and experienced her first real peace with a man in her young life. While Greg was in his business meetings she wandered Fifth and Madison Avenues as if she had entered a fairyland. The stores were endless and filled with elegant clothes and sparkling jewels. And the bustle, the energy, the constant flow of people, all in a hurry, going this way and that way, weaving through each other as harmlessly as if it were a rehearsed dance. I've never seen so many people. Where are they all going, she asked herself? And the soaring buildings and cars and trucks and buses, some double-decked, and taxis and dark-windowed vehicles, some of which seemed as long as train cars. She tingled with excitement. I have to come here. I have to live here. The wish gripped her like a bulldog. And there was Greg, the hero who brought her here, who introduced her to all these wonders, who cared for her, who held her gently, who let her be herself without fear of the dominating male she had experienced so often. On the plane she caught herself looking at him reading his iPad, thinking how heavenly it would be to share with him that magical place, this wonderful dream. The thought was so overwhelming she shook her head as if it had frightened her.

They took a cab from Lambert-St. Louis to Hetty's new apartment on the Illinois side of the Mississippi, minutes from the Golden Swan. As the cab approached she leaned to him in the back seat.

"Greg, I can't thank you enough. It was a wonderful,

wonderful trip. I've never had a trip like it."

She looked at him, hoping to hear him say they would repeat it. Instead, he kissed her hard and said,

"It was wonderful for me, too. I'll be in touch. Maybe I'll stop by for a rehearsal."

He kissed her again less aggressively and she slid out of the cab. The driver took her bag to the door of the apartment house. She turned for one last look at Greg, but he was focused on his iPad.

The next morning she arrived at the Swan early to view the progress of her new Show Boat cabaret. Another week to its opening, said Jerry. He also told her that Isa and Jonah's return from their Chicago trip would be delayed. There was business in New York Isa had to attend to and he wanted Jonah with him. New York. There it was again. The day after she returned! It was a good omen, she thought. Was Isa setting up a nightclub there, was he involved somehow in a Broadway show, was he doing something she could be a part of? He was involved in so many things she hoped something in New York was one of them.

"We missed you, Hetty," said Jerry with a trace of pining.

She smiled at him. "It's good to be back, Jerry" was all she said. A woman senses when a man is drawn to her and she didn't want to hurt Jerry by spewing out the thrills of her trip, especially the sexual ones.

"I set up a room near the stern for you to rehearse. It's small, but it's better than nothing. Practice is necessary."

She looked at him. "Are you a singer, Jerry?"

"No, a pianist, a once-was pianist. I haven't played for probably two years. The last time I sat down I played between the keys."

She grinned. "Can you play for me?"

"Not until I practice."

"The piano is available. Let's make a date. One week from today you'll play a song and I'll sing it. Okay?"

"Okay, but no listening while I practice."

"Fair enough."

She wandered off to see her new stage. It was done, but it looked so tiny compared to what she had seen in New York. Little me. What was I thinking? I'm just a country singer, a small-stage performer…No I'm not! Damn, damn, damn, I'm not! I'll wow 'em even more here and then…and then I'll get an agent. I've had calls and I've read the reviews. The contract. Maybe Isa will let me out of it, maybe he'll let me sing somewhere else part time. As long as I come back here. Maybe I can build a better career. Maybe get to New York.

Three days went by without hearing from Greg. Not a call or an email on her new iPhone. She didn't have his phone number or email. All she remembered was part of the name of the bank where he worked when Isa mentioned it at that first dinner. Another day passed and she could no longer handle the tension. She saw Jerry doing his rounds of the boat and went to him.

"Jerry, I need a favor."

"Of course."

"The man who came to our table when Isa and Jonah were here, do you know the name of the bank where he works?"

Jerry's face darkened. "Yes, I do."

"Can you give it to me? I want to…"

Jerry knew what she wanted.

"Hetty, I don't think…"

"Jerry, I need it."

He looked at her in a melancholy way and said, "Hetty, come with me."

She followed him mystified. It's a simple question. Why all the fuss?

He led her into his office and unfolded a copy of the

Sunday edition of the *Post Dispatch.* The society section was exposed. Jerry sat in his chair and nodded for her to pick it up. She skimmed across the array of pictures of men and women dressed formally at a charity affair. She looked at Jerry with a question mark. He bowed his head.

She focused more intensely. There was Greg in a tuxedo standing close to a beautiful woman in a strapless gown. Beneath the picture was the caption, "Among the attendees were Mr. and Mrs. Greg Roberts…"

She let out a gasp and reached for Jerry's desk to balance herself. "Oh, God..."

Jerry stood and helped her into his chair. She was limp. Her face was paper white. She dropped her head to the desk and tried to let out a cry, but her eyes only stared at the wooden top. Her stomach jerked, then again. Jerry rushed for a waste basket and handed it to her. She vomited in it once, twice. Her mind went numb at the first sight of the picture, but now it was alive and awash in pain, memory pain, as they all flooded in: the concerts and hockey games in St. Louis, the sexual tension that built between them, the whispers in bed when it was finally released, the holding hands, the walks, the dinners, the fun they had with a French menu, the intimate smiles, the shared laughter, the joy of the theater and opera, the City, the future…she vomited again.

"Hetty, I'm sorry. Let me get you a glass of water." She nodded.

He returned and knelt next to her. She drank some of the water and uttered,

"Jerry, I've been a fool. For three days…"

"I know, Hetty. Take another drink." She swallowed more water.

"I fell for…the...the son of a bitch."

"That's it, Hetty, that's it. More, more…"

She was tearful now. "He...he made love to me, showed me New York, took me to a fancy hotel and everything, he led me on…he's a bastard, Jerry."

"Yes, he is. Drink some more water."

A thought froze her.

"Does Jonah know about my trip and Greg…married?"

"Yes."

"On dear Jesus, dear Jesus. When are they back?"

"Day after tomorrow."

"Jerry, get me Greg's number."

He hesitated.

"Please, Jerry. You don't know…please…"

Isa and Jonah boarded a plane at LaGuardia for St. Louis a day later than planned. Certain loose ends had to be attended to. To leave a job as fraught with repercussions as the two they had just finished without knowing that all the doors were closed would disturb Isa's sleep, a nightly refreshment he guarded jealously. Everything had to be attended to before a project was done and, now, he was satisfied that this one was complete. The painting stolen from the murdered Chicago conservator was sent by private car to New York, as agreed with the man on the park bench. The two similarly stolen paintings in New York were sent by private courier to the same destination. This completed Isa's part of the venture. Now, the art would go to a buyer or buyers he had no interest in knowing. His only interest – demand – was that the sales be made quickly and that the proceeds be disbursed immediately thereafter. His contact in the park had argued for additional thefts, but Isa had refused. He wanted to see the first endeavor go full circle before any expansion was planned. If there was a problem or a suspicious delay in getting his twenty percent, he would drop out of the venture and would not be responsible for any consequences that followed.

But the test did go full circle. Isa's money, roughly fourteen million dollars, was wire transferred as instructed into three St. Louis banks. The test was successful. Isa was pleased, but not happy.

Nor was Jonah, but for a different reason. When he heard about Hetty's condition after she learned that Greg was married, he became withdrawn, distant, as an artist might musing over a creative project he or she was contemplating. Isa had to ask for his attention twice instead of once. The man is not all there, thought Isa, but he didn't probe. It was Hetty who brought Isa into reality.

"Isa, Jonah knows Greg took me to New York. Now, he knows how upset I was when I found out he was married."

"He's married. Huh. I didn't know. Oh, well. I wouldn't worry about it. There are plenty of men who will knock on your door. You're a beauty. If I were younger…"

"Isa!"

He started. People didn't speak to him that way, especially an employee. His eyes narrowed.

"What?"

"He's going to kill Greg!"

Isa stared blankly, but he understood instantly. The forty-year-old banker had cheated Hetty, hurt her, but she didn't want him dead. Isa knew Jonah well, but this woman actually lived with him. Jonah didn't ask me to give her a job. He told me to give her one. There was a special relationship somewhere in Jonah's mind. Isa was thinking fast. Given the relationship, she would know if his killing Greg was a real possibility. Her fear also explained his moody behavior since we returned from New York. The bastard's planning the kill, he concluded. He would be careful, but if he slipped, it could backfire on me. Will he really do it? Yeah. He has this goddam code. He'll kill on my instructions, but he'll also kill on what he sees as an injustice to him. "He who does unto my children does also unto me," or some idiocy like that was surely running through the brute's mind. Isa thought it was nuts, but he knew with Jonah it was real. Hetty exclaimed,

"You have to stop him!"

Isa kept his professional stare. I agree, he thought, but he had no idea how. He had never interfered with Jonah for that very reason – he didn't know how he would respond. Would he turn on him? He wasn't going to take the chance. He looked hard at her.

"I can't sway him. You have to."

She slumped into a chair in front of his desk.

"Isa, you set me up with Greg, remember? Don't tell me you didn't know he was married. You used me to get the loan from his bank."

Smart ass, thought Isa. I've got to get rid of her, but it has to be smooth as ice or my ass is dead. His mind was racing.

"Okay. We do it together."

"How?"

"I don't know. Let me think."

He got up and walked to the bay window facing the towering St. Louis arch. How do I tell Greg his life is in danger? Why, he would ask? Because I have a professional killer working for me who gets pissed off when something upsets the goddam hillbilly you screwed in New York. Jesus! Can I send Jonah somewhere? Can I send Greg somewhere until Jonah cools off? He won't cool. He'll wait twenty years, if he has to. Goddam it! A diversion. I need some kind of diversion or at least a way to delay him and hope something happens. In the meantime, she has to show him she's as happy as a giggling nutcase. He turned back to Hetty.

"Go to Jonah and give him the best goddam smile in your book. Ask him to have lunch with you, shop together for something. Christ, I'll pay for whatever you buy. Show him that the crying incident is over, water off your back. You had fun. Ah…" he paused.

"Tell him that you plan to hurt him, that's it. You plan to take care of Greg yourself."

"How can I hurt him?"

"Jesus, woman! You tell his wife. Make Jonah believe this will ruin Greg, put him down the sewer. His wife will take everything he has. Let him think you're his executioner, not Jonah."

The idea struck Hetty on two levels. It just might satisfy Jonah and save Greg, and it had the side effect of getting back at Greg for not telling her he was married. But she was not the woman scorned that blabs to a wife. She would take her hurt and deal with it; but, now, she had no choice. Greg's life was at stake. She was angry, but not that angry.

Isa watched her thinking it though. She's got to do it, but she's waffling.

"Hetty, do this and I'll shorten your contract."

That triggered an instinct in the worldly thirty-year old. A man like Isa didn't give anything away unless he was worried about his own survival. He's afraid of Jonah; afraid he can't handle him in a situation like this, but he also fears some personal disaster, if Jonah kills Greg.

"I want it cancelled completely."

Goddam her! The anger ran up his spine like a flame, but he kept a calm-face.

"I'll reduce it to six more months."

I'm right, she thought. He's afraid. She went for more.

"With a twenty-thousand dollar bonus, payable now."

He almost lost it. I'll kill her myself was his first reaction! But it quickly quieted, for at that moment the full impact of her position hit him. The damned woman's invulnerable. Jonah would kill anyone who hurt her. It wouldn't surprise me if he would kill someone as a *favor* for her. Does she know that? I don't think so. I think the balls are coming from her days on the road, fending for herself. But what if she does! Then I'm not bargaining with a hillbilly singer, I'm dealing with the manager of a psychopathic killer. She's me!

"Okay, young lady. Now, get to Jonah before all this back and forth means nothing."

"I will."

She planned to do that and more. First, she would tell the agents who had contacted her about her new circumstances; then she would bargain for a larger stage somewhere, then a larger one. Eventually, she would get to New York where the twenty thousand would pay the bills until she no longer cared about bills.

She left a worried but smiling-as-usual Isa. He also had a plan that served two purposes – a distraction that, hopefully, would pull Jonah off Greg and accomplish a business objective at the same time. He took out his cell phone and punched in a number. The man he met in the park answered.

"I am pleased with our initial venture. Everyone performed as promised. But changes must be made, if we are to continue. I recommend we meet in St. Louis. My office is in the Golden Swan on the Mississippi. You can't miss it."

"Give me a couple of weeks," said the man from the park.

CHAPTER 24

"Okay Arnie what do you have on construction Jack?"

The big Scot plopped on the couch across from my desk, taking it one plop closer to death.

" 'is business is iffy. A sergeant I know is married to the senior clerk in the Planning Office downtown. I asked 'im if 'is wife would mind checking on 'arris and Jacobs, any permits pending, applications, anything that would say if the firm's active. 'e called me last night. There 'asn't been one submission of any kind for three years."

"Does he have anything in progress? Any Certificates of Occupancy pending or issued?"

"Nae, not one."

"He's out of business."

"Or into another kind."

"Like robbery and murder."

'Aye, it could be."

"Or massaging his sister-in-law's shoulders and parts beyond."

"She's fifteen million richer now."

"And a lot richer than that, if her husband Gerald is dead. The apartment on Park Avenue is probably worth thirty million."

"Do ye think 'e's dead?"

"My gut says yes, but I don't know."

"No word from 'im at all?"

"He called his wife, Mona, a week ago from St. Louis. That's the last she's heard from him."

" 'as she called the police?"

"No."

"I wonder why not."

"Private lives. She sleeps with her husband's brother and he sleeps with professionals."

I thought of telling Arnie about my half-brother, Ronald Mason's apparent involvement in this mess, but held back. Later, if I have to.

"Where do we go from 'ere, 'ank?"

"I wish it were different, but I think there's only one way. Our job is to find Gabriel's killer by the end of the year. That's less than six weeks away. All this other stuff – Mona and her brother-in law having a fling; her lover's failed or failing construction company; her missing husband, Gerald; Harris and Jacobs' transfers of money to Bermuda and onto a front for Hamas; the sales of the three art thefts, also transferred to Bermuda – it's all related, I believe, but damned if I know how. According to Bill Sanchez the money marked for Hamas ceased flowing to Bermuda some time ago. We can probably scratch that connection to Gabriel's murder, if there ever was one.

"More important, there's no real money in all this unless we catch Gabriel's killer by year end. How do we do that? The only way I know is the tethered goat strategy. Wait for the pro to show up, nab him and forget all the other stuff. Any other ideas?"

"I'm afraid not. But I'm across the street from ye, 'ank."

I smiled. "I know, it's risky, but we can't afford to chase our tails forever. We either get the guy in the next three weeks or the hell with the whole lot. We have the hundred and fifty from Mona and our standard fee from Patterson and now one from Mona to find Gerald. That should buy some Christmas presents for us. I'm going to tell both of them three weeks more and no killer or husband and we're out."

"Aye, 'ank, but I 'ave to be across the street from ye."

"I know, Arnie. I know."

I paused.

"Holden told me they got one print from the Gabriel murder scene. On the toilet lever. Absolutely no match in any known data base. In today's world that makes our catch a non-entity."

" 'e shot Gabriel then peed in 'is toilet?"

"That's what Holden told me. Balls that cool make a very dangerous adversary. Even the most confident pro would want to get away from the scene as fast as possible. This guy took a leak! Ever hear of that, Arnie?"

"Nae. 'e's a psycho. No feelings or fear."

"And no record."

I hit Holden's number to tell him his goat was going back on duty *gratis*. His two-week contract had expired, but if he could renew it, we wouldn't object.

CHAPTER 25

Jonah was studying a dealer at a Twenty-One table when Hetty entered the huge gambling room. It was mid-morning and the area was an eerie quiet. No beeping slots, no rattle of steel balls bumping into the numbered holes in the roulette wheels. He saw her coming and looked away from the table.

"Isa told me you were back from your trip to New York."

There was no show of welcome or anger. Just indifferent eyes.

"It was wonderful, Jonah. I heard you and Isa were there, too. What did you think of it?"

His stare seemed to pierce her skull looking for truth. Is he still wonderful, Hetty, now that you know he's married? She felt the question and addressed it.

"When we got back I discovered he was married."

He kept his stare, waiting.

"It pissed me off, but what the hell. He paid for everything and I got to see New York. The hell with him."

The right side of his mouth rose a couple of millimeters. He's not buying it, thought Hetty.

"I guess you heard I was upset. Well, I was for a few minutes, but I'm all right now. Women get over these things quickly."

She shrugged her shoulders and smiled her best, at the same time studying him. The slightly raised lip slipped back into its regular home.

No anger. Just a statement. "He lied to you."

She shivered. Her effort had gotten nowhere.

"Yes, and he's going to pay for it. I'm telling his

wife."

Jonah shrugged.

"It will ruin him, Jonah. She'll divorce him and take all his money. He'll be penniless and out of a job."

He looked back at the dealer sliding cards out of the shoe.

Jesus, he's counting cards. Did he hear anything I've said? He looked back at her.

"Will he lose his job?"

She didn't know if he would or wouldn't. Divorce isn't grounds for dismissal.

"I…I don't know for sure, but he'll be broke once his wife sues him."

"Will she?"

"After I'm through talking to her she will."

"Maybe she won't."

Holy shit! I'm making it worse.

"It's possible, but Jonah, I'm all right. Truly I am. I'm ready and anxious to sing on the new stage."

"I like to hear you sing. Your voice is…wonderful, Hetty."

A thought. "Your guitar. Are you still playing it?"

"I have all the important chords in my head."

"Let's go to the stage. Let me sing with you, like we did that one night."

"Okay. I'll be through here in an hour."

She smiled as brightly as she could. "I'll see you there."

He stepped back to watch the dealer sliding hole cards to three players. She was convinced she hadn't defused him. I'd better tell Isa right away, she thought. He has to arrange a trip for Greg, hide him, get him out of town. She entered without knocking. Isa was going over an Excel sheet spread across his desk. Hetty could see "Weekly" something printed at the top.

"Isa…"

He looked up with a disturbed face that slowly changed into a half smile.

"If you're back for more money, the answer's no, double no. I'll take my chances before I…"

"No, Isa. It's Jonah. We need to talk about Jonah."

The half-smile faded. "It didn't work."

"No. I have one more shot, but I can't count on it. You need to get Greg out of town right away."

"He works for a bank. I can't…"

"Don't say that. Tell him you need another loan, something. I can't think straight right now. But Greg has to get out of here."

He agreed. She might be a hillbilly, but her instincts were Ph.D. material.

"You have to keep Jonah here on the Swan until Greg's gone."

That's not a problem, thought Isa. I need him for…

"I can try," he said.

"Try! Don't try. Do it!"

That ran a hot flash up his back. This, this…this singer telling me what to do! But Isa's self-control was pig iron. Fanning the fire of a hysterical woman was not the call of the moment.

"I'll find a way to keep him here. And you keep working him. Did you tell him you were squealing to the wife?"

"His reaction was 'So what?'"

"I see. Okay. As soon as I finish this…"

She lowered her voice to a plea. "Isa, please. He's in danger."

I'll be goddamned, he thought. She's in love with the pretty boy. He lies to her, bangs her, drops her…and she's protecting him. If someone did that to me, I'd push them off a cliff.

"I'm meeting Jonah at the new stage. He plays the guitar…"

"My god, really?"

"I'm going to sing with him."

"Good, soothe the beast. I'll call your lover now. Do you want to stay?"

"No."

I was right. She's in love with the guy.

"Then go."

Hetty left filled with apprehension. "Your lover," he had said. The earlier pain filled her stomach once more. Her lower lip trembled. I can't let Jonah see me like this, she thought. She went into a Ladies Room and sitting inside a stall, lowered her head in her hands and sobbed.

Isa knew the straightest path to a person's brain was through his bank account. He also knew Greg went to New York to interview for a bigger job than the one he had in St. Louis. What if he were being considered for an even bigger job in L.A.? The lie must have substance. Lover boy isn't stupid. Isa knew a highly-placed banker in L.A. he could lean on, using a past misadventure the man would not want known. I'll force him to act as an interviewer working quietly on behalf of the Board of Directors of L.A.'s largest bank. He won't refuse, not with what I could reveal. When Greg learns he lost the job, I'll give him some chips and console him like a father. An opening as Executive Vice President should satisfy Greggie boy's ambition.

It was 8:45 in L.A. when he reached for the phone. A half hour later, Isa's banker-friend called Greg in St. Louis. At noon St. Louis time, Greg had a ticket to Los Angeles and a two-night reservation in a hotel. Then Isa made another call.

"My plane lands at 4:55 p.m.," said the man he had met in the park. "I can be at your office between six and six-thirty p.m. I've never been to St. Louis. Would you book a room for me in a luxury hotel near the Golden Swan? Whatever is on your mind about our venture, I am sure we can work out. Our first three installments went very smoothly. I also believe we should talk again about the Renoir in New York. As I said, once it's repaired it could be worth as much as…

Isa was aware of the amount. He agreed to talk about it again, but didn't commit any services. He did say he would make an arrangement for a fine hotel and guarantee the man's late arrival. But come here first, he said. Isa felt it was important they meet as soon as he was off the plane.

Hetty pulled herself together, washed the tears from her face, combed her hair, smoothed her new skirt to her hips and talked to herself in the mirror.

I have to appear calm and happy. I have to *act* calm and happy. I can do it. If we don't linger and talk before I sing, I'll be okay. Once I'm singing I kind'a go somewhere else.

Sing. I need an upbeat song, one Jonah can handle on his guitar. Christmas is only a few weeks away. Maybe a Christmas song, with chord progressions he can manage. She took deep breathes and left for the new stage Isa had built for her. Jonah arrived a few minutes later.

"Can you put a chair on the stage for me, Jonah? Get one for yourself. We'll sit next to each other."

She asked him if he had a song in mind.

"Yes, I want to play your favorite, the one the audience always wants you to sing at least twice. I've practiced it."

His face was childlike in its innocence as he sat looking at her, holding his guitar across his lap, waiting to start. She stared at him and thought, how could this man do what I think he does? His pose, his face, body, posture all conveyed blamelessness, and yet she was almost certain he…

He wanted to do the one song she didn't, "Can't Help Lovin' Dat Man," her signature piece, the one she always threw herself into, the one that always got an encore. Was he testing her apparent cheerfulness? It didn't matter, she had no choice. He was sitting with his guitar at the ready with an expression that said there was nothing but peace in the world.

"In C, Jonah."

He strummed a G-7th and she began.

"Fish gotta swim, birds gotta fly. I gotta love one man till I die…"

His eyes were locked on her. He never looked at the guitar as he strummed it. It was now part of him, as integrated as a limb. He kept in perfect time with her delivery. She thought she would break down singing this quintessential torch song, but the emotion went the other way. It gave her strength, a cathartic release from her hurt. She sang with a deep throaty timbre, moving her eyes on and off of Jonah. He, too, seemed to have entered another world. He was smile-less, but his face had a dim glow. Was there a human being in there somewhere, she asked herself? If so, she knew it was only a visitor.

"When he goes away…dat's a rainy day…"

His eyes never left her as he played. The chords were simple ones, D-minor, A-minor, D-7, G-7 and so on, but the simplicity of his rendering allowed her voice to excel. She soared into hope

"…and when he comes back, dat day is fine…"

and then lowered her voice into a feminine happiness as she sang

"...de sun will shine."

They finished and gazed at each other, not as lovers, as musicians look at each other for a moment when they realize their music had created a magic they didn't expect. Hetty had never left her chair while she sang. Was that part of the new sensation she felt? Usually, she moved about the stage when she sang the song. Maybe that's too much energy, too much display for the song's meaning. Sitting is more intimate, adds to the heartache the soulful lyrics intend. She made a note of it for her act.

Jonah wasn't thinking professional notes. He was fixed on her. Not romantically, with interested indifference, as a sated predator looks at a vulnerable creature. He saw she was whole again. And she was. The song, his soft accompaniment, the new staging washed away her previous mood. Her spirit hardened. Her music, her career, were what mattered, not some smooth-talking, splashy married man. She would not let him upset her path. She would sing the best she could and the hell with the bastard. She was not alone in her conclusion. Seeing her perform, Jonah decided killing Greg wasn't worth the trouble. He saw Hetty was okay. She was herself.

A messenger called out to him.

"Mr. Hajjar would like to see you in his office, Jonah."

He rose and Hetty gave him an air kiss on the cheek.

"Jonah that was the best I've sung since I've been here, maybe ever. You have to do it for me again!"

"I will. It was good, Hetty."

It was a fleeting moment of normalcy for Jonah, for he knew why Isa wanted him. As he walked toward the elevator, he fingered the garrote in his coat pocket.

CHAPTER 26

"News, Tower. I need news" was how his gravel voice greeted me on my cell.

"Harold, I don't have any damned news. As soon as I do, you'll get it."

"My nose. It smells something's missing."

"Well, it's right about that. It's missing your help. If Fidelity insured the paintings stolen in Soho and Chicago, give me the beneficiaries and I'll have something to go on."

I saw him leaning back in his chair, looking out that fantastic window.

"Right now I'm in a dead-end alley. My only lead is a fingerprint with no owner."

"How's that possible?"

I explained it couldn't be traced.

"I don't believe it. Everybody's fingerprinted today, especially crooks."

"Our killer wasn't. The police searched every data base for a match."

"Interesting."

"Yes. But not helpful. Harold, I keep my promises, if I have something, I'll give it to you."

I imagined the leg going up on the desk.

"Tower, I said I can't reveal policies. Lay off asking me about beneficiaries."

"Right. Well, let me ask you this. I own a valuable painting that's gotten dirty or has a scratch. I hire a conservator to fix it for me, but he needs the painting in his studio. Is there a rider to cover that?"

"Tower, I said…"

"Pretend it's a billion dollar painting."

My mind saw him leaning forward, shoe back on the floor.

"You're a persistent chap."

"That's not an answer."

"It's not intended to be. I have only one interest – finding the killer who stole the Picasso so he doesn't steal anything else."

"Or kill anyone else."

"Yes, but I'm more interested in his not stealing anything else I have insured."

"So you do have other paintings insured."

Patronizingly, "Tower, I have bridges insured, airports insured, diamonds insured, I once had an actress's legs insured. I gave the Harris woman a fast payout on the Picasso because I want you tracking down the thief. So knock off the who's who on my client list. It's proprietary and confidential. Ask around, if you don't believe me. Call me when you have something. If it's solid, I'll see what I can do to help within my confinements."

I imagined his teeth clamping down on a cigar, signaling end-of-conversation. I rang off.

I put my own leg on my desk. I held back telling him about Gerald's call from St. Louis. If the cranky bastard wasn't going to cooperate with me, I wasn't going to cooperate with him. Not that Gerald mattered to him. He had already paid out the insurance money to Mona. Unless Gerald was part of a larger scheme. That he would be interested in. Anyway, screw him. I'll call him when I feel like it.

I bellowed out,

"Freddie, have you heard from your Aunt Lydia?"

He looked into my office.

"She says she's comfortable in the assisted living home and enjoying the attention. The oxygen bag helps, but she says it's hard to get used to."

"Send more flowers and sign it from you, Arnie and me. What about the name I gave you to check out?"

"I have a folder. Do you want to go over it now?"

"No. Keep working on it. Here's something else, a phone number with a St. Louis area code. Can you find out where the call came from?"

He took the number and sprung back toward his desk anxious to dig in.

I called Mona and asked her if she had heard from husband Gerald since his last call. She hadn't.

"Is there any way he could know about your fifteen million?"

"No, and I'm not going to tell him. The last he heard the insurance payment was months off."

"Please call me if…"

"I will, Hank."

Dead ends. Frustration. But a case is a case, not just for the money, for the engagement. Sitting and waiting for some rich or wretched soul to come in the door is… well, it might not be as bad as Hellfire, but if Dante's right about layers in Hell, the eternal waiting room won't be far from the hottest furnace.

Freddie returned.

"It came from a cell phone. If I had the time and day it was made…"

"I have that."

"Even then I don't think I could trace it to where it came from. Only NSA has that ability."

"Really? Stay with the name I gave you. I'll see what I can do."

I punched in Bill Sanchez's number.

He had already done a favor for me on the Harris and Jacobs transfers; asking for another this invasive would not be easy. I asked for a similar one some time ago when he was traveling back from Washington after a contentious Congressional hearing on the vast reach and abuses, according to some, of the National Security Agency. He was not in a good mood. "Do people really believe we're interested in their private lives? Do they think we give a damn about their petty gossips and fornications? All we care about is the safety of our country, period." For Bill these rhetorical questions were radical departures from a temperament as steady as the horizon. His answer at that time was "No favors until this cools off. Maybe not even then." But that was several months ago and my newspaper reading suggested the heat on NSA had cooled. Maybe I could get this favor.

He answered right away. That aspect of our relationship was intact.

"We enjoyed the dinner, Bill. You and Nora look great. The conversation. The food. All of it. You and Nora looked so happy..."

"Hank..."

"At the table I could tell the pressure of those distant hearings had disappeared. Things were back to normal at the NSA. You looked relaxed, happy. Nora looked more at ease, too."

"Hank..."

"Okay, I need a favor."

Silence.

"Only the omniscient NSA can provide it. It's quite innocent. No national security implications, but it will help prevent another murder."

Silence.

"I need to know from where a phone call was made. I have the number it came from and the day and time. Could you fish out of your ocean of calls and ID its location? Really, Bill, it could save a life. After all, that's what the program is intended to do, right?"

Silence.

If he says no, I lose. It was my best pitch.

"What's the number?"

"A St. Louis area code."

I gave the data to him.

"I have decided that from now on you have two favors a year. Choose them carefully. I'll call you in a few minutes."

A few minutes. Such is the computer power of the NSA. Two a year. Calendar or fiscal? I could work the dates.

"Mr. Tow…Hank, are you ready for the folder?"

"Not yet, Freddie. Stay with it. Is Lydia taken care of?"

"Yes. A dozen yellow roses."

"Good."

"When you think you have the folder full, get Arnie's input."

"Okay."

My cell rang.

"The call was made from the phone of a Gerald Harris. It came from a gambling boat on the Mississippi called the Golden Swan."

CHAPTER 27

Gerald Harris landed at Lambert-St. Louis and took a cab to the wide gangplank leading into the Golden Swan.

"I'm here to see Mr. Hajjar," he announced to the guard whose job was to verify the ages of youthful-looking customers.

"Straight ahead to the elevator on the right. Top floor, St. Louis side."

So this is where Isa steals his money, thought Gerald. He did a cursory examination of the large open room to get an idea of the size of its profit. You can't know until you see the numbers, but I bet the fourteen-plus million he made in one week on the three thefts was more than he makes in six months here. Yeah, he'll want a bigger share of the deal, but he's in. And his sergeant is very good. The papers had nothing that suggested a clue to the killer. If I can get the seller to drop to forty percent and chip in five points of my twenty, Isa would have thirty-five percent instead of twenty. That burns, but the trouble is he's necessary. I wouldn't know where to go to replicate what he does, if he dropped out. But he doesn't know that and he won't drop out. Then, again, he doesn't know where to go for the sale. Without a private sale the whole thing is pointless. All he has in that regard is White Falcon. Gerald grinned. It sounds like a restaurant or the title of a B movie. I'll take the odds that he can't trace it. The final sale is my real leverage, my only leverage.

Then there's the Renoir. The smart-ass in New York says it's too risky a job. Shit. It's a low-hanging apple, a golden apple. It's a lark compared to what Isa's killer has already accomplished. A set up by the police? I don't believe it. Even if it is, it's the killer who takes the hit. He won't be taken alive, not after three murders and who knows how many others. He'll go down with a bullet and our names will die with him. I don't want to get worked up, but the stupidity of it! It could be worth a hundred million! Maybe more! I bet Isa will feel the same about it as I do.

Gerald stepped out of the elevator and went to the St. Louis side of the ship. He hadn't called Mona for three weeks and was afraid she might report him missing. The last thing he needed was the police finding him here with Isa. It also gave him a moment to catch his breath before confronting Isa and his hired killer. They exchanged a perfunctory conversation and he hung up. He went to Isa's office door.

Jerry let him in. The Lebanese was sitting erect behind his desk, smiling. Jonah was sitting in a leather chair to the right of the huge bay window that framed the majestic arch. It was particularly striking at this hour. Its curved steel was glistening from the bright lights beaming up from below. Jonah had a leg hanging over the side of his chair. It was 6:30, dark outside, and too early inside for a sizable gambling crowd.

Standing, "Hello, Gerald. Take a chair. A drink? I've got them all."

"No. Later maybe."

"Jerry, you can go. Please check on table four. Jonah says the cards need replacing."

"Will do."

"And don't hold a table for us in the restaurant. I know an Italian place near Busch Stadium I want to show Gerald. Fantastic food. The veal lasagna is worth ten times the price."

Jerry left the room.

"Gerald, that's Jonah sitting at the window. That's

all you need to know. But take a look out. Isn't the thing magnificent? Sparkles like a giant necklace. Gateway to the West it's called. St. Louis was the last cultured city before the cowboys and Indians took over. Lots of history. Here, please, have a seat."

Gerald was more interested in Jonah-the-killer draped over the chair than the arch across the river. He was clearly a psycho. There was no feeling in his face. His eyes were empty, dead. Would he take a self-inflicted bullet rather than life in prison or a needle? There was no way to tell. He was an empty stage. Gerald backed away from the window and took the chair across from Isa. Jonah remained static.

"Gerald, we can discuss everything in front of Jonah, but nothing in front of Jerry."

"I understand."

"Now, where shall we start?"

"You said you wanted to meet, Isa."

"Of course. First, I want to tell you and all your associates that I am pleased with the test we ran on the first three thefts. It was flawless. My share was delivered promptly as I wished. I sensed your helpful hand saw to that, Gerald. But you said you want to try for another painting, one that's even more valuable than the first three combined. Can you elaborate?"

"The word among a few dealers is that it's a lost Renoir. If that's true, we're talking at least a hundred million dollars."

"I see. Money that size carries more risk, don't you agree?"

Gerald was boxed. He couldn't advance his sacrifice the killer theory – he was in the room – if the theft were botched. So he took another tack.

"The one in Chicago and the two in New York were done so professionally I can't imagine a fourth would fail. I scanned every newspaper that reported the killings and there was never a mention of a clue, a witness, video, a lead of any kind. Every report suggested hopelessness."

He looked over at Jonah. "All three were masterfully done, Jonah."

"Still," said Isa "as Confucius said, 'The cautious seldom err.'"

That sent a chill up Gerald's spine. It was exactly what his hidden partner had said about the Renoir in the New York restaurant. Did Isa know the person? Had they talked? Was his use of the aphorism only a coincidence? If Isa knew who his ace in the hole was, his leverage on keeping even part of the profits was gone. There was no need for him. The identity of that person he had dinner with was a lock on his role in the arrangement. He had to know if Isa knew who that person was before he went any further.

"It's an interesting saying. Maybe I should pay more attention to it. Where did you hear it?"

"Hear it? I've lived by it since boyhood. Only the foolish dismiss caution. A knee-jerk conclusion in my business can be fatal."

It wasn't as definitive an answer as Gerald wished, but it helped him believe his contact was unknown to Isa.

"What is your answer, Isa, about the Renoir?"

The sly Lebanese leaned back in his chair.

"Risk and reward have to balance, counselor. It's the law of success."

"I'm listening."

Isa smiled deviously. "The real reason we're here is to discuss the allocation of profit. Once that is resolved we can move on to the pros and cons of the Renoir. I feel the see-saw is out of balance."

"I have given it thought, too. I can speak to the seller about the fifty percent share. I believe I can get it down closer to the industry standard. Regarding my own share, I am willing to reduce it. If I'm successful with the seller, you're share would rise to thirty-five percent."

"I see. Of course, the seller might not see these sales are subject to the industry standard. They're on the black market, aren't they? I suspect that's why the seller wants half of the proceeds."

Gerald felt the situation slipping away from him.

"I'm confident I can reduce it."

"To thirty percent?"

Gerald stiffened. "That would stretch it too far. Why risk that? Without the sale there's no money."

"You're right." He stopped and turned to Jonah.

"Jonah, get that folder I left on the table over there."

Jonah unraveled himself from the leather chair and strolled slowly to a side table near the office door.

"I put together some figures for us to review. I'm happy to see you haven't lost your sense of fairness, Gerald..."

Jonah locked the office door.

"...your willingness to accept less than your current share shows cooperation. I'm sure we can..."

Jonah removed the garrote from his pocket.

"...come to a deal suitable for everyone."

Jonah handed a manila folder to Isa. He opened it. Gerald leaned toward it.

"Let's see now..."

Like a whip the garrote was lashed around Gerald's neck. Jonah's strong arms twisted it into his skin, crushing Gerald's' windpipe. He uttered a low gagging sound and reached for the wire. His eyes were bulging and he started to kick at Isa's desk. Jonah pulled him away, his chair fell from under him. Jonah pulled him away from the chair and onto the floor, tightening the garrote as he pulled. He looked down at him to see if more pressure was needed, but he was already lifeless. Isa came from behind the desk.

"Let's get him into my bathroom..."

They carried the dead man into Isa's private lavatory. Jonah emptied his pockets and propped him between the commode and a wall. Isa took Gerald's wallet, comb and other items in his pockets and put them in a bag saying,

"There's a large elevator box used to move food up here from the kitchen. Meet me at three and we'll send Gerald down it for a pre-dawn swim. Burn the bag in the boiler. Greed, greed, greed. It eventually catches up with you. Won't people ever learn?"

CHAPTER 28

What was Gerald Harris doing on a gambling boat on the Mississippi? Was he a high roller as well as a woman shopper? One of those habits can be expensive; two can break the bank. Anyway, what relevance did Gerald have to finding Gabriel's killer? Mona owned the Picasso and Mona has the fifteen million. The only relevance I could think of was Gerald knocking her off for the fifteen. Was that even relevant to my case? No, but it was relevant to Mona. I called her.

"Mona, I have located Gerald. Interested?"

"Of course, Hank. Where is he?"

"He made his last call from St. Louis from a gambling boat on the Mississippi called the Golden Swan. Ever hear of it?"

"No. I haven't been west of the Hudson for twenty years."

"Mona, paid-for women and gambling can get a man in deep. What happens to the fifteen million if you die?"

"Hank! Are you suggesting..."

"It's my mind, Mona. It wanders."

"Gerald has his business one hundred percent. I have the apartment and its furnishings. Once I serve the divorce papers..."

"You plan to?"

"As soon as he returns."

"May I wander into another area?"

Silence. She knew where I was going, but I went there anyway.

"Jack's construction business is in the tank. There

hasn't been a request for a building permit in three years."

"Hank..."

"Just be careful, Mona. Just be careful. An old friend once told me that nice guys and girls can finish first as long as they don't think everyone is a nice guy or girl."

"If Jack and I do get together, I will insist on a prenup."

"Good."

Why I get myself into other people's lives – when there's no money in it for me – is a habit I need to kick. Life has enough crap in it without inviting more. We logged off.

Arnie came into my office. I explained the Golden Swan call and gave him a "Should I go to St. Louis?" look.

"Aye, 'ank. Gerald seems a bit off the main track, but 'e's the only lead we have to the killer. Can ye think of any other opening?"

"Only waiting in that goddam cellar."

"What if I waited and you followed up on Gerald?"

I looked at him.

"No one knows what the restorer looks like. 'e could be me as easy as ye."

"You'd go nuts, Arnie."

"Aye, yer probably right, but I've been promising the missus for months that I would fix a wooden chair that goes back a century in 'er family. I could do it there. Some of the tools might fit."

I grinned. "Arnie, it's a good idea. But don't let the project dull your antennae. The guy we're after is clever."

"I won't."

"There's something I have to tell you."

He listened intently as I explained Ronald Mason and the Bermuda connection to him.

"I thought he was out of my life, but he's not. I suspect he's the seller of the stolen art. He has international contacts..."

"Didn't ye say Gerald Harris was an international lawyer?"

"Yes, I did. He and Ronald could have crossed paths."

"It's another reason to find Gerald in St. Louis."

"Yes, it is."

"Arnie, Ronald Mason is about ten years older, but at a distance he's a dead ringer for me. But for the age difference, he's a twin. He fooled Jake at the Thirsty Tongue. He was cleaning glasses and Mason was only ten feet away. He thought it was me. If you think you see me on the street, be careful. It might be Mason."

"Do you think 'e's a killer, 'ank?"

"No, but that could be wishful thinking. The truth is, I don't know. The worse truth is there's a conflict – he saved my life."

Arnie did a deep head bow. "If it comes up, 'ank, maybe I should 'andle it."

"I hope it doesn't." I paused and said sincerely,

"It's a relief sharing it, Arnie. No one else knows, not even Carol."

"Aye, 'ank. I understand."

Carol comes from St. Louis. Her fatherly uncle – both her parents are dead – lives there as well as a severely depressed sister. She could come with me and stay with her uncle, Jack Tomkin. That would keep a distance between us and prevent another blending of vacation and business – and the horrific results it produced last time. Still, this is St. Louis, not the Caribbean.

No. It's a bad idea. I could be walking into something I don't know enough about. Carol has to stay in

New York.

And those eyes in the Venetian blinds when we were having dinner at 'good.' My gut said they belonged to Ronald – he has the necessary height – but I couldn't be sure. Besides, Ronald wasn't to be feared by me or Carol. I felt he would even protect her, if necessary. No, I go; Carol stays.

Golden Swan. Riverboat. Gambling. Action. The anticipation of it triggered another reason I wanted to go alone – the rush of possible danger.

I asked Iroquois-Freddie, who still had the lonely row of corn stalks running down the middle of his head, to book me in a hotel near the riverfront on the St. Louis side of the Mississippi for two nights and get a plane ticket for tomorrow morning. I handed him my .38 to FedEx overnight with a "Hold for arrival" note to the hotel. He was fascinated as I unloaded it.

Gerald, my peripatetic friend, you can't be places unknown for a month without something big swimming in your head. You don't go to St. Louis to get laid or gamble. Both of those recreations can be pleasantly satisfied in New York. The best explanation for being in St. Louis is that you're part of this scam.

I phoned Mona, told her what I was doing and asked her to email me a picture of her philandering husband.

CHAPTER 29

When Hetty saw the source of the incoming call on her iPhone, her fingers trembled. She let it ring a few times while she collected herself.

"Hello, Greg."

"Hetty, I've been in meetings for days. Please forgive me. They seem to start when it's dark and end when it's dark. I've wanted to call you two or three times and something always got in the way. Are you all right?"

She felt her stomach churning.

"Yes, I'm fine."

"I have to see you. You're on my mind. I…I…"

"What is it, Greg?"

"I have to talk to you, but not on the phone. Can we meet? Can I take you to dinner tonight?"

The tremble increased. Oh, god, I thought he was out of my system.

"I don't know. I can't…"

"Please, Hetty. Tonight I'm free…"

"Aren't you free every night, Greg?"

"Sometimes the office keeps me late and I can't…"

"Is that the only reason?"

He went quiet.

"You saw the paper."

"It was a knife in my stomach, Greg. I can't see you…now that I know. It's too painful…she's beautiful…"

"And as warm as a drill sergeant. We were kids married out of college. We have no children. We've grown apart. Neither of us understands the other…"

"Oh, god, Greg. Do you know how many times I've heard that?"

"Hetty…" He went quiet for a moment.

"Can we see each other? I'm going nuts. Those three nights in New York…they were Heaven to me. You enjoyed them, too, didn't you?"

"Yes, I did. I'll never forget them, but…"

"Don't say 'but' Hetty, It scares me to death. I'm going to Los Angeles tomorrow about a new job. I want you to come with me. It's for two nights. We can be together and talk and…and hold each other. I only need a few months to work it out with Ellen and if the job in L.A. works out we could..."

Perhaps it was the "few months" or the "neither of us understands the other" that echoed similar pleadings from past married men. She had turned down all but one of them and the pain of that affair told her not to repeat the mistake. The heartache lasted for months. She interrupted him.

"Greg, I care for you, but unless you're free I can't see you. It would hurt too much. My stomach's a mess even talking to you."

Greg seized on it.

"You care, Hetty. I know you do. Those nights we made love…they were magic. Give me some time to work it out, but see me while I do. Let's have dinner tonight and go to Los Angeles tomorrow…"

Oh god, she thought. If I do that, I am truly lost. No, no, no. Married men always go back to their wives. She remembered that one time, despite being warned over and over by friends to avoid it. She braced herself.

"Greg, I can't. There's no one else in my life. Do what you have to do, then we can have dinner every night, but not before that."

It was hard to say, but she meant it. Her attraction to him was powerful and understandable. He towered over the other men in her life, Billy, in particular, and she knew he was sincere in his need to see her. It wasn't just sex. There was the fun they had. The laughs. The holding hands. But she also felt deep in her soul that it would lead nowhere. There would be a month, two months filled with excuses explaining another delay; and the pleasure would be exquisitely unnerving along the way. Then another month would pass filed with excuses of a different kind and then one day he would explain tenderly, over dinner most likely, why he had to go back to his wife. "She loves me," he would say. "I can't hurt her. We've been through so much together over the years"...and so on. No, no, no. I won't let it happen to me. I can't let it happen. I have my future, my career...

Plaintively, "Hetty, I need you...I'll call. I understand you're hurt. I'm sorry."

She had a tear on her cheek, but she clicked off the phone and stood quietly for a moment. She might not have expressed it concisely, but there is dignity in saying no. It warms as well as relieves.

A noise behind her.

"Are you all right, Hetty?" asked Jonah. He was holding his guitar at his side.

His expression was an open face, devoid of ruse or suspicion, a sheet of paper.

She turned slowly and smiled.

"Yes, Jonah. I never felt better. The last of it is gone. Let's go to the stage, but this time I want to pick the song. I've had an idea in my head for an audience participation song. Ever hear of the "Beer Barrel Polka"?

"No."

"I learned it from a salesman traveling through Abilene. He sang me the words and gave me fifty dollars to sing it. The whole place joined in. They loved it. It's easy. Key of C and F. One time through is all you'll need. It's a happy song, Jonah, a very happy song. It'll send everyone home smiling."

She grinned at him.

"And wait 'til you see what I plan to wear!"

Jonah knocked on Isa's office door at 2:55 a.m. The Lebanese was leaning back in the large, black leather chair behind his desk, dozing without a care. Jonah repeated his knock. Isa shook himself awake, went to the door, quietly unlocked it and shut it behind Jonah. The only light in the room was from the bridge and the arch across the river. Jonah pulled a heavy curtain across the window and turned on a dim light near the bathroom door. He opened it, gripped Gerald under the shoulders and dragged him into the room.

"Over here," said Isa. He was standing next to a four by-four locked door in the wall to the left of the darkened window. He pressed a button on it and heard a grinding sound. A minute later there was a click. Isa opened the door, revealing a large cavity used to transport items back and forth from the kitchen at the boat's water line to his office on the top deck. He signaled Jonah to bring the body to it.

"Head first," said Isa. Jonah's strong shoulders held up Gerald's while Isa pushed his legs into Gerald's chest. In one coordinated shove, they pushed Gerald's sitting corpse inside the four-by-four cube.

"Go down to the kitchen. Ring me if it's clear. I'll join you once this greedy bastard is on his way down."

Isa turned off the one dim light in the room and waited. Five minutes later his phone rang. It was Jonah. He pushed a button on the box elevator and the grinding sound resumed as Gerald started his journey to the kitchen. Isa followed on the passenger elevator.

The kitchen was empty at this hour, but to avoid a surprise Isa locked the entrance door. The two men pulled Gerald out of the box and with Jonah holding him under the shoulders and Isa holding the lighter end they carried him out a back entrance that led to an outside garbage area. They were on the St. Louis side of the boat only six feet above the river racing past them.

"Check his pockets one more time." Jonah obeyed.

"They're empty."

"Wristwatch, ring?"

"I have them."

"Throw them overboard and when it's safe, burn the bag with his other stuff in the boiler."

Jonah took the bag and set it aside.

"Okay. Launch time."

They picked up the dead man and swung him over the side. The dark, undulating river swallowed him immediately. The current bounced the body off the side of the riverboat then an eddy spun it toward the middle of the current to begin its journey south.

"You leave first. Be sure you're not..." Isa avoided completing the sentence. It was unnecessary.

"I'll follow. If we're asked, we were checking the cleanliness of the kitchen."

Jonah nodded and with a careful look into the passageway, found a place to rest until the night guard took a bathroom break, then went to his car. Isa would sleep on the couch in his office, as he often did.

It was 4:00 a.m. when they finished their grisly task. At 6:00 a.m. in New York Hank Tower rose, refreshed himself, packed a light suitcase and took a cab to La Guardia for a 9:05 flight. By 1:00 p.m. he would be checked into his riverfront hotel and have his .38 snuggly holstered in the small of his back. After a much-needed lunch, he would try his luck at the tables on the Golden Swan.

CHAPTER 30

Jonah shook himself awake after six hours of sleep. After the disposal of Gerald Harris, he had gone directly to his apartment, but he didn't retire. For hours he practiced the polka Hetty had shown him. He wanted to get it absolutely right and give it various tempos. At 2:00 p.m. he reentered the Swan. At that hour of the afternoon the tables are sparsely attended and easier to inspect. He made his routine rounds, checking the newness of the cards and the condition of the shoes that delivered them and other devices the Swan used to keep the odds of winning on its side.

He checked the kitchen. It was short-staffed, but running smoothly and all the cutting and serving tables were orderly. From there, he went to the boiler room where some of the boat's waste was incinerated and from where part of the Swan's heat was generated. The temperature is unbearable in the boiler room during a St. Louis summer, but in November it was comfortable. He opened a small hatch to the boiler and tossed in the bag Isa had given him, ending the last of Gerald Harris's personal belongings.

Jonah knew Gerald's departure had expanded Isa's share of the profits from the three thefts. Did Isa want to expand it even further, he wondered? If so, he would have to locate the pointer and the all-important seller to arrange a new deal with them. He would want me for that, thought Jonah. Isa knew who the pointer was from the meeting he had with Gerald on the park bench in Chicago, but all he had for the seller was "White Falcon," a name that puzzled both men. As always, the next move was up to the boss, thought Jonah.

It was 4:00 p.m., another slow time for the casino, when Jonah noticed a face not among the hundreds of others he had stored in his fathomless memory. The man was a good size: six-one, about one-hundred and eighty pounds, lean and muscular. He was walking nonchalantly among the gaming tables with what appeared to be a half-interest in their offerings. Jonah was suspicious of newcomers. Was he a cop? Did Gerald's corpse wash ashore near the Swan instead of flowing down river with the current? Unlikely, thought Jonah. The river was high and running fast, and he had seen the body bounce away from the Swan toward midstream before it went under.

The man finally sat at the roulette table, alone, and placed a twenty dollar chip on red and another one on the number fourteen. He broke even, winning the color bet, but losing the numbered one. He left for the Twenty-One table and laid down two twenty dollar chips. He won with a picture hole card and a nine showing. He pocketed the eighty dollars in chips and resumed strolling.

He's looking for something or someone, thought Jonah. He told a waitress to ask the man if he needed anything.

"Yes," he responded, "I'm looking for a Mr. Gerald Harris. I was to meet him here at four thirty. Do you know him?"

"I don't know the name."

"Here's his picture. Have you seen him?"

She studied the photograph. "I'm afraid not."

"Is there someone else who could help me?"

The woman glanced at Jonah, standing out of Tower's vision. He nodded for her to join him and quickly left. She told Tower she'd get someone to help him.

Out of Tower's sight she told Jonah,

"He's looking for a Gerald Harris. He showed me a picture. I said I didn't recognize the name or the picture."

"Thank you, Tina. Wait five minutes and ask him if he wants a drink. Watch where he goes, but don't follow him."

She left on her mission and Jonah went immediately to the elevator to Isa's office. Tower continued walking the floor, stopping a few times to play a twenty dollar chip. The craps table would have been his choice, but it was unattended at this hour, so he traded in a chip for quarters and sat in front of one of the monster slot machines and slowly fed it. To an interested eye, he was clearly dallying, waiting for someone to approach him.

The room held hundreds of people when it was full. Now, there were only thirty or so and they were mostly white-haired women. Tower stood out.

Jonah was about to step into the elevator when Isa stepped out and pulled him aside.

"I've been watching from above. I don't think he's a cop. Too slick, too well-dressed. Note the shoes. Cops wear baggy clothes and thick shoes. Insurance inspector? Gaming Commission? If so, he's new, but I doubt it. He's definitely East, probably New York."

"He's looking for Gerald."

He grinned. "Is that right? Now how did he know to come here?"

Isa did not like the unexpected. He thought hard. Could this be a law partner looking for him, a client? It didn't matter. He knew Gerald would never reveal what they were doing. The bastard was greedy, but not stupid. Was he here because of the art thefts? He couldn't be sure. If I'm going to find out why he's roaming my casino, I have to hide any knowledge of Gerald.

Tower was even more in need of a story to hide behind than Isa. If his gut was correct, Gerald was dead, murdered, and his killer was on this boat.

Isa looked at Jonah.

"Has he seen you?"

"No."

"Good. Stay out of sight. Let me handle it."

Isa strolled up to Tower and said genially,

"Isa Hajjar. I'm the owner of the Golden Swan. The waitress asked me to see you. You are looking for someone?"

Tower stopped dropping quarters into the bottomless machine and faced him.

"Hank Tower. Yes, I'm looking for Gerald Harris, an attorney from New York. My company insured a painting he owned for a large sum. There are questions we need to ask him before we can disburse the funds. I've been looking for him for three weeks."

"I see. Why here?"

Tower dodged it.

"Here's a picture of him. Ever see him in your casino?"

Isa noted the dodge, faked a study of the picture and said,

"No. Not here."

"It's a large room. When it's full…"

"We keep close track of our clientele a number of ways. I've never seen him."

Tower looked at the ceiling, recognizing one of the ways.

"May I ask again, why are you looking here?"

That registered with Tower. Repeating the question meant it was important for this Isa guy to know.

"According to his wife, Gerald liked to gamble. You're the fifteenth casino I've visited looking for him. She's anxious for the money."

Isa was tempted to say, "Well, keep looking," but refrained. He had already gone too far repeating the question. If this guy's sharp, he picked up on it. He simply said,

"I see."

Isa felt Tower's eyes studying him. There's danger here he thought.

Isa gave Tower his signature smile and said,

"Let me suggest taking a break from your Odyssey. We just redid our entire entertainment room and opening night is tonight. Why don't you come? Our singer is famous. Las Vegas, Broadway, etc. etc."

"I'd love to. The only casinos left for me are in Las Vegas and Reno. I'll never find him there. I'll probably go back to New York. Tonight is open."

Widening the smile,

"Good. The show is at nine. Come early. We need the customers. The goddam redo cost a fortune."

Tower gave a soft laugh. "I'll put my remaining chips on double zero. That should help a bit."

"Not if you win!"

The two parted. Isa was convinced Tower was a risky sniffer. Insurance company? Which one? He didn't say. But asking the question would have made him appear too interested in Gerald's wife's problem.

Tower also left convinced he was onto something... that Gerald and this Isa person were connected. Isa didn't add up as the pointer in the game. A casino owner isn't usually wired into the high-end art market. If he's not the pointer, that means he's the killer. He tried double zero on the roulette table, lost, and took a cab to his hotel.

Hetty was nervous for the first time in her show biz career. She was standing in front of a full length mirror in her new dressing room, examining her new outfit: an eighteenth century bonnet, a shoulder-less blouse that exposed most of the upper hemisphere of her breasts and a full skirt adorned with roses, daffodils and other designs from yesteryear. She could have joined a square dance or served steins in a German beer garden. She cocked her head, spun around causing the skirt to fly horizontally, revealing her shapely legs and her pink panties. She untied the bonnet, spun again and let her blonde hair fly loose. It was her costume for the new polka number, the final act of her show. She left the dressing room and went to the new stage where Jerry played the piano while she rehearsed. He was enthralled.

"It will leave them smiling and panting, Hetty. Every male eye will be waiting for your next spin. Don't disappoint them."

"I won't. Do you really like it?"

"Absolutely."

"Then play it for me during the show."

"What about the regular pianist?"

"I'll ask him to sit out the last number."

He smiled. "Okay. I'd love to."

"It will help me, Jerry, if you're there. I'm a bit nervous. I'm more comfortable with the slower songs, country and torch."

"Nonsense, besides once you start spinning, I doubt any male in the audience will hear you."

She smiled and sat next to him on the piano stool. She kissed his cheek. "Thanks, Jerry."

He sat quietly for a while after she left, letting his fingers roam the keys in free association. A number from Hetty's Showboat routine emerged.

"We could make believe I love you...we could make believe that you love me..."

Tower spread himself across the king size bed and

gazed at the ceiling. The more thinking he gave the encounter with Isa Hajjar the more his suspicion hardened into conviction. This is the killer part of the formula and Gerald was its most recent victim, he thought. But the smooth Lebanese didn't fit as a hit man. There was no way to be sure of that, of course, but I'd give odds he isn't. He's not a loner, not that the trait is necessary for a professional, but it helps. Nor was there roughness or swagger or other macho signs. But then only an outsized insensitivity to life was required for the job. Still... Isa was smooth and his manner was alert for nuance in what I said. He was not in the blunt instrument business. He was management. He hired his killers. A knock on the door woke him from his musings.

"A package, sir."

Tower took it and tipped the young man excessively. His .38 had arrived. He napped for two hours, rose, dressed, holstered the gun in the small of his back underneath his sport coat and went to the lobby for a cab to the Golden Swan. It was dinner time.

Ronald Mason, Hank Tower's half-brother, was also looking for Attorney Gerald Harris. He was his only connection to the thieving part of the scam. When they last met Gerald was excited about a Renoir under repair. "It's worth a hundred million," he had said rambunctiously. He even had the address of where it was being repaired. At the time Mason demurred. "Too risky, too soon," he had warned. He felt that even more certainly after checking the address Gerald had given him. He saw two cameras aimed at the entrance to the studio, waiting to record the thief.

But a hundred million, half his! Such a score would finish his involvement in this particular scam on a remarkably high note. Ronald's rule was always to leave a situation before it was fully exploited. Not so with Gerald Harris. Gerald would exploit it until he got caught. He always went too far in all his adventures, even a paid for woman would eventually give him trouble. "Never wait for the top. Get out before it" was a philosophy that had kept Ronald and his sister out of jail their entire adult years.

But fifty million! Half his and, as always, half the Countess's. There had to be a way to the Renoir that kept the odds in his favor. He had no intention of stealing it himself – a violation of another rule – but even the best of the thieves in his address book seemed inadequate to the challenge. He knew it was a set up. So let's say someone gets in, he thought. Who's inside waiting? Not a weak-wristed artist. It would be a top-gun officer, maybe two.

A possible solution came to him while he was shaving. Hank Tower, his look-alike half-brother. He was a known and trusted ally of the police. He could get by the cameras and into the studio without suspicion; and if he could, so could a face as closely matched to his as mine is.

But that means I would have to participate in the actual theft. That I will not risk. If someone were with me while I establish myself as Tower to the cameras, he could go inside while I either waited for him on the sidewalk or simply left. Then what? He'd have to deal with the policeman inside. Disable him with a stun gun. Then what? Have the accomplice carry out the painting on camera? The police would be there in a moment.

But what if he carried out something with the painting inside it? Better yet, what if "Tower" were delivering something, a table, say, with a helper. The helper takes it inside and emerges with a table with a missing leg – with the painting secured underneath it. A simple replacement of a broken piece of furniture with a healthy one under the watchful eye of good guy, Hank Tower. Yes, I could disappear once the accomplice was inside, but that might not be necessary in this scenario. In fact, it might make it look suspicions, if I were not there helping the other man load the injured table. Was such a scheme worth the risk?

Mason washed his face, dressed and went to the White Falcon's paneled den to have cocktails with the Countess. There was another issue on his mind. Like Tower, Ronald had kept his half-brother to himself. Revealing it to her would mean the Countess would know he was only her half-brother. He knew he was uncomfortable with that knowledge when he first learned about Tower. It dropped a thin curtain between him and the Countess in his mind. Would it have the same effect on her? He didn't know and he didn't want to find out. Their relationship had been extremely close for forty-eight years. No, he would keep his secret a secret. He would talk only about the Renoir and the risk and reward it presented to them. Deep in the wallet of his mind, he already knew what their conclusion would be. Money has its ways and the larger the amount the more persuasive those ways become. They would discuss it, but he knew it was a done deal.

At the same time Ronald Mason was walking to the ship's paneled room to meet the Countess, the real Hank Tower was in a cab crossing the Mississippi to the Golden Swan for dinner and a 9:00 show. His only inherited asset, his deceased father's five-shot, Smith and Wesson .38, was tucked in its holster. He had a premonition that the legacy had arrived just in time.

CHAPTER 31

"You have a PI looking for Gerald?' asked Jack Harris a bit startled.

"Yes. For all I know he could be dead. If he is, I want to know."

Jack rolled over on his back and looked at the ceiling of their hotel room.

"No more sneaking around, if he is."

"We don't sneak very well. The PI knew about our last rendezvous."

"That means he was following you."

"Not him, a hired hand. He's after the restorer's murderer."

"And he thinks you killed him?"

"I doubt that. I suspect it's part of his job. Speaking of that, you need a job, Jack."

He rolled over on top of her.

"My job is to keep you hungering for me."

"A kept man?"

"It's my best option at the moment."

"And if it weren't an option?"

"But it is. You love me and I fell in love with you at your wedding. If my dealing brother's dead, my heart won't hurt much."

She said teasingly, "Well, I didn't fall for you that early. It took about ..."

"About what? Tell me."

She ran her hand down the front of his naked body and held him.

"When we danced at the reception and I felt you against me."

"So it wasn't love. It was my body."

"No, it scared me. I was just married and my brother-in-law's pressing his masculinity against me."

"I didn't press. It just grew."

She laughed and squeezed him. He said,

"You didn't back away."

"Yes, I did."

"But you came back. I remember."

"If you hadn't moved to California, things might have turned out differently. I would have divorced Gerald."

Mona ran her fingernails up and down his inner thigh.

"My body is not backing away now."

He slid his hand under her back and pulled her to him. Ten minutes later he was sitting on the side of the bed. He said thoughtfully.

"In the past when Gerald disappeared it usually meant he was into something besides other women. This time he might have gotten out of his league."

"The detective traced him to St. Louis."

He turned to her. "What in hell would he do there?"

"I don't know, Jack. I don't know. But I..."

"What?"

"Intuition."

"What intuition? Tell me."

"I'm almost certain he's dead. It somehow fits. I can't prove it."

"Let's hope your man can. I want to take you places."

"Who's taking whom, Jack?"

He dropped his head to his chest. "Please, Mona. I have some leads. I'll get back on my feet. It's not easy..."

She spun him around to her, a deep concern on her face.

"Jack, forgive me. I know it's hard. I'm with you,

honey, I'm with you. It's not knowing about Gerald that's driving me silly."

She held out her arms.

"Hold me."

He looked at her.

"Please."

"Let's get dressed."

"Jack, please."

She slid to the side of the bed and dangled her legs over the side, but he was already slipping on his underwear.

Jack didn't dare reveal it to her, but he actually did have a lead, a very sizable one. The fake partner's account, the Jacobs of Harris and Jacobs, was the receiver and distributor of the proceeds from the sale of the three pieces of stolen art. Half went to the Countess in Bermuda for finding the buyers and the other half to various numbered accounts. Jack had made all the distributions as agreed with his brother, except for Gerald's share. Jack didn't know where to send it. If his brother were truly dead, Jack would not only have the pleasure of his wife's body and her insurance money from the stolen Picasso, he'd also have Gerald's fourteen million. Best to keep the unknowing Mona thinking he was broke until Gerald – or his remains – showed up.

Isa watched Tower walk into the large casino room, stop and look around. He went to him.

"You're in time for dinner, Mr. Tower. Good. I recommend the veal scaloppini. Our chef is from one of Rome's greatest restaurants. He's a true master of Italian cuisine, all kinds of awards. Follow me."

The two went into an adjoining dining room filled to capacity, but for a few tables for two. Isa led Tower to one alongside a window that faced the arch across the river. White tablecloths, handsome cutlery, flowers, candles, wine buckets, crystal chandeliers overhead – all new and tastefully done.

"I'll have a waiter for you in a moment," said Isa. "You're staying for the show?"

"Yes. I look forward to it."

Smiling mischievously, "Would you like to meet the star?"

Why the attention, thought Tower? Isa picked it up.

"I want you to tell all your New York friends about the Golden Swan. I've got to pay for these damned renovations."

It was weak, but saying nothing would have been worse.

"Here she is now."

Hetty was standing at the door to the room. Isa waved her to Tower's table. She had on the same striking outfit she had worn when she met Isa for the first time. Every male eye followed her across the room.

"Mr. Tower, meet Hetty Staar."

Tower rose and took her hand.

Isa beamed. "What a couple! Handsome and beautiful."

Hetty smiled demurely. Tower nodded to the compliment.

"Now, I'm expected on the casino floor. The two of you enjoy yourselves. The dinner's on me, but the wine's on you."

Hetty looked at Tower and smiled pleasantly.

"Do you think I showed up accidentally?"

"It was right on cue. Why am I so important?"

"I don't know, but I am instructed to keep you happy."

Her long blonde hair was folded neatly over her shoulders and the tight, red sweater made her upper figure impossible to ignore.

"I can't think of a better jackpot than you."

"Well, I'm not to go too far."

"Relax, Hetty, I'm not thinking that way. It's always enjoyable for a man to have a beautiful woman at his side. It pumps up our delicate egos."

Hetty smiled inside. Her male experiences didn't include delicate egos. But the thought relaxed her.

"I'm sure the same is true of women." She blushed. "About men, I mean."

She's genuine, thought Tower. Las Vegas, Broadway? No. Isa's most likely a habitual liar. The waiter arrived and they both ordered the veal scaloppini. Tower added a bottle of their best pinot noir, slightly chilled. They chatted small talk while they ate, each warming to the other. Hetty was quick to admit she had never been to Las Vegas or Broadway. Tower nodded with a smile. She said she was born on a farm in Kansas, a large one that grew acres of wheat, had two brothers, couldn't stand it and escaped by teaching herself how to sing and perform and read music. She said she had ambitions, so does every other showbiz person, thought Tower, and said she was determined to achieve them. After they finished a small dessert she realized she had been doing all the talking. She was supposed to learn about Tower, not spill her past and dreamy future. She admitted it to him.

"I have more practice getting other people to talk, Hetty. The reason I'm here is to find a person who has come into a lot of money. He appears missing."

"That's an exciting job. How much?"

"It's in the millions. Here's his picture. Do you recognize him?"

"No."

"His name is Gerald Harris, a lawyer from New York. His last call home was from the Golden Swan about a week ago. No one's heard from him since."

No one's heard from him since. The phrase had a deadly ring that reached into her street smarts. She thought of Jonah. And shuffled in her seat.

"What is it, Hetty?"

"I can't…nothing."

"No one's heard from him since sounds like he's dead, doesn't it?"

"Yes, I mean, no." She looked at Tower with a plea.

"I don't know what I mean."

Tower backed off. She's afraid.

He leaned back in his chair and smiled.

"Tell me. What can I expect in the show? Tap dancing, hoop juggling, seals balancing balls on their noses?"

She smiled widely. "No, none of that. It's mostly me with an accompaniment. I have a new number I'm introducing tonight and I'm a bit scared…"

"Naw. I'm sure everyone in the room will stand and cheer. If they don't, I won't let them out until they do."

She grinned weakly. "Thanks. It's just when it's new you're never sure."

"What is it that's new?"

"I'm singing The Beer Barrel Polka in a low cut blouse and a dress that swirls revealing a good part of me. Will you be there?"

"Hetty, I wouldn't miss it if I had to climb that huge arch across the river to see it."

Her eyes twinkled. "I'll look for you afterwards."

"I'll be there."

She excused herself and started for her dressing room. Tower took a good sip of the pinot and concluded that Gerald was dead and she knows who killed him. He took another sip and smiled at his next thought. Sometimes in this job seeking the truth can have side benefits. He kept his eyes on the back of

Hetty's splendid figure as she left the room.

In the casino,

"What did you learn?"

She looked at Isa. "He's looking for someone."

"Who?"

"A lawyer named Gerald Harris. He says he has money coming to him, but he can't find him. He had a picture."

She almost said that his last call home was from here and no one's heard from him since, but held back.

"I'll see him after the show."

Isa's highly sensitive antennae wiggled. "Keep it business, Hetty."

She lifted her chin in protest and left.

The bitch. If it weren't for Jonah, I'd... Jesus! If he sees her cuddling up to this guy, I'm...I'm tied like a hog. I can't ask him to waste the nosey bastard. If I get Jonah off the boat, maybe I can..."

He called Jonah on his cell phone.

"Jonah, I'd like you to deposit the receipts tonight to First City about nine. Meet me in my office at eight-thirty."

"I want to see Hetty's show at nine."

"You can watch the eleven."

"The nine is the first time she does the new song. I want to see both shows."

"Okay. I'll get Jerry."

"He's playing the piano for her."

"What's wrong with the regular player?"

"Hetty wants Jerry."

Hetty wants Jerry! Goddam it, this woman has to go! She taking over my business!

But a larger concern quickly cooled his temper. An argument with Jonah could take more than my business. I'll deal with the country girl later, but she's got to go. Maybe a job in New York – or Nigeria. I'm not going to let a pushy broad screw up my life.

"Okay, I'll get someone else."

Like Tower, Isa had also come to conclusions. The first was that the fake insurance man knew that Gerald Harris was no more. Otherwise, he would continue searching for him, not return to New York. Add in that an expensive piece of art was involved and all doubt left Isa's mind. That was a mistake, Mr. Tower, using insurance money for a painting as cover. It tipped off your involvement. The question now was what to do with him before he spilled a story that could send me to life in prison. What to do is not the issue, he thought, and neither was when. It had to be now, tonight. A phone call by Tower to the police and... He shook off the thought. How to get rid of him was the issue.

Jonah would be riveted to Hetty during her 9:00 show. That lasted until 10:00, except her new act probably extended it. If it did, he could never pry Jonah loose between shows. He would not leave the cabaret, knowing he might miss part of the second one. Then he would want to see Hetty after the show. The brute has this weird, goddam devotion to her. To use Jonah, he would have to wait until well after the last show and hope Tower was still around. The whole thing was iffy, but the after-show solution eased his mind. Then another thunderclap.

What if Tower had already relayed his conviction about Gerald to the police? If so, he was screwed. But something told his gut that he hadn't. His eyes and most likely his thoughts were on Hetty. But he couldn't assume he wouldn't call the police after the first show. Shit!

Isa walked back and forth looking at the Twenty-One tables, fretting over the problem. It was too late to accomplish anything before the show began at 9:00 and even though his fear of Tower doing anything before that show ended had subsided, the problem was still there. I have to get to him between shows before he walks away to make "a personal call." Isa kept a revolver in his desk drawer, but he didn't have a silencer. I'll have to lure him somewhere separated from people and sound-proofed by thick bulkheads. The solution gelled. Get him to the rear of the boat to see the huge stern wheel that once propelled it, shoot him and hide his body until Jonah could help him dispose of it.

He nodded his head in half inches as he continued walking among the tables. Yes, it was the way out. Get rid of Tower and release Hetty from her contract. She leaves. Jonah's pleased with her good fortune. Tower's gone. Problem solved.

He stepped into the elevator to his office to retrieve the nine-millimeter locked in his desk drawer.

Hetty's looks had stirred Tower's out-of-town testosterone, but it was more than her looks that accounted for it. It was also the hard innocence she projected. Here was a farm girl who had left the wheat fields for others to handle and pursued a singing career with no formal training; who surely had to bargain her pay with cheating bosses and fend off scores of slobbering satyrs. In the midst of all this, she had polished her talent, learned to read music and to sing different styles of music and, now, created a personalized show. He was impressed. There was spunk as well as beauty. After she left the dining room, he had sipped another glass of the pinot and wondered as much about her as the case. I have to see her afterwards. Those lovely blue eyes know something I need to know. He checked his watch. Thirty minutes to show time. He checked his voice mail. Arnie:

"I'm seeing the woman in Brooklyn early tomorrow

morning, the one who 'ad 'er Cezanne stolen from the conservator in Soho. After that, I'm going to the studio. No word from Patterson."

He clicked off the phone and strolled to a nearby Twenty-One table to kill some time. He bought fifty dollars in chips from the dealer and laid down thirty. A deuce in the hole and a five up. Not bad. He took a card, a ten for seventeen. The dealer was showing a seven. Tower waved off another card. The dealer flipped over an ace. Eighteen. Tower tried the remaining twenty and lost it, too.

He wandered into the already half-full cabaret room. Hetty's going to have standing room only for her opening night, he smiled. He found a table for two just a few feet from the stage.

From an indentation in the back wall of the room a pair of eyes had followed him from his entrance to his chair.

On the top deck, in his office, Isa hid his Glock nine-millimeter underneath a collection of blank papers in a small briefcase and left to watch the show.

CHAPTER 32

At 8:55 the cabaret room was filled to capacity. Tower sat at his table for two just off the right side of the stage and Jonah sat on a high stool inside the darkness of an indentation in the back wall. The stool and his natural height gave him a panoramic view over the audience to the stage. The four piece band was in place. The piano player went center stage holding a small microphone.

"Ladies and gentlemen, tonight I have the pleasure of introducing the first performance in the Golden Swan's new cabaret club. We have a show for you I believe you'll talk about for many days and nights to come. You're going to hear a medley of songs from Hammerstein and Kern's immortal *Showboat* sung by someone you will have the right to claim you saw before she conquered Hollywood and Broadway, Miss Hetty Staar!"

He paused and got a light applause.

"But there's more than a few songs from *Showboat*. Hetty has prepared a *grande finale* that will blow the suds off your beer. I'll say no more, except hold on to your hats! And, now, here she is. Please welcome, Miss Hetty Staar!"

Hetty, dressed in a long, off-the-shoulder, white gown, entered to a strong applause. She went to the side of the piano and bowed her head demurely, then smiled and waited for the audience to settle. She said.

"Tonight, I'm going to sing a song that's a deep part of American culture, but… but I don't think it's ever been sung by a woman. If I'm right, you'll be the first to hear it. I hope you like it."

She looked at the pianist and on a soft, low note she began to sing *'Ol' Man River."*

The contrast of a white, blonde female, dressed in a formal, white gown, delivering a song created for and historically sung by a black, baritone male dressed in shaggy, workman's clothes achieved the striking distinction she had hoped for. It captured the audience. They were mesmerized. The applause overpowered her wish to remain in character at the end. She bowed and smiled back proudly. From there she segued into the wishful, longing refrains of "Make Believe" and taking the clue from her session with Jonah, she sat in a chair and rendered her signature piece, the soulful, yearning *"Can't Help Lovin' Dat Man of Mine."*

At the end, she got those precious few seconds of silence every artist hopes for. The brief quiet that means the audience is still caught in his or her performance, even though it has ended. A wild applause followed. Hetty remained seated and held down her head. There was no bow. The pianist waited for the clapping to fade and stepped in front of her. The stage lights dimmed and Hetty escaped to her dressing room. The pianist beamed…

"Thank you, thank you. Now, order another drink and hold on to your chairs. In a few minutes we're going to rock!"

Five minutes later Hetty twirled to center stage in her *Beer Barrel Polka* outfit and Jerry took the piano. Before the two had finished the first rendering of the song people were on their feet singing with Hetty. "Roll out the barrel, we'll have a barrel of fun…."

Hetty walked the stage as she sung. When she swirled her skirt, it went horizontal, revealing her shapely legs and pink panties. Male voices bellowed, "More! More!"

Tower was amazed at the performance. She's a natural, a pro, he thought. This is only a quick stop. She's New York material. Jonah was transfixed, caught in an emotion as close to pride and admiration as his neuter soul permitted. Isa was leaning against a side wall, watching Tower, holding his briefcase at his side. He was going to show Tower how a boat the size of the Golden Swan could navigate the changing depths of the Mississippi River.

A young girl dropped a note on his table as she passed by. It was from Hetty.

"Hank, please meet me on the rear of the boat near the paddle wheel. Be sure you're not followed."

He pocketed the note. She knows something and she's scared. "Be sure you're not followed." He would try to accommodate that, but once you left the public areas, the boat became a labyrinth of passageways, doors and steel ladders. All he knew was that he was one deck above river level and about mid-ship. If he were followed, it would be by someone in this room. He waited for the crowd to rise and shift about and slipped through the middle of it into the casino. There was a door that faced the aft end of the boat. He passed through it as covertly as he could. A ladder. He hurried down it, keeping to his aft direction. It was hot. The laundry was just ahead. Another door. The heat changed into the strong smell of the river. A passageway took him further aft into an open space in front of a huge paddle wheel. The river was rushing by only a few feet below the lowest deck of the flat-bottomed vessel. It was an eerie, isolated place with the rolling water alongside it blinking flickers of moonlight off its wavelets. He unbuttoned his jacket and waited. He was standing next to a four-foot metal bannister too short to lean on safely that wrapped itself around the stern of the boat. Behind it loomed a huge paddle wheel. Hetty arrived breathless.

"I only have a few minutes. I had to see you."

"Hetty, your show, it was fantastic..."

"Thank you, but please let me talk. I need your help."

Tower nodded.

"I want out of here...I'm scared to death. There are things I know that I don't want to know...things I want to get away from. You're from New York. When are you going back?"

"Tomorrow."

"Please take me with you. Isa...Isa...he's, I don't know. But I think he's a..."

"A what, Hetty? Say it."

"A killer, maybe not him, but..."

"But someone who works for him."

"Yes, someone I...in a strange way I like. He looks out for me."

"Looks out for you?"

"Yes. I think if he wasn't here, Isa would have me killed. I know he wants to get rid of me."

"Hetty, those are strong words."

"I know. I've never said them before, even thought them; but now...now with this Gerald person missing and I know..."

"You think he's been killed by Isa and the other man?"

"Yes. It's easy to throw someone overboard. Look, we're only a few feet from the water. It's so fast it would carry anything far way before it was discovered. If it ever was."

"Of course you can come with me, but first I need to make a call. I believe Gerald Harris was murdered and dumped, too. One murder usually requires another one."

Tower took his cell from his pocket.

"Toss it over the side, Tower."

Isa was standing at the passageway, pointing the nine-millimeter at Tower. Hetty gasped with her hand over her mouth. Tower looked at him coolly.

"You know how to use that, Isa? It's got quite a kick."

Isa added his other hand to the gun and kept it trained on Tower.

"Over the side, I said."

Tower shifted the phone to his left hand.

"Now!"

"Let the girl alone, Isa. I'm the one who's going to turn you in for Gerald's murder."

"Bullshit. I'll handle her later. Toss the phone over the side." Tower obeyed.

"Now, step away from her."

"I'll do better."

He wrapped his left arm behind Hetty and shoved her forward at an angle away from Isa. It distracted him for the split second Tower needed to draw his .38 from behind his back. He shot Isa in his gun shoulder. Isa cried out, but he still had the gun dangling in his hand. He was aflame with anger and pain. A careful man, he had lost his steadiness. He was blazing at the thought that this…this country hillbilly could send him to prison. He pointed his gun at Hetty.

"You bitch! You're the one behind this."

He was ready to pull the trigger when a much stronger arm caught his wrist and pushed the gun into the air. The shot pinged off of one of the stern wheel's large blades.

"No, Isa, No."

Tower tried to see the man holding Isa, to get his gun on him, but he was standing in the long shadow of the passageway and Isa was between the two of them. He forced the gun out of Isa's hand onto the deck and now had his own in his free hand. But he wasn't pointing it at anyone. Hetty was poised to bolt. Jonah said, calmly,

"Stay here for a moment, Hetty."

She looked at Tower, questioning. He nodded. She stood at the door to the passageway, Tower started for Isa. Jonah's gun came up at him.

"No. stay there."

The tone was one of unruffled, deadly composure. Tower recognized the tone from an earlier near fatal encounter. It was uttered by a professional killer who would have shot him, but for Arnie killing him first. But Arnie wasn't here. He stood still as ordered, holding his .38 at his side.

"Put your gun away."

Tower holstered it.

In the same monotone,

"I want you to take Hetty to New York. If she is harmed, I will find you. I will deal with Mr. Hajjar."

Isa eyes widened in fear. Jonah loosened his arm around his neck, but Isa knew it was fruitless to pull free.

"Hetty, go with this man to the entrance and take a cab away from here. Jerry will explain it to the audience."

Isa struggled, mixing his anger with his fright. Jonah tightened his grip on his throat and said calmly,

"Go, Hetty. It's all right."

He stepped back out of Tower's line of sight. Hetty grabbed Tower's hand and pulled him running through doors and passageways up to the main deck and out the Swan's entrance. There was a line of cabs waiting at the end of the gangway. She dragged Tower into the first one in line. Frantically,

"Tell the driver your hotel."

Tower hesitated and looked back at the boat.

"Please, Hank, please. We've got to get out of here. You don't' know..."

He gave the driver the name of the hotel.

When the cab turned onto the Eads Bridge high above the Golden Swan, Hetty broke into violet shivers and pulled herself tightly to him as a three-year-old might grasp a teddy bear in a lightning storm. She still wore her polka dress beneath a light topcoat.

Once Hetty and Tower were gone, Jonah released Isa. He picked up his gun and threw it far out into the river.

"Take off your jacket and shirt."

Isa obeyed. There was blood on both from the shoulder wound. Jonah looked at it. The bullet was still in the flesh. He flipped open his switch knife, pinned Isa to the railing and dug it out point first. Isa let out a scream as shrill as the squeals from the many pigs Jonah had butchered on the farm. He wrapped the shirt around Isa's bleeding shoulder and helped him slip on his jacket. He called the boat's doctor.

"Mr. Hajjar has cut his shoulder badly on a piece of steel in the engine room. I'm bringing him to the infirmary."

Moments later the doctor had Isa on a table in the small room, cleaning the wound. He didn't ask for any information beyond what Jonah had told him.

Jonah watched the entire procedure without a sign of emotion, despite his boss's anguish. But Isa's fear didn't interfere with his smarts. His mind was whirling, for he knew he had committed a cardinal crime – attempting to shoot the only thing in the Universe Jonah cared a whit about. He was still alive because his once faithful employee hadn't figured out how to dispose of him, yet.

Tower rushed Hetty through the lobby to the elevator and up to his room. From the moment they left the

Golden Swan he had watched to see if they had been followed. Now, safely in the hotel room, he had to figure out what to do with her.

The shelter of the room and Tower's presence had quieted Hetty's shivers. She shed her overcoat, wrapped her arms around herself and went to the window. The drapes were drawn back, revealing the uppermost section of the arch and the oscillating red warning at its tip. Tower asked,

"Who was the man behind Isa, Hetty?"

She turned to him. "Please don't ask me, Hank. He saved my life."

"He's a killer."

"He might be, but he saved my life."

"Yes, he did, and maybe mine."

The conflict wasn't new to Tower. There was his half-brother Mason…

But Isa was a different matter. He picked up the hotel phone and started to dial Tom Holden in New York.

"Wait, Hank."

She looked deliciously silly standing there in her off-shoulder blouse, flowing blonde hair and full skirt. Only the bonnet was missing.

"You saved my life, too."

"I guess we saved each other's lives, Hetty." Tower smiled at all the life savers.

"I need to report Isa. He's an accomplice to murder and he attempted to kill both of us. My police captain friend can contact the East St. Louis police…"

"Please wait."

She went into the bathroom.

Danger frightens us. It reveals our fragileness; but it also excites us when we face danger and survive it. Both of their lives were seconds from death's claim and both beat it. It's like winning the ultimate gold medal and both of them felt a hot rush.

Hetty emerged from the bathroom dressed only in a towel, as she had in the motel room with Jonah after fleeing Billy. Only this time she knew her hero was a full man. Tower was sitting on the side of the bed with the hotel phone in his hand about to call Tom Holden when she stepped in front of him and spread his legs with her knees.

"Hold me, Hank, please hold me."

The towel came down slowly and the phone was returned to its cradle. Perhaps an aged monk would have responded differently, but with the blood rush of survival still heating his veins, this time Hetty's gratitude was not ignored.

Tower called and said he would be in the office midafternoon and to ask Freddie to get a new phone for him. Oh, he said, also reserve a hotel room for a young woman who's returning with me. Details to follow. Then he called Captain Tom Holden with the Isa story and gave him his hotel phone number. Hetty and Tower were dressed and about to leave when Holden called the room.

"I spoke with the East St. Louis police. A body has been found washed ashore about ten miles north of Chester, Illinois. Its fingerprints matched an SEC file. Gerald Harris, an attorney from New York."

That news was important financially to Gerald's widow, Mona, but it just confirmed what Tower already knew. Isa and his hired hand had murdered him.

CHAPTER 33

The doctor bandaged Isa's shoulder wound and gave him some pain-killing pills.

"I need to change that bandage in three days, Isa. Keep it dry. Just be careful with your movements. It was a very jagged piece of steel you ran into. Jonah was smart getting you here before it got infected."

Isa nodded yes and slid off the table. Jonah was standing aside, watching.

Attempting to regain his authority, Isa said with firmness,

"Let's go to my office, Jonah."

Neither man spoke until Isa was standing behind his desk.

"I lost my temper, Jonah. It won't happen again. You did me a large favor being there. I won't let it go unrewarded."

Jonah's expression remained unmoved. Isa asked,

"Are we okay?"

Jonah was standing a few feet in front of his desk, his eyes unknowable. But there was a tiny nod. Isa would have given Jonah whatever earthly thing he wanted at that moment, but he had no idea what it could be. Money? Isa knew that money was not important to him. He accepted it for his services perfunctorily. As far as Isa knew, he never spent a dollar of what he had, nor did he know or ask where he kept what must be a considerable horde. Besides, if he ever needed money, he could go to one or more of his banks – the thousands of Twenty-One tables spread across the country – and with his talent withdraw hundreds or thousands of dollars. Women? He clearly wasn't interested in sex, male or female. What the hell else is there besides money and women, complained Isa, mystified.

Isa kept a managerial tone, as if life hadn't changed.

"You'd better see Jerry. It's almost eleven. Tell him she'll be out for a few weeks...that she slipped on a wet staircase and broke her ankle or leg. Make it an ankle. It's more believable. That gives us time to find someone else."

Jonah left without saying anything. When he gave the news about Hetty to Jerry a score of desperate questions ensued that only a face as fixed as Jonah's could scare away. Jonah's shadowy patrols on the Golden Swan – he was there, but he wasn't there – produced opinions that ranged from "He's just a person doing his job" to "He's spooky. Stay away." Jerry was in the latter camp and refrained from pressing Jonah. He would find out more about Hetty some other way. He went to the cabaret and made the announcement to the 11:00 audience.

Isa leaned back in his chair and considered his position. It was tenuous and frustrating. I can't read the bastard, he thought. He's a map without towns or cities. He finally gave up trying to psyche out his paid killer and called a contact in New York. He went straight to the point.

"I disagreed with your arguments at the time, but circumstances have changed. I believe we should go ahead. Give me every detail you have and I'll take care of it."

The other person responded with continued skepticism, but at Isa's insistence produced the details he needed. He called Jonah's cell.

"We're flying to New York tomorrow. I'll get the tickets."

He explained the purpose.

"As soon as I have a hotel, UPS your gun to it with a

'Hold for arrival' note. You can address it to me or yourself."

Jonah quickly chose himself.

Isa's paranoia flared. He either doesn't trust me with a gun or wants to use it on me. Shit! I just can't get into the son of a bitch and I'm good at psyching people. I don't know if he sees me as business as usual or his next prey. The wiser conclusion is the latter. All that "Jonah saved you from infection." Bullshit! He enjoyed digging that bullet out of me. He would have given a piece of wood more care. Why did he do it? Why not shove me over the side? Because I'd be missing and he'd be the last one with me. He's waiting for a better time and place to finish me. I could run and hide. I've never done that in my life and I'm not going to do it now. If money and women won't redeem me, maybe this New York action will succeed. It would at least keep him focused for a few days while I figure out how to kill the bastard.

But for a disappointed 11:00 crowd, the remainder of the night went without incident. The casino room peaked at the usual 1:00 a.m. and by 4:00 was empty for the cleaning crew. Jonah retired at his usual time, as did Isa. Isa's two plane reservations were in the airline's computer and the tickets were to be picked up and paid for at the airport. Flight time was 1:00 p.m.

At 10:00 a.m. Jonah placed his small bag in the back seat of a cab between where he and Isa would sit. Isa arrived moments later. The driver put Isa's larger bag in the trunk and they departed. The cab drove onto Front Street and wound its way onto the Eads Bridge. Neither Isa nor Jonah spoke. About midway across the bridge, the MetroLink started blasting its thunderous clacking sounds from the track beneath them while a fifty-five foot trailer truck geared down with a loud, menacing growl alongside. Jonah reached into the bag.

Inside, among thickly packed wads of discarded green felt, was his gun. He raised the bag to Isa's heart level and pulled the trigger. A muffled report and Isa began falling forward. Jonah propped him upright. The driver started at the noise.

"The truck backfired when it changed gears," said Jonah.

The cab left the bridge and weaved its way onto U.S. 70 north toward the airport.

"Driver, wait! We've forgotten something important. Go back to the Golden Swan as quickly as you can. We should have enough time."

"The quickest way back is over the Martin Luther King."

"Okay. Take it."

The small, bearded man with an Indian accent turned so quickly to catch the bridge, Jonah was forced to grab Isa's body to keep it from falling on him. Near the Illinois end of the bridge, Jonah pressed the muzzle of his gun to the back of the man's head.

"Get off and take Front Street north."

"Hey, what are you doing? Get that gun off me."

Jonah pressed harder. "Quiet."

About a mile north on a virtually empty Front Street on the right side of the road appeared a thick forest of trees. Jonah waited for zero traffic.

"Pull to the side of the road."

The driver obeyed.

"Drive into the trees."

"Mister, I can't do that…"

"Do it or I'll shoot you."

The man's hands were trembling on the steering wheel. He eased the cab down a slight incline and carefully weaved it through narrow openings until the thicket became too dense to proceed any farther. Jonah pushed Isa's body on the floor. The driver turned his head to speak and Jonah shot him in the forehead. He fell back over the wheel. Jonah got out and laid him across the two front seats. He closed the cab's doors, wiped clean whatever he had touched and walked unseen through the trees and behind derelict railroad buildings to his car parked near the Golden Swan. A few minutes later he and his six-figure cache of hundred dollar bills were on U.S. 40 driving east toward New York.

While we waited to board our plane to New York, I called my now *very* rich client, Mona Harris, on Hetty's phone. With husband Gerald's death now proven, she would inherit the co-op in the "Tower of Power" on Park Avenue. However, my finding Gerald also ends her daily fee.

"Mona, I'm in St. Louis getting ready to return to New York. I have news about Gerald."

"He's dead."

"Yes, he is. His body was found..."

With a slight catch in the throat,

"Hank, can you take care of this for me? I can't...I'm not strong enough...the arrangements...will you?"

"I'll need the name of the funeral home you want to use."

"I'll email it, but please deal with the police for me."

"How do you know the police are involved?"

"He was murdered, wasn't he?"

"Yes, but how do you know..."

"I just knew. His absences had grown longer and his calls were fewer and fewer. He had to be involved in something worse than his other deals. When you said his body was found...I knew."

"How are you?"

"I'm okay. Learning I was right was a jolt, but I'll be

all right. I told you about our marital situation. And you know about Jack."

"Include my associate in your email. He'll start what has to be done. Am I still on your payroll?'

"Yes."

"Okay."

I gave her Arnie's email and Hetty and I boarded. She was still dressed in her polka outfit underneath her top coat. She attracted eyes and smiles when she shed it going through Security. We had two cozy seats in coach.

"Hetty, we're getting you a hotel room. Do you know anyone in New York?"

"Just you."

I was afraid of that.

"Last night...we were hyped after the shooting. I don't regret it. You're beautiful, but I have a lovely woman in my life..."

She took my hand. "I don't regret it either. I understand. As soon as I'm under a roof and have some clothes, I'm calling the agents who were after me. I have money I squeezed out of Isa, but I need a job as soon as possible."

"I'll see if I can help."

We went quiet while the plane roared off the runway. Minutes later I asked,

"What do you think Jonah will do?"

Her face darkened. "He'll kill Isa and leave the Swan."

It was a straight forward, unhedged answer.

"Then what?"

"I suspect he'll come looking for me."

"And me?"

"I don't know."

With her head on my shoulder her hand holding mine she drifted off.

It seems Jonah has issues with anyone who mistreats Hetty and expresses his unhappiness in a lasting way. I wondered if having a woman in my life qualified as mistreating Hetty.

"I don't like the smell of it," said the Countess to Ronald Mason.

"It has an aroma, but a Renoir...you could sell it in a blink."

"Yes, I could, and a hundred million is not out of the question. But that's not the right question. What are the odds on a missing Renoir showing up? A hundred to one, a thousand?"

"Probably somewhere in between."

"Do you want to play odds like that? You've never gambled anywhere close to that."

"I think my plan will work. The jackpot is huge."

"Your plans always work, dear brother. That's not my point. What if it's a fake?"

"Then I'm screwed. Lots of work for nothing."

"Ronald, don't do it. We have the profit from the three sales. There will be other chances for a win. We both know that. You say there are cameras watching the place. Have you thought about the consequences of that? The police will have your face on tape. They could spread it worldwide."

The moment of truth had arrived. The argument against that possibility required that Mason disclose his look-alike, half-brother, Hank Tower. It would be his name under the face the police would have on tape. Revealing that to his sister, friend, cohort and confidant since childhood was the issue at stake. Did he want to risk their relationship? It had always been a strong bond. Did he want to risk weakening it? He looked at her then scanned the expensively paneled room filled with pictures of Bermuda and other world harbors they had visited together. And the numerous artifacts – a tiny gold anchor from Antigua, a ceremonial sword from Bora Bora – that added to the room's warmth and memories.

He turned to a large picture of their shared father and onetime Earl standing with his mother, both regally dressed at some gala affair – *her* mother; that is – but his, too, for she was the only mother he knew. He started to feel an overpowering sense of belonging. The pictures, the artifacts, the White Falcon where they sat now, weaved themselves into an upper class tapestry that had been tightly stitched over his forty-eight years. He and the Countess were the threads that kept it beautiful, not the Earl or his late "mother." Dropping such a thunderbolt wouldn't unweave the tapestry, but it would require a patching. Could even the most sensitive conversation make the patch unnoticeable? Was it worth finding out?

What did I feel when I learned the Countess was my half-sister? Was there a sense of a diminishment? Yes, but it wasn't deep. Would she, a woman, feel a more intense diminishment? I don't know. Then there was the pull Tower had on him. He knew even an occasional drink with him was not realistic despite the blood sharing. We are on different life paths. And he has a woman, a very attractive woman, from what I could see through the window at that restaurant near his apartment. Best I leave him alone.

He stood and poured himself two ounces of a fifty-year-old rum. She watched, waiting. Telling him she would refuse to sell it was not an option. He had to decide. If he succeeded in stealing the painting and it proved to be an original, she would benefit from its sale as much as he, but she said nothing. She looked and waited. He sipped.

"Damn, it's good."

He sipped again, paused, and asked,

"What would the Earl do?"

"The Earl? He'd plunge ahead, of course."

He smiled warmly and said,

"It's a bad idea. Let's drop it."

She walked over to him with her arm in a hook. With a loving smile she said,

"Please escort me to dinner, Mr. Mason."

Mona called Jack Harris immediately after hearing from Tower.

"He's dead, Jack. I just heard. Tower will have his body shipped back from St. Louis."

"St. Louis…how…?"

"I don't know. We'll find out all the details as soon as Tower's back, probably tomorrow."

Like Mona, Jack felt a moment of sadness, but it was brief. The money consequences of Gerald's death shouldered out any brotherly pain. The millions in the Jacobs account were now his, as were the Park Avenue apartment and its furnishings now Mona's. Together, they would be quite a financial force. But now he didn't need her money. Did he need her? Yes, somewhat, but his mind was already fantasizing expanding his knowledge of the other gender. In time, he thought, in time. First, the transition. Then, too, he thought, Mona might want to expand her social reach as well. We'll see. We'll see. A little time must pass.

"Jack, I need to see you. Can you come to the apartment?"

Teasing, "But it's only eleven o'clock?"

"I feel vulnerable, weak. A long history has ended…"

"For me, too, Mona. I'll be there in a half hour."

At 11:45 they were in bed together, each clutching

the other tightly. Mona's need was a desperate and honest search for love. Jack's need was sexual.

CHAPTER 34

I brought Hetty to the office with me from LaGuardia. Arnie was doing guard duty in the fake artist studio, but Freddie was present and quickly went on full alert. After I introduced her, she took off the topcoat and sat across from him, revealing her off-the-shoulders blouse and legs barely covered by her polka skirt. The poor guy nearly had a heart attack. He was still gaping when I asked,

"Any luck with a hotel room for Hetty?"

"Uh? Yes." Composing himself, "It's a small one on the Upper Eastside with a galley kitchen and a separate bedroom. I hope the price isn't too high. Here take a look."

I showed the price to Hetty. She said it was fine.

"I would check in right away and then go to some of the stores on Second Avenue for clothes. Freddie can show you the way."

"Uh? Oh, yeah. It's not far from here. An easy walk."

"Did you get a phone for me, Freddie?"

"Yes, it's on your desk. Same number."

I handed Hetty's phone back to her.

"Good. Go to it. I have some calls to make."

A grateful Hetty and a rattled Freddie went out the door together. She was still taking in everything she saw, buildings, stores, people; Freddie was brushing his blonde hair with his hand, trying to make it longer. It was stubble length, but the cut was even, suggesting a more traditional style would emerge. I called Patterson.

"Hugh, I don't have Gabriel's killer in custody, but I am ninety-five percent certain I know who it is."

"Who, Hank, who?"

"A psycho named Jonah Flood. I'm told by good authority that he's on his way from St. Louis to New York. He may be looking for me so I'd appreciate it if you would get caught up on any outstanding bills. I don't have a good idea what he looks like because he was hidden behind another person when we met. I plan to get a police picture from someone who does know what he looks like."

"My bonus still stands, Hank."

And I wanted to collect it; but I didn't say that.

"Good. You had three paintings stolen from your gallery some years back. I believe one was an Andy Warhol."

"Yes."

"You bought them from a man named John Smith,"

"Yes, I told you."

"Is his real name Ronald Mason?"

"I don't know. Truly, I don't. I didn't want to know. The insurance covered most of what I lost so I dropped it."

"I see. Do you remember the insurance company?"

He gave the name to me.

"I'll be in touch, Hugh."

I had only a few weeks to land Jonah Flood for my hundred grand bonus. On my desk were the research folder I had asked Freddie to prepare and a note from Arnie stating that the painting the murdered Soho restorer was working on was insured by Indemnity Assurance, Harold Bullard's company; so were the three paintings stolen years ago from my client, Hugh Patterson.

In a small town in eastern Pennsylvania Jonah swapped his BMW for a Toyota and attached his "safe" underneath it. After one night's rest during the nine-hundred mile drive from East St. Louis, he was now only two hours from Manhattan. His destination was the art studio where Isa had told him a valuable piece of art was being restored. Isa had finally decided they should steal it. Jonah knew where to send the piece for resale from the painting he had stolen in Chicago and the two he stole in New York. He would send this one to the same address with a note to direct the payment to a Miss Hetty Staar. He would include how the mysterious seller should do that in a separate note as soon as he found Hetty. His plan to locate her was through the "insurance man" who shot Isa in the shoulder. Isa said his name was Hank Tower. Through a series of instructions from service station attendants, he was able to navigate the labyrinth of roads that lead into Manhattan where he found a parking garage on the upper Westside. From there he was walking distance from the art studio Isa had described to him.

"Curiosity killed the cat burglar" would have been appropriate advice, if the Countess hadn't thought Mason's craving for the Renoir had ended with "The Earl? He'd have plunged ahead!" The craving had left, but a burning curiosity remained. Was it real or fake?

Dinner included the two of them and a woman friend of the Countess from Spain. After dining the three chatted for a while in the paneled room before the two women retired to their staterooms. Mason lingered behind, thinking. He was convinced the odds on the painting being genuine were weighted too heavily against the risk of trying to steal it, but his mind was playing with him. Was the damn thing real? Unlikely. Could he have stolen it the way he had planned? Yes. He was sure of that. Fifty percent of a hundred million…the idea of such a sum was squeezing his temporal soul. How can I be absolutely certain if it's real or not? There's only one way – look at it. I know enough about art to recognize a fake.

The Countess was taking the White Falcon to the Bahamas the day after tomorrow. "It's gotten chilly here," she said. I can go with her, thought Mason, but I'd be helpless for days aboard ship and going slightly nuts with the is-it-or-isn't-it question. He sipped the last of a snifter of cognac and started for his stateroom. No, I'll stay in New York and pay a visit to that art studio. The police have it under surveillance, but I'm sure they won't mind if their partner in crime prevention, my look-alike half-brother, dropped in. He set down the snifter. I'll have to deal with whoever is inside, but posing as Tower will give me the advantage of surprise. I'll have Cain stand by to pick it up, if it's real. If it's not, I'm off to the Bahamas. He turned off the lamp at his side and fell asleep.

Tower confirmed that Hetty had her new clothes and was safely in residence in the hotel Freddie had found for her. He also made sure Freddie had his nerdiness back on duty. He needed a cyber ace, not a drooling, stage-door Johnny. Arnie said he would leave the art studio at 7:00 and go straight home. With all seemingly in order, Tower got Carol's agreement for dinner, locked the office door and took the subway to their apartment. Later, the two were in a restaurant nearby.

"I hope to wind up the case in a few days. How would you like a vacation to, say, Rome or the Amalfi Coast. It's warm there."

Quickly, "I'd love it. I can spare at least a week. Can you stay free long enough…"

"Things usually go dead after a case, but if someone walks in offering me Venus de Milo in gold, I promise

I will say no, no. I'm taking a beautiful woman to a warm place with a small bed."

"Venus de Milo?"

"A metaphor for my enduring love."

It got a raised eyebrow.

The two finished dinner and walked home. Tower's arm was tight around Carol's waist, but his mind was in last night's hotel room watching Hetty's towel slipping down her front.

He called Arnie from home.

"I'm going to call Holden first thing in the morning and ask him to shut down the studio operation. I also need a police artist. The woman who came back with me knows what the killer looks like. I know who he is, but couldn't see him in the dark. I know this, though. He's not an art aficionado. There's no need for you to go there tomorrow, Arnie. I'm only going there to collect the Renoir Holden promised me."

"Aye, 'ank. I'll be in the office with Freddie."

"Please check on Lydia for all of us."

"Aye. I will."

At 10:00 the next morning an armed Jonah was walking to the studio from four blocks away. Ronald Mason, also armed, was one block away. Tower was in a cab turning onto the street, his .38 tucked in the small of his back. The fake Renoir was sitting on its easel like a Roman emperor in his box, waiting for the lions and the Christians to enter the arena.

Mason walked down the street toward the studio, wearing a jacket, but no hat. At the top of the steps that led down to its entrance he hesitated and looked around in a casual way to be sure the cameras caught his face. He went down the stairs to the studio's door located in the small alcove beneath the stoop above. He took out his revolver and tapped on the door.

Nothing. He tried again. Nothing.

Five steps up at street level a cab stopped and Tower stepped out. Mason heard the cab's door shut and huddled in the darkest corner of the alcove. Tower descended the steps in a lively manner and was aiming his key at the door…

"Hello, Hank."

Tower froze. It was too tight a space to draw his gun and whirl around to face the voice.

"It's Ronald. I come in peace."

Tower half turned to him.

"Can I come in?"

Tower pushed open the door and stepped inside. Mason pocketed his gun and followed him. He said,

"I came to see the Renoir. I didn't know you would be here."

Tower stepped behind him and pulled the door shut. He faced his visitor.

"I didn't know you were in the country."

Ronald walked nonchalantly to a chair.

"It's temporary."

"So why are you here?"

"A curiosity of mine that was too determined to defeat. I picked up word that a new Renoir had been found and was under repair by a conservator at this address. I knew the odds on it being real were gargantuan, but I had to see for myself. May I look at it?"

Tower waved his hand at the easel.

It took Mason a minute to see it was a fake. He turned to Tower, smiling.

"Whoever did it deserves a compliment. The uninitiated wouldn't know the difference."

"Ronald, do you know that in one week three conservators were murdered in their studios?'

"What do you mean?"

"Three art treasures were stolen and the restorers were killed."

Mason's face went dark. "I didn't know..."

Tower studied him closely. An instinct honed by dealing with hundreds of both innocent and guilty as a spy and a PI said he was telling the truth. Tower took a chair and faced his half-brother. He said,

"Were you involved in the sale of those pieces?"

Without any sign of wrongdoing,

"Yes."

He drifted off, then said,

"So this is a trap to catch the killer."

Tower nodded. "I'm closing it down. I know who the killer is. I can't ID him, but I have someone who can. She'll work with a police computer technician."

"If it's the guy who did this, you'll have a picture worthy of an art gallery."

"Did you sell paintings to an art collector named Hugh Patterson, using the name John Smith?"

"Good Lord, no."

Ronald looked around the room with the easiness of a guiltless man and changed the subject. He looked at Tower with concern.

"Can I help in any way?"

Tower ignored the question.

"Half of the seventy-one million from the sales went to an account in Bermuda. From there it went to three European accounts."

"I see."

Tower kept his stare fixed on Mason and said,

"The scam needed a pointer, a killer, a seller and an organizer. The person I believe organized it was murdered in St. Louis."

"I see. You have a client?"

"An art dealer. He was buddy-buddy with one of the murdered conservators."

"I see."

"Four men dead, one in Chicago, two in New York, one in St. Louis. So far."

"Are you safe, Hank?"

"I believe the killer's on his way here from St. Louis."

Tower's stare was still fastened on Mason.

"He's psycho. The only person he seems to care about came here with me from St. Louis."

"A woman."

"Yes, a beautiful one. If he thought I mistreated her…"

"It would not be pleasant."

Tower remained in his chair a few feet from the easel. Mason said,

"I want to help."

"I need to know for sure…"

"I knew nothing about the murders. The paintings were sold to private collectors. If they weren't insured, the owners were stupid."

"You saved my life the last time we met…"

The door swung open and Jonah stepped in poker-faced with his gun pointed into the room. The two look-alikes, Mason standing, Tower sitting only feet from each other, threw off his concentration. His shot hit Tower's shoulder as he was reaching for his .38, dropping Tower off his chair to the floor. Mason dove to the floor, reaching for his gun as he went down. Jonah fired at him. The bullet caromed off the floor, missing his head by inches. He kept rolling, his gun caught in his belt. Jonah looked quickly at Tower and then longer at Mason. He stood over Mason lying on the floor still trying to free his gun and leveled his gun at his head. Mason was frozen, looking up into the dark barrel of Jonah's weapon, his eyes locked in a death stare.

A shot filled the room. Jonah fell to the floor only a

few feet from Tower, blood gushing from his neck. Their eyes were level with each other's for an eternal second, then Jonah wiggled enough to train his gun back on Mason's head. Tower clenched his teeth, gripped his .38 and fired a shot into the back of Jonah's head, killing him instantly.

Blood was spreading over Tower's shirt and jacket. He tried to raise himself and fell back on the floor. Mason rolled over and leapt to his feet, kicked Jonah's gun aside and lifted Tower under his good arm to a chair. He removed his jacket and shirt and tied the shirt into a tourniquet to stop the bleeding.

"I'll call an ambulance. It looks fleshy, but it's bleeding like a hydrant."

"Call 911. Use my phone. In my jacket pocket. Use my voice, then get out of here. I'll handle the police."

Mason hit 911. "I'm reporting a shooting at…" He spoke as one wounded.

"I can't leave here with you bleeding…"

"You can't stay. A police captain knows I'm here, so does my Associate. The dead guy's the killer we're after. Case closed. Get out of here."

Mason looked at him intently. "You saved my life. He was an instant from pulling the trigger."

Tower mustered a half smile. "Next time be more careful with your curiosity."

Mason nodded.

"Go!"

"I'll be in touch, brother."

As Mason went out the door. Tower thought,

"I saved yours and Jonah spared mine."

Moments later three armed policemen in body armor broke into the room. Tower nodded at Jonah on the floor.

"I'm a licensed PI, Hank Tower. The dead man's a murderer. You'll find his fingerprint in the studio of one of his victims. Call Captain Holden of the Seventeenth. He'll know what to..."

He leaned forward and fainted.

CHAPTER 35

I smelled like a hospital and looked like a half-finished mummy. My right shoulder was in a sling which a nurse had bandaged to my chest to keep me from disturbing the wound. Ronald was right. It was fleshy and bloody. It took a transfusion to keep my tank full. Carol showed up about 1:00 with a look that conflated worry, pain, sorrow and depression. "Another scar for me to look at," was one of her comments. I assured her I would be home for dinner. Hospitals don't coddle their patients anymore, even if they want to be coddled. They fix and toss.

I knew seeing me once again bundled in tape would not bode well. How much of this near death can she take? If Jonah hadn't hesitated that half-second that let me duck a few inches, his shot would have gone to my heart. If she finally said enough is enough, I want normalcy, I wouldn't have much of an argument to come back with. Her insistence on sleeping on the couch "... to give you more room," was a loving gesture, but anger and frustration were also part of the motive.

My first office chore after a long conversation with Arnie was an even longer one with Captain Tom Holden. It seems Jonah had a parking garage stub in his pocket. The police had retrieved the car, searched it and found a cache of bills totaling two hundred and sixty thousand dollars. There was also a piece of paper with "For Hetty" written on it. "Who's Hetty?" Holden asked reasonably. I explained and asked if the note comprised a will.

"It's evidence until a judge says otherwise."

We rang off and I called my hundred-thousand-dollar client.

"Hugh, Gabriel's killer is dead. His name was Jonah Flood, a floater with no file anywhere. No DNA, no birth certificate, no credit card, nothing, except one of his fingerprints matched the one found on the toilet lever in Gabriel's studio. He was a professional killer. More bodies will probably show up that belong to him. I wanted you to know right away."

"There was mention of a shooting on the Westside on the news this morning."

"Four shots. The killer fired two. I fired two."

"You killed Gabriel's killer."

"Yes."

"I'm dropping off my check this morning."

"I won't be here. Please give it to Freddie at the reception desk."

Arnie was sitting on my suffering sofa, waiting for me to hang up.

"Yer even with yer half-brother, 'ank."

"Yes. He saved me and I saved him. You know, I think Jonah saved me, too. When we were eye to eye on the floor his gun was still on me. He could have shot me far more easily than Mason; yet he went for Mason. He had a soulful look in his eyes that reminded me of a small dog I had as a kid. It was hit by a car in front of our house. It was lying in the street dying and looked at me with the same kind of eyes. Surprise, pain, can you help me? I'm not trying to whitewash the guy. He was a cold-blooded murderer, but the look he gave me…"

" 'e wanted Mason even though ye were easier."

"Yes. He had me cold. I can't figure out…"

"Can I try 'ank?"

"Of course."

" 'etty."

"Hetty?"

" 'e needed ye alive to look after 'er."

"Oh, come on."

"Ye said 'e gave each of ye a 'ard look and then went for Mason. 'e saw ye were the one who was with 'etty in St. Louis. It's the only way to see it."

That slow-falling towel came back on my screen.

" 'ave ye told 'er yet?"

"No. I will. Hetty can take care of herself. I'm not necessary."

"I'm sure yer right, 'ank."

The subject made me a bit uncomfortable. I changed it.

"Let me go through the dossier Freddie prepared."

Twenty minutes later I was in an elevator on my way to the offices of Indemnity Assurance high up in the Seagram Building on Park Avenue.

Harold Bullard's assistant waved me in and closed the door. There he was behind his desk as I had imagined him from Day One: Edward G. Robinson, the insurance executive in *Double Indemnity,* chomping on a cigar.

"Sit down, Tower. Tell me a story."

"Do you actually smoke that thing, Harold?"

"No. Used to, but the evidence is too strong. I chew."

He leaned back in his high-back chair.

"What the hell happened to you?"

"You'll see it on the news."

"Ah, the shooting on the Westside. Tell me what's not on the news."

I gave it all to him as concisely as I could.

"So crime pays. The seventy-one million has been distributed and can't be recovered."

"Well, that's not entirely true."

He squinted his eyes and wiggled the cigar to the

other side of his mouth.

"Go on."

"I'll have to speculate how the cartel divided the money. Let's say a big part went to the person who sold the art to the private market. That money would be the most difficult to recover. Then there's the organizer of the scam, Gerald Harris, who, by the way, is on his way back to New York in a box."

With narrowed eyes. "I see."

"A victim of greed, I suspect. If so, his cut could still be in a bank account somewhere. If I were still on the case, I would look into the accounts of Harris and Jacobs. If the money's there, it's recoverable; if not, it can be traced.

"Then there's the killer, or killers. I suspect a man named Isa Hajjar was the manipulator. According to a good source, he's probably dead – killed by his hired gun. Their money can also be traced through, I'm guessing, wire transfers to a St. Louis bank or banks."

I paused.

"Tower, now I know for sure. You're a spy. Well, it's over. I'm sure justice will prevail."

"Analyst, Harold. But there has to be another player."

"Why's that?"

"Gerald Harris had art in his apartment, but he wasn't interested in the day-to-day life of the business. Nor were the killers. One was a casino owner; the other a hit man. Art was not part of their world. The organizer, Gerald Harris, knew who could sell the pieces, but it's a stretch to think he knew where expensive art was being repaired. He was a lawyer. Lawyers deal with many kinds of people, stock people, banking people, insurance people. I suspect he knew someone in a business he needed and they set it up. Let's call that someone the pointer."

I left my chair and went to that panoramic, floor-to-ceiling window and waited. The room was silent.

"What a view, Harold."

I turned to look at him. He had his leg on his desk, holding the cigar between his thumb and forefinger as if he were about to flip its ashes.

"Am I supposed to ask a question?"

"Harold, you're the pointer."

His face was a poker player's, deciding whether to call or raise.

"I know you insured the two paintings stolen in New York and most likely the one stolen in Chicago. You sold the riders, or more likely, pretended to sell the riders, to insure the paintings while they were off-premise. You knew where the paintings were going to be repaired, who would do the work and when."

"That's your analysis?"

"I believe your share of the seventy-one million can be traced and recovered."

I was still standing at the window; he had the cigar back in his mouth, staring at me, undecided on his next move. I said with a supercilious grin,

"You know, it's a bit like that movie, *Double Indemnity*. You and I, I mean. Do you know it?"

He nodded suspiciously. His eyes were piercing me.

"Fred MacMurray played an insurance salesman trying to cheat his company. Edward G. Robinson was the insurance executive who found him out. Now reverse that. Here we have the executive as the cheater and the salesman, me, finds you out. See what I mean? Just the reverse of the movie. Fascinating, isn't it? I've always admired old movie classics."

"Tower, rein in your imagination. What you're saying, even it were true, would be impossible to prove."

"Yes, it's circumstantial, I admit, unless a sudden bump in your wealth, let's say, about fourteen million, was discovered and traced back to a Harris and Jacobs bank account. That would be a direct link to the murdered Gerald and from there to the killers of three men."

"You're bluffing."

"It all fits, Harold. I asked the police to trace all the transactions that have gone through the Jacobs account. It's hard to hide money today. It drives the drug people nuts trying to do it. I know because I used to trace millions as a government analyst."

The cigar was clamped in his teeth, pointing at me like a rifle on a tripod.

"Harold, I would call a good criminal lawyer."

I looked back out the window.

"And enjoy this view. Your next one will be different."

And so I left my fantasized Edward G. Robinson insurance executive with a cigar fastened between his teeth and a leg on his desk for the police to arrest.

Hetty: "Come in, Hank. The door's open."

She was in her hotel room, standing in front of a full length mirror. Her back was bare from neck to heel. In the mirror's reflection I could see she was holding a strikingly beautiful blue and white dress that ended well above the knees. I caught my breath.

"Hetty..."

She spun around to me. "Oh, I thought, well, the other night we were both..."

"Can I see the dress on you?"

She wiggled her nakedness into it and let her blonde hair fall loose over her shoulders.

"Hank, what happened?!"

"Let's sit on the couch. I'll explain."

She curled in her legs and snuggled up on my working side.

"Jonah is dead, Hetty. There was a shooting..."

"He shot you!"

"Yes, but..."

She looked away from me.

"You shot him."

"I had to, Hetty."

"It's best. He was a..."

"He was a killer, Hetty."

Dropping her head, "Yes, I know, but I tried not to. He always treated me well from the first time we met."

"It will be on TV and in the tabloids. Did you know he had thousands of dollars in a case under his car?"

"No...I had no idea."

"The police have the car and the money. There was a note in the case 'For Hetty.'"

"My god, Hank. I swear I had no idea."

"It was probably his bank. His only connection to the normal world was an expired driver's license with a picture that looked nothing like him."

"You...are you okay, your arm, the bandage..."

"Yes. It comes off in two weeks, maybe less. I'll be able to..."

"...to hold me again like you did."

"Hetty, I have a..."

She didn't hear me.

"He almost killed you....Jonah almost killed you."

She pressed her lips hard on mine and ran her hand across my stomach.

"I can be careful not to hurt your arm."

My brain started whirling, sending powerful signals southward.

"No, Hetty, not now. I...maybe..."

"I know. I'm sorry. I shouldn't have."

She pulled away her hand and uncurled her legs.

"Let me model my new dress. I bought five outfits."

She stood in front of me barefoot and bare-shouldered and turned her body sensually this way and that. It intensified the signals that already had my blood on fire. I needed an escape.

"Hetty, I know a few people I can call for a job. Let me do that and I'll call you. If the police call, let me know. I'm late for a..."

I couldn't think of anything to be late for. She looked at me apologetically.

"I know, Hank. I know. Another time."

I stood up, she came into me. I kissed her on the forehead before she could raise her face to mine and left, shutting the door quietly behind me.

I walked back to the office in the brisk, early December air with my jacket open to fumigate the last of my hospital smell. Beautiful, educated, smart Carol was in my mind, then luscious, less educated, street-smart Hetty, then Carol again... My cell rang.

"I have air reservations to Rome and a hotel booked on the Amalfi Coast."

"When?"

"A week from now. Are you sure you can go with the arm? I can cancel."

"No, I want to go...I want to go."

I need to go.

I clicked off the phone. Maybe I can straighten out my libido in Italy with beautiful, educated Carol. And think about my job, if possible. I'm beginning to think that my job and libido are interlocked. Each is feeding the other, strengthening the partnership. If so, that's bad for Carol's happiness if she stays with me. I've hurt her in the past with my libidinal failings and frightened her with my cuts and wounds. What if it's true that I'm more of a threat to her future than a blessing? The air, the view, the blue water, the beauty of the Amalfi Coast will be a welcomed diversion, but wherever you go in the world your head goes with you. And when I come back. What then? I don't want to hurt her...God, I really don't...

EPILOGUE

'ank asked me to do some checking while 'e's away in Italy. Don't email me, 'e said, tell me when I'm back. 'e's right about forgetting. After ye 'ave looked down the barrel of a gun, ye need to think elsewhere as fast as ye can. 'e wanted to know about Isa Hajjar. I can tell 'im that 'is body was found with a cab driver's by some young lads passing through thick trees near the Golden Swan casino. I'll 'ave to tell 'im that I came up empty with 'is 'alf-brother, Ronald Mason. 'e must 'ave left the country in a private jet. I 'ad some of my old friends on the force check their sources and they couldn't find a trace of 'im.

'e wanted to know about our ex-client, Mona Harris. I asked Mona if there was anything we could do now that Jack Harris was under arrest. She said she posted bail for 'im. I kept my thinking inside, but if I were the lass...well, it's not my business.

'ank said 'etty wanted to know about Greg Roberts, a friend from St. Louis. After a bit of phoning, I learned 'e had lost 'is job at a bank in St. Louis. The man said when the President found out 'e was job interviewing in LA, 'e decided to "...free 'im up for fulltime looking." That was the way 'e put it.

The money in Jonah's car will probably go into New York City's General Fund. I was told the note with it 'ad no legal status.

Yesterday, 'etty stopped by looking for 'ank. I said 'e was gone for a few more days. She's a pretty lass – genuine and 'onest. She 'as what Mrs. Macgregor would call a winning way. There's a feeling in the lass for 'ank, but I've seen it before in others. I sometimes wonder 'ow Carol feels about it. But it's not my way to speculate on such matters.

ABOUT THE AUTHOR

Born and educated in St. Louis, Missouri, Charlie Horn was a Naval Officer, a corporate "Mad Man" in New York, a writer of numerous successful "How to" financial books, a Registered Investment Advisor, publisher of an investment newsletter subscribed to by thirty-thousand people and one of the top direct-response copywriters in the country. His DR ads sold $200,000,000 worth of his own products. Now, he is an accomplished writer of crime fiction.

His Hank Tower PI series includes a variety of human insights in the fast-moving world of who-dun-its. His fresh style moves a reader smoothly from page to page.

Horn targets two Hank Tower novels a year. His work is available in bookstores everywhere, from amazon.com and on Kindle, Nook, Kobo and iBook. Currently in print are:

DEATH VISITS THE CARIBBEAN
THE BONE DEALERS
FINAL INHERITANCE
THE BRIDE KILLER
MURDER IN VENICE
THE DEATH CHIP
THE BENNINGTON MURDERS
WALL STREET KILLERS

Horn lives with his wife in Connecticut and has a daughter, son-in-law and three young grandchildren.

ACKNOWLEDGEMENTS

To Barbara for her professional critiques and advice.

To all the heavy readers of the genre for their positive playback.

To Nancy for her ability to see what I can't.

To Linda for her expert editing eye and wifely overview.

To Doug for his designs and formatting patience.

To Michaela for her Internet expertise.

CPSIA information can be obtained at www.ICGtesting.com
Printed in the USA
LVOW04s1740150915

454265LV00017B/658/P

9 780991 512881